THE

INVESTMENT
TRUSTS
HANDBOOK

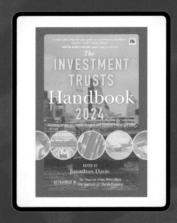

THE
INVESTMENT
TRUSTS
HANDBOOK

2024

*Investing essentials, expert insights
and powerful trends and data*

EDITED BY
JONATHAN DAVIS

www.ITHB.co.uk

HARRIMAN HOUSE LTD
3 Viceroy Court
Bedford Road
Petersfield
Hampshire
GU32 3LJ
GREAT BRITAIN
Tel: +44 (0)1730 233870

Email: enquiries@harriman-house.com
Website: harriman.house

First published in 2023.
Copyright © Harriman House Ltd.

The right of the authors to be identified as the Authors has been asserted in accordance with the
Copyright, Design and Patents Act 1988.

Hardback ISBN: 978-1-80409-071-8
eBook ISBN: 978-1-80409-072-5

British Library Cataloguing in Publication Data
A CIP catalogue record for this book can be obtained from the British Library.

www.ITHB.co.uk

CONTENTS

INTRODUCTION

The darkest hour?

THIS IS THE seventh annual edition of *The Investment Trusts Handbook* and looking back over the period in which the publication has appeared (2018 to 2023), it is striking what a rollercoaster ride it has been. We have gone from two years in which we said "you have never had it so good" (2018 and 2019) as an investment trust investor to the crisis of the Covid-19 pandemic, then a remarkable euphoric recovery in 2020/21, followed by a surge in inflation, the Russian invasion of Ukraine, a winter of energy shortages and great hardship, and two years of the most dramatic rise in interest rates that anyone can remember.

As I write this introduction, we are faced with another sudden geopolitical crisis too, the threat of an escalating war in the Middle East, following a shockingly bloodthirsty incursion by Hamas terrorists into Israel. The war in Ukraine has meanwhile morphed into a drawn-out stalemate and governments across the developed world are struggling with what increasingly looks like unsustainable levels of debt. The risk of a global recession, although it has yet to materialise, hangs menacingly in the air.

Far from being a case of "never had it so good", the questions for shareholders in investment trusts today are therefore "has it ever been this bad?" and "will it ever improve?". The honest answers are "rarely" to the first (the global financial crisis was the last time) but definitely "yes, of course" to the second, although in the latter case it may take a little longer yet for improvement to become apparent.

Investment trusts have certainly been in the eye of the recent storms, with discounts widening across the whole universe, compounding a more general decline in net asset values driven by higher bond yields, mixed equity market returns and the use of gearing, which adds value in good times but magnifies declines during periods of falling asset values.

Only 16 out of more than 300 trusts that I follow on a regular basis now trade at a premium. The average discount has widened to 18%, its widest level since the global financial crisis. Two years ago the equivalent figure was 2%. A striking 75% of trusts have produced negative total returns since the Russian invasion of Ukraine. As a result an increasing number of trusts are opting to merge or wind up. The sector is shrinking, and the process is far from complete, so these are certainly challenging times.

1

Future opportunities

This latest edition of *The Investment Trusts Handbook* chronicles these dramatic changes in detail, but also looks forward to the future and the opportunities which such a turnaround in sentiment towards the investment trust sector is creating. It may be scant immediate consolation for investors looking at splashes of red ink across their portfolios, but history is clear that it is from these dark periods in the investment cycle that the best future results can be obtained, at least for those brave enough to take them.

A year ago I noted that one of the great strengths of the investment trust sector has been its ability to adapt to a changing environment, but that it would require "patience and fortitude from shareholders and resolute action from boards of directors". Even if the response of boards in many cases has been slower this year than I (and other contributors to this year's *Handbook*) would like to have seen, I see no reason to change that opinion.

I think it is healthy that the investment trust industry is being challenged to show that its response to the dramatic downturn in performance is sufficiently bold and decisive to make a difference. Ben Conway, a young fund manager at Hawksmoor Investment Management, has done us all a service by asking pertinent questions about some of the ways in which the industry operates (see page 91). These questions need to be addressed and answered.

While I remain as convinced as ever of the merits of the investment trust structure as a means to grow your wealth effectively, it does not mean that all investment trusts are good and above criticism. A good number, perhaps as many as a quarter of today's current crop are either too small to be viable, too undistinguished to be trusted or too poorly governed to merit survival. The coming cull of trusts that are past their sell by date will be an important and positive element in its future revival.

In the Handbook this year

The Investment Trusts Handbook is an independent editorial publication in which we look to pull together all the most important developments of the past 12 months into a single, handy reference volume, on its way, I would like to think, to becoming recognised as the *Wisden* of the investment trust world. It has already been bought or downloaded more than 45,000 times and the publishers and I remain grateful for your continued support.

The 2024 edition follows a now-familiar pattern:

- a detailed review of the last 12 months by our resident experts;

- a look ahead to an unusually uncertain future and what it may bring;

- Q&As, profiles and conversations with analysts and fund managers;

- my own thoughts on the year just gone and the one that lies ahead;

- reviews of trust performance and the model portfolios I monitor for readers; and

- a detailed how-to/data section at the end of the book, completely revised and updated.

I am happy to report that many of the readers of the *Handbook* continue to listen to the free *Money Makers* investment trust podcast, a weekly roundup of all the news from the investment trust world. We have now clocked up more than 180 episodes and listener numbers continue to rise.

Nearly 500 of you also now subscribe to the *Money Makers Circle*, a subscription service which, for a modest monthly or annual fee (equivalent to just £2 a week), gives you access to a range of premium content relevant to an investment trust investor. These include in-depth profiles of more than 120 trusts, regular summaries of the latest results and market movements, portfolio updates and commentary by myself and others.

You can find out more about both the podcast and the subscription service from the *Money Makers* website (www.money-makers.co). My thanks again to the many readers who have come up to introduce themselves to me at events, including the AIC's annual Investment Trust Showcase event, the annual *Master Investor* show and J.P. Morgan's new private investor event.

Performance in context

Turbulent periods like the last 18 months pose real challenges for shareholders in investment trusts because of the way that discounts can widen dramatically in times of market weakness. The risk of discount volatility has been repeatedly flagged in more recent editions of the *Handbook*. You should never invest in investment trusts unless you understand how discount movements will affect your portfolio.

Regular readers will know that I have been advocating a more defensive posture since the end of 2021, given the excesses of monetary policy and the unsustainably strong performance of almost every kind of asset we witnessed over the previous decade of low and even negative interest rate policies. The current surge in inflation is the inevitable consequence of that foolish and unsustainable policy stance.

There is little pleasure in being vindicated by recent developments. A year ago I reiterated my view that defensiveness remained the most appropriate stance going into the first half of 2023, but hoped that we would be beginning to see the light at the end of the tunnel as this latest edition came round. We may still be in the tunnel, but the light is definitely getting brighter.

In the event, while bonds have continued to sell off sharply this year, some parts of the equity market have proved more resilient than many expected, with the US stock market in particular continuing to defy gravity, helped by enthusiasm for the revolutionary breakthrough that artificial intelligence may prove to be. It is fair to say, however, that the results from the most defensive investment trusts, which aim to protect you against market falls, have been disappointing this year.

The headline facts, however, are that the investment trust index, which tracks around 190 of the trusts that are listed in the FTSE All-Share Index, has fallen for the second year running, and by just under 10% this year (at the date of writing). Since the completion of the last edition of the *Handbook* 12 months ago, the figures are a little better thanks to the recovery we saw in equity markets in the final quarter of 2022.

This performance needs to be seen in the broader context of market movements, summarised most simply in the chart below. This shows the five-year total returns from equities (UK and World indices) and the gilts market, together with a line tracking cumulative inflation over the same period. The inverse relationship between inflation and the price of gilts could not be more clear. Equity markets have been pleasingly resilient, at least in nominal terms.

Asset class five-year performance

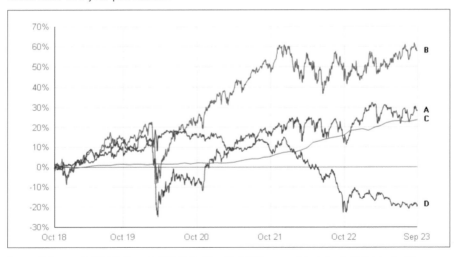

Source: FE Trustnet. A: FTSE All-Share, B: FTSE All-World ex UK, C: UK Consumer Price Index, D: FTSE Actuaries UK Conventional Gilts All Stocks.

The continued rise in interest rates – and the speed with which they have increased – has been the single most important factor in driving down asset price returns. The bear market in bonds, which move in inverse proportion to their yields, is the most sudden and brutal in living memory and possibly in history, according to Bank of America analysts.

It is not surprising in the circumstances that asset prices generally should fall; they typically do when faced with higher interest rates for any sustained period of time. Investors are paying the price as central banks persist in their efforts to control the inflation that they signally failed to forecast or anticipate with policy action in earlier years. 2023 has been the year when 'higher for longer' replaced 'lower for longer' as the prevailing narrative for where interest rates are headed.

The impact of interest rates

A second point to make is that the majority of investment trusts are doubly exposed to the impact of higher rates. In the case of equity trusts, many of them are geared plays on their asset class, and so when equity markets fall, on average they will tend to fall further and faster than the indices. The cost of debt will also tend to rise as and when any borrowings need to be refinanced.

At the same time alternative asset trusts, which have been the growth engine of the investment trust sector for the last decade, thanks mainly to their attractive yields, are in a competition for investor attention against other interest-bearing assets. When the returns investors can get from a short-dated government bond rise from under 1% to 5%, as they have done, it is no surprise that investors are being tempted to pull their money out of the trusts and move it into gilts or money market funds.

This is exactly what we have witnessed over the course of the past 12 months. The impact on many trusts in the alternatives space has been compounded by the fact that their ability to deliver good yields is dependent on higher levels of borrowing than you will find in a conventional equity trust. Those who have failed to take advantage of cheap borrowing costs in the zero-interest-rate era, or have borrowed too much to be comfortable, face the prospect of lower income and, in some cases, balance sheet stress in this new era.

It is no surprise, therefore, that the derating that has affected all investment trusts has been particularly marked in the alternatives sectors, as the chart overleaf shows. Having been sold initially on their ability to produce inflation-beating income streams, they have suffered more than conventional equity trusts in share price terms from comparisons with competing interest-bearing investments.

Absolute discounts over 10 years

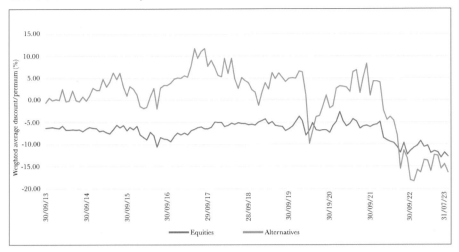

Source: theaic.co.uk.

Bear in mind, however, that what we have observed over the last two years is merely the flip side of the positive and superior returns that investment trusts produced in the low-interest-rate era of the previous decade. As the tables of 10-, 20- and 30-year performance in the Analysis section show, long-term investors in the best investment trusts have still generated excellent annualised double-digit returns, well above the 2–3% average annual rate of inflation.

Another factor to consider when looking at investment trust performance is how and where they choose to invest. Historically the majority of conventional equity investment trusts have always looked for opportunities in global equity markets rather than the UK market. This is reflected in the way that different sectors have performed in recent years, since global markets, with the exception of emerging markets, have offered much better returns on average. Share price total returns from global sectors have been between 2x and 3x greater than from UK sectors over the past 10 years.

Within the UK market too, domestic economy companies have suffered more than the larger global businesses in the FTSE 100 index. Investment style is another important differentiating factor. Smaller companies generally have been out of favour and the discounts across smaller company trusts of all kinds are currently wider, and their performance somewhat worse, than larger company equivalents. Trusts with an equity income focus meanwhile currently trade on a lower discount than the average 10%–14% observable across the equity trust universe.

Sectors in demand

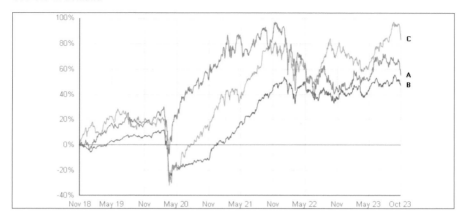

Source: FE Trustnet. A: IT technology and technology innovation, B: IT private equity, C: IT India/Indian subcontinent.

Sectors losing ground

Source: FE Trustnets. A: IT smaller companies, B: IT renewable energy infrastructure, C: IT growth capital.

Compensating factors

The widening of discounts, dramatic as it has been, does come with compensations. Trusts whose shares have derated will, if they pay dividends, automatically see their dividend yields rise. Only if those dividends are cut will the yields not go up, and even if that appears necessary, then boards have the option to use their reserves to maintain them, one of the unique advantages that investment trusts enjoy in comparison with open-ended equivalents.

Investment company yields are rising

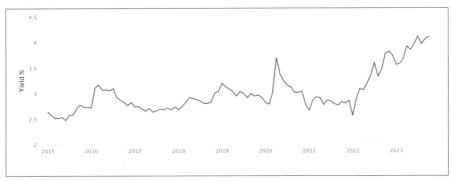

Source: theaic.co.uk.

Of course it may be that the reason why discounts have widened is that the net asset values (NAV) against which trust share prices are being compared are simply wrong. Whether that is in fact the case has been much debated this year, with particular reference to trusts in commercial property, private equity and infrastructure. Unlike conventional equity trusts, whose shares are 'marked to market' every day, NAVs in these areas are calculated by formula and with lags, meaning that they can never by definition be precise or definitive.

One of the corrective mechanisms that help to bring discounts closer to NAV is the possibility of bids coming in at a premium to the share price when discounts have widened too far. This year has seen a number of those in the property sector (Industrials REIT, Civitas Social Housing, CT Property Income). These have made useful gains for shareholders although all have been pitched below the last reported NAV. Given that property trust NAVs have been marked down in most cases, whereas those of many infrastructure and private equity trusts have not, or to the same degree, it does provide some *prima facie* evidence that NAVs as reported may indeed be too high.

The onus though is on the boards of trusts which are trading at a big discount to take action to redress the problem. They are not short of options, whether that takes the form of share buybacks, debt repayment or asset disposals. The one prediction that can be made with confidence is that the next 12 months will see a continued flow of announcements from trusts that are attempting to take action in this way.

The arrival of professional activist funds on many share registers in recent weeks underlines the fact that those trusts which fail to respond to concerns about their discounts will find themselves at risk of being forced to sell or wind down. It is reasonable therefore for shareholders in underperforming trusts to expect that if their companies cannot reform themselves, then the market will do it for them – which is a good reason for thinking that discounts this wide are unsustainable.

Personal highlights

Notwithstanding a difficult 12 months since the last *Handbook* was completed, and the contrasting behaviour of different sectors on style and geographic focus, there have still been a number of pleasing individual trust performances to note. 3i and Literacy Capital have performed notably well in the private equity universe. JPMorgan Global Growth & Income has been particularly impressive in the global sector and a number of UK equity income trusts, led by the evergreen City of London, have continued to deliver what they promise, just as I hoped last year that they would. Nippon Active Value is another trust whose performance has particularly pleased me.

On the negative side, having proved their worth so well in 2022, it has been disappointing to see the likes of Capital Gearing, Ruffer and Personal Assets (the best performer of the three), fail to preserve the value of their shareholders' capital again this year, as they aspire to do over every 12-month period. BH Macro has miserably underperformed after its capital raising back in February. Making it my trust of the year for 2022 was obviously the kiss of death. RIT Capital is another trust, although one I haven't owned for a while, whose strong past reputation has not prevented its shares moving to an unprecedentedly large discount and which has plenty of work to do to show that it has not lost its touch since its founder, Jacob (Lord) Rothschild, stepped back from his frontline role. The poor performance of most UK small cap trusts, traditionally one of the strongest performing investment trust sectors, has however not been much of a surprise given the prevailing headwinds they have been facing, and they do now look very cheap.

The disasters that have afflicted shareholders in Home REIT and ThomasLloyd Energy Impact, both of whose shares remain suspended as I write, have not done any good to the reputation of the investment trust community. While the inquest into what went wrong is ongoing in both cases, it seems fairly clear that the seeds of the damage were already in place before the trusts came to market. Questions need to be answered by the promoters who brought such flawed vehicles to the market in the first place, by the boards which did not properly challenge them and by the investors who failed to spot those flaws at the outset.

I was never tempted by either of those two, but I do still have a holding in Hipgnosis Songs Fund, where similar criticisms may perhaps be levied at those involved. The difference in this case is that there is still an interesting and potentially valuable business in there somewhere, despite the conflicts of interest that were, unwisely from a shareholder's perspective, written into the arrangements with the fund management company at the outset. The contrast with the experience of those who bought shares in Round Hill Music Fund, which was sold this year at a significant premium to the share price (though not the reported NAV), is an informative illustration of the difference that a well structured and proactive board can make.

Turning to other alternative asset sectors, hanging on to a number of the trusts that I owned going into the great derating of the past two years looks now like a mistake, as the value of their handsome dividend yields has been more than eroded by the declines in their share prices. However, even in a higher-for-longer interest rate world, with new investment opportunities constrained by the inability to issue more capital, the best of the renewables, such as Greencoat UK Wind and Bluefield Solar, and infrastructure trusts, such as BBGI and 3i Infrastructure, remain excellent core holdings, in my view, and I have doubled down in the last few weeks on one or two situations as their yields have risen to offer a similar premium to comparable index-linked gilts.

Amongst the private equity names, even if the NAVs do still look suspect in a number of cases, the likes of Oakley Capital and Intermediate Capital Group can justifiably point to their strong long-term performance records as evidence that their future remains positive, while Pantheon International's commendable attempts to resolve its discount with buybacks and tenders sets an example that other trusts could do well to emulate. I remain less clear about the immediate scope for commercial property trusts to re-rate, although the case that Marcus Phayre-Mudge, manager of TR Property, makes in his article elsewhere in the *Handbook* for improved longer-term performance on valuation grounds strikes me as a strong one.

I do not have space to analyse the performance of the *Money Makers* model portfolios in detail, and given my advice last year to bias your holdings towards defensives and income-generating trusts while the downturn continues, these lists of the quality holdings in different style categories (growth, income etc.) are not particularly representative of how I think trust portfolios should be structured at present. Suffice it to say that they have all performed pretty much as expected, with total returns down by between 5% and 10% over the last 12 months, similar to the investment trust index. The general point I would make is probably that while buy and hold is generally the ideal way to invest in investment trusts, there are periods, typically once in a decade or so, when some wholesale rethinking may be necessary to maximise future potential returns. We have just been through – and have yet to emerge from – one of those periods, during which until now short-term capital preservation has been the priority.

The case for optimism

The final point to make is that the level of discounts we are seeing today, while painful for existing shareholders, is creating exceptional opportunities for those with new money to invest. In many sectors discounts are wider than at any point since the global financial crisis. Even in those sectors where discounts are the norm, such as private equity and commercial property, the extent of the derating is producing plenty of potential bargains. According to Nick Greenwood, manager of MIGO Opportunities (MIGO), a trust that hunts for bargains in the investment trust sector: "We are likely to look back to the autumn of 2023 as the perfect time to invest in investment trusts".

Those who follow Warren Buffett's advice to "wait for the fat pitch", meaning that if you are interested in making exceptional returns you need to have the patience to wait until share prices are not just cheap but glaringly cheap, should now be looking closely at the discount tables. While there will be casualties, trusts which never return to former glories, there are once-in-a-generation opportunities out there that are too good to miss.

"Even if markets remain volatile and difficult for a little longer, they will revive at some point in the near future", I also said a year ago. "Investors who have the patience to sit out this difficult phase will in due course reap the rewards in superior performance over time. It has always happened in the past – 2009, the year in which the markets finally started to recover from the global financial crisis – was one of the greatest money-making opportunities in my lifetime. And it will happen again".

I stand by this conclusion too, noting that at today's discounted prices the best investment trusts offer many opportunities for good performance as and when markets recover. In many sectors, there is scope for improving performance to be reinforced by narrowing discounts, reversing the relentless trend of the past two years. The direction of interest rates will be key to that happening and there are encouraging signs that we are close to the peak in interest rates, although I am not sure that we are quite there yet.

While we will undoubtedly lose a significant segment of the investment trust universe over the coming months as the fallout from a riskier, higher-interest-rate world calls time on weaker funds, the important thing is to keep your faith in the ability of investment trusts to create real positive returns, as they have done through history. They will rise again, just as they have always done in the past, and the rise could be impressive when it comes.

JONATHAN DAVIS

25 OCTOBER 2023

JONATHAN DAVIS *is one of the UK's leading stock market authors and commentators. A qualified professional investor, his books include* Money Makers, Investing with Anthony Bolton *and* Templeton's Way with Money. *After writing columns for* The Independent *and* Financial Times *for many years, he now writes the private circulation* Money Makers *newsletter. Find out more from the* Money Makers *website: www.money-makers.co.*

Trusted counsel, pragmatic implementation, measured results.

Quill PR is a leading UK financial services media relations consultancy, with specific expertise in the investment trust sector.

Creative yet practical, Quill delivers effective public relations campaigns tailored to meet each client's specific communications objectives.

The team's many years' industry experience means that Quill is an invaluable adviser, guiding clients through today's fast-moving media environment.

Quill is a trustworthy business partner combining senior level service with original strategic thinking ensuring high quality, targeted media relations.

Call us - +44 (0)20 7466 5050

Email us - sarah@quillpr.com

Drop in - 107 Cheapside, London, EC2V 6DN

www.quillpr.com

ACKNOWLEDGEMENTS

Producing *The Investment Trusts Handbook 2024* is, as it has been for the last seven years, an intensive and collective effort. Thanks to all of those who have helped to bring it to fruition, whether as contributors or handmaidens to the production process.

At Harriman House: Myles Hunt, Sally Tickner, Nick Fletcher, Tracy Bundey, Victoria Lawson-McKittrick, Christopher Parker. Thank you also to Chris Wild.

At the publishing partners: Rob Austen and Manish Chavda (Columbia Threadneedle), Louise Bouverat (abrdn), Alexander Denny (Pantheon), Lucy Draper (AssetCo), John Ennis (Fidelity International), Vik Heerah (Polar Capital), Sunil Kler (Schroders), Kimmberly Lau (Asset Value Investors), Alexandra O'Brien (Invesco) and Vicky Toshney (Baillie Gifford).

Contributors: Robin Angus (much missed), John Baron, Emma Bird, Alan Brierley, James Carthew, Ben Conway, Richard Curling, Alex Davies, Simon Edelsten, Simon Elliott, Nick Greenwood, Peter Hewitt, Max King, Alastair Laing, Anthony Leatham, Ewan Lovett-Turner, Andrew McHattie, Richard Stone and Stuart Watson.

Interviewees: Joe Bauernfreund, Rhys Davies, Kate Fox, Abby Glennie, Stephen Lilley, Gaurav Narain, Marcus Phayre-Mudge, Nicholas Price, Ben Rogoff, Richard Sem, Helen Steers, Ali Unwin.

Research: Ewan Lovett-Turner and Colette Ord (Numis), Kieran Drake and Emma Bird (Winterflood Securities), Christopher Brown (J.P. Morgan Cazenove), Alan Brierley (Investec), Richard Pavry (Devon Equity Management), William Heathcoat Amory (Kepler Intelligence), Ed Marten and James Carthew (QuotedData).

Statistics: big thanks again this year to David Michael and Sophie Driscoll at the AIC for all their help in providing the performance statistics and a lot of other data.

Important information

Please note that everything you read in these pages is independently edited and provided for information and research purposes. Without knowledge of your individual circumstances and tolerance for risk, it is impossible – and prohibited by the Financial Conduct Authority – to give individual investment advice. However, all the opinions expressed here are honestly held and believed to be accurate at the time of writing. Please remember also that past performance, while helpful, is not a reliable guide to future performance. The value of investments and the income from them can go down as well as up.

YEAR IN
REVIEW

TRUST PERFORMANCE DATA

W E SUMMARISE HERE the most important trends in quarterly investment trust performance since the last *Handbook* was published. The tables cover share price, NAV and discount data for both individual trusts and for sectors, together with a summary of inflows and outflows. The data is drawn from the invaluable monthly and quarterly round-ups of investment trust news produced by research firm QuotedData and free to private investors (www.quoteddata.com).

2022 TOTAL

Figure 1: Best performing funds in price terms in 2022

	%
Doric Nimrod Air One	159.9
Doric Nimrod Air Three	73.7
Doric Nimrod Air Two	70.8
Amedeo Air Four Plus	56.1
Riverstone Energy	45.8
JZ Capital Partners	44.7
SME Credit Realisation	37.7
BlackRock Energy and Resources income	36.6
CQS Natural Resources Growth and Income	30.2
Gresham house Energy Storage	29.6

Figure 2: Best performing funds in NAV terms in 2022

	%
Amedeo Air Four Plus	72.3
Rockwood Strategic	53.7
Riverstone Energy	42.3
Taylor Maritime	42.3
Literacy Capital	38.9
Gresham house Energy Storage	36.7
BlackRock Energy and Resources income	36.0
BH Macro (USD)	35.7
Hipgnosis Songs	34.5
Riverstone Credit Opportunities	32.9

Source: Morningstar, QuotedData. Note: excludes trusts with market caps below £15m at 31/12/22.

Figure 3: Worst performing funds in price terms in 2022

	%
JPMorgan Emerging Europe, Middle East and Africa	(87.7)
Chrysalis Investments	(68.6)
Home REIT	(68.6)
Seraphim Space	(64.0)
Schiehallion Fund	(62.6)
EPE Special opportunities	(56.3)
Schroder UK Public Private	(53.3)
Baillie Gifford US Growth	(52.8)
Scottish Mortgage	(45.7)
Tritax EuroBox	(44.6)

Figure 4: Worst performing funds in NAV terms in 2022

	%
JPMorgan Emerging Europe, Middle East and Africa	(94.3)
EPE Special opportunities	(52.8)
Baillie Gifford US Growth	(44.1)
Scottish Mortgage	(41.4)
River & Mercantile Micro Cap	(40.2)
Baillie Gifford European Growth	(38.7)
Manchester & London	(38.0)
Chrysalis Investments	(37.9)
UIL	(37.2)
abrdn UK Smaller Companies Growth	(37.2)

Source: Morningstar, QuotedData. Note: excludes trusts with market caps below £15m at 31/12/22.

Figure 5: Money raised in 2022

	£m
Ruffer Investment Company	369.3
Capital Gearing Trust	357.0
International Public Partnerships	311.0
Cordiant Digital Infrastructure	307.0
The Renewables Infrastructure Group	280.3
Supermarket Income REIT	263.6

Figure 6: Money returned in 2022

	£m
Pershing Square Holdings	(237.7)
Scottish Mortgage	(206.7)
Monks	(180.0)
F&C Investment Trust	(164.8)
Alliance Trust	(147.3)
Witan	(128.8)

Source: Morningstar, QuotedData. Note: based on approximate value of shares at 31/12/22.

FIRST QUARTER 2023

Figure 7: Best performing sectors by total price return over Q1

	Median share price TR (%)	Median NAV TR (%)	Median discount 31/03/23 (%)	Median sector market cap 31/03/23 (£m)	No. of companies in the sector
Technology and media	12.9	17.7	(13.9)	1728.0	2
Europe	9.5	10.2	(10.7)	408.4	7
European smaller companies	4.7	6.6	(14.1)	485.4	3
Latin America	2.8	4.8	(10.9)	68.0	2
Global	2.5	4.2	(10.2)	896.0	16

Figure 8: Worst performing sectors by total price return over Q1

	Median share price TR (%)	Median NAV TR (%)	Median discount 31/03/23 (%)	Median sector market cap 31/03/23 (£m)	No. of companies in the sector
Growth capital	(18.4)	0.0	(54.2)	113.9	7
Property – UK residential	(13.0)	1.1	(55.0)	236.4	7
Property – UK healthcare	(10.8)	1.6	(26.2)	404.0	2
Biotechnology and healthcare	(10.2)	(1.2)	(8.7)	567.0	6
Commodities and natural resources	(10.2)	(0.4)	(13.2)	117.3	9

Source: Morningstar, Marten & Co. Note: inclusive of sectors with at least two companies.
Note: Many alternative asset sector funds release NAV performance on a quarterly basis.

Figure 9: Best performing funds in NAV terms over Q1

	%
Polar Capital Technology	19.1
Manchester & London	17.3
Allianz Technology Trust	16.4
Martin Currie Global Portfolio	16.1
Aurora	14.7
BlackRock Greater Europe	14.1
Marble Point Loan Financing	13.3
Geiger Counter	13.2
Fidelity European Trust	13.1
Baillie Gifford European Growth	12.2

Figure 10: Best performing funds in price terms over Q1

	%
Livermore Investments	24.6
JPMorgan Emerging Europe, ME & Africa	19.0
Amedeo Air Force Plus	18.8
Nippon Active Value	17.4
Polar Capital Technology	16.0
Martin Currie Global Portfolio	15.5
Blackstone Loan Financing	13.5
BlackRock Greater Europe	12.9
Pollen Street	12.6
Doric Nimrod Air Two	12.1

Source: Morningstar, Marten & Co. Note: excludes trusts with market caps below £15m at 31/03/23.

Figure 11: Worst performing funds in NAV terms over Q1

	%
Biotech Growth	(16.5)
Crystal Amber	(13.7)
Riverstone Energy	(12.9)
CQS Natural Resources G&I	(9.3)
Greencoat Renewables	(9.3)
UIL	(8.6)
Greencoat UK Wind	(8.6)
Miton UK Microcap	(8.5)
Third Point Investors USD	(7.8)
India Capital Growth	(7.6)

Figure 12: Worst performing funds in price terms over Q1

	%
HydrogenOne Capital Growth	(40.4)
Schiehallion Fund	(29.6)
Triple Point Social Housing REIT	(28.3)
Digital 9 Infrastructure	(27.9)
Phoenix Spree Deutschland	(24.9)
Chrysalis Investments	(23.7)
Aseana Properties	(23.6)
Residential Secure Income	(23.3)
Globalworth Real Estate Investments	(21.7)
UIL	(18.6)

Source: Morningstar, Marten & Co. Note: excludes trusts with market caps below £15m at 31/03/23.

Figure 13: Money raised over Q1

	£m
BH Macro GBP	304.7
KPMorgan Global Growth & Income	292.0
3i Infrastructure	96.8
City of London	58.3
Ruffer Investment Company	45.1
TwentyFour Income	20.4
Harmony Energy Income Trust	19.7
Merchants Trust	16.8

Figure 14: Money returned over Q1

	£m
Trian Investors 1	(419.8)
Scottish Mortgage	(65.7)
Finsbury Growth & Income	(50.9)
Worldwide Healthcare	(47.4)
RIT Capital Partners	(45.8)
Polar Capital Technology	(39.5)
Smithson Investment Trust	(37.2)
JPMorgan American	(33.1)

Source: Morningstar, Marten & Co. Note: value of shares issued/repurchased as at 31/03/23.

SECOND QUARTER 2023

Figure 15: Best performing sectors by total price return over Q2

	Median share price TR (%)	Median NAV TR (%)	Median discount 30/06/23 (%)	Median sector market cap 30/06/23 (£m)	No. of companies in the sector
India/Indian subcontinent	12.1	11.1	(11.5)	271.0	4
Technology and technology innovation	12.0	11.0	(13.6)	1899.8	2
Private equity	6.9	0.0	(39.2)	344.6	19
Japan	6.7	2.7	(5.9)	246.3	6
Royalties	6.2	(0.9)	(46.1)	601.9	2

Figure 16: Worst performing sectors by total price return over Q2

	Median share price TR (%)	Median NAV TR (%)	Median discount 30/06/23 (%)	Median sector market cap 30/06/23 (£m)	No. of companies in the sector
China/Greater China	(16.9)	(16.3)	(11.6)	204.8	4
Property – UK Logistics	(9.6)	1.3	(33.7)	528.6	3
Commodities and natural resources	(8.6)	(3.3)	(17.4)	49.1	9
Renewable energy infrastructure	(6.8)	1.2	(15.2)	420.5	22
Debt – direct lending	(6.7)	0.2	(28.6)	192.6	8

Source: Morningstar, Marten & Co. Note: inclusive of sectors with at least two companies.
Note: Many alternative asset sector funds release NAV performance on a quarterly basis.

Figure 17: Best performing funds in NAV terms over Q2

	%
BlackRock Latin America	17.7
India Capital Growth	15.9
Manchester & London	15.1
Ashoka India Equity Investments	14.2
Gulf Investment Fund	13.1
RTW Biotech Opportunities	12.3
Allianz Technology Trust	11.9
Polar Capital Technology	10.1
Greencoat Renewables	9.7
JPMorgan American	8.9

Figure 18: Best performing funds in price terms over Q2

	%
Civitas Social Housing	51.4
HydrogenOne Capital Growth	34.9
Manchester & London	22.2
Gulf Investment Fund	21.9
CT Property Trust	19.3
Apax Global Alpha	19.1
India Capital Growth	19.0
abrdn Japan Investment Trust	18.7
Triple Point Social Housing REIT	17.5
Chrysalis Investments Limited	16.9

Source: Morningstar, Marten & Co.

Figure 19: Worst performing funds in NAV terms over Q2

	%
JPMorgan China Growth & Income	(18.5)
abrdn China Investment	(16.6)
Baillie Gifford China Growth Trust	(16.0)
Fidelity China Special	(13.0)
Livermore Investments	(11.9)
Aseana Properties	(10.0)
Schroders Capital Global Innovation Trust	(8.9)
Asia Dragon	(8.4)
Baker Steel Resources	(7.6)
JPMorgan Emerging Europe, ME & Africa	(7.5)

Figure 20: Worst performing funds in price terms over Q2

	%
Seraphim Space Investment Trust	(40.4)
Ecofin US Renewables Infrastructure	(29.6)
Livermore Investments	(28.3)
Warehouse REIT	(27.9)
JPMorgan China Growth & Income	(24.9)
Aquila Energy Efficiency Trust	(23.7)
Balanced Commercial Property	(23.6)
abrdn China Investment	(23.3)
Baillie Gifford China Growth Trust	(21.7)
Tufton Oceanic Assets	(18.6)

Source: Morningstar, Marten & Co. Note: excludes trusts with market caps below £15m at 30/06/23.

Figure 21: Money raised over Q2

	£m
Castelnau Group	101.6
JPMorgan Global Growth & Income	48.4
Gresham House Energy Storage	46.6
TwentyFour Income	29.5
City of London	27.6
Merchants Trust	21.2
Ruffer Investment Company	10.4
Scottish American	7.6

Figure 22: Money returned over Q2

	£m
Worldwide Healthcare	(67.1)
RIT Capital Partners	(59.4)
Alliance Trust	(41.2)
Capital Gearing	(41.1)
Monks	(36.8)
Polar Capital Technology	(34.8)
NB Global Monthly Income Fund Ltd GBP	(34.5)
Witan	(33.8)

Source: Morningstar, Marten & Co. Note: value of shares issued/repurchased as at 30/06/2023.

THIRD QUARTER 2023

Figure 23: Best performing sectors by total price return over Q3

	Median share price TR (%)	Median NAV TR (%)	Median discount 30/09/23 (%)	Median sector market cap 30/09/23 (£m)	No. of companies in the sector
Royalties	32.0	2.2	(44.7)	675.0	2
India/Indian subcontinent	7.1	7.2	(11.7)	293.0	4
Debt – loans and bonds	5.5	4.8	(6.6)	117.0	12
Property – UK logistics	5.4	0.0	(36.2)	518.0	3
Property – UK commercial	4.3	1.4	(28.2)	194.0	15

Figure 24: Worst performing sectors by total price return over Q3

	Median share price TR (%)	Median NAV TR (%)	Median discount 30/06/23 (%)	Median sector market cap 30/06/23 (£m)	No. of companies in the sector
Infrastructure securities	(12.6)	(15.0)	(11.9)	140.0	2
Property – rest of world	(11.9)	0.9	(61.8)	105.0	3
Property – Europe	(11.5)	1.4	(41.6)	30.0	4
Renewable energy infrastructure	(6.2)	1.5	(14.1)	258.0	22
North American smaller companies	(5.3)	(3.2)	(12.7)	352.0	2

Source: Morningstar, Marten & Co. Note: inclusive of sectors with at least two companies.
Note: Many alternative asset sector funds release NAV performance on a quarterly basis.

Figure 25: Best performing funds in NAV terms over Q3

	%
Geiger Counter	48.2
India Capital Growth	14.4
Ashoka India Equity Investment	9.8
CVC Income & Growth EUR	9.6
VietNam Holding	8.5
CQS Natural Resources G&I	7.9
Nippon Active Value	7.3
Temple Bar	7.0
VPC Speciality Lending Investments	6.8
BH Macro USD	6.7

Figure 26: Best performing funds in price terms over Q3

	%
Round Hill Music Royalty	62.0
Seraphim Space Investment Trust	60.2
Geiger Counter	42.5
Symphony International Holding	24.2
Ediston Property Investment Company	23.2
Schroders Capital Global Innovation Trust	19.9
Pantheon international	14.5
Riverstone Energy	14.1
EPE Special Opportunities	13.8
Tritax Big Box	13.2

Source: Morningstar, Marten & Co. Note: excludes trusts with market caps below £15m at 30/09/23.

Figure 27: Worst performing funds in NAV terms over Q3

	%
Premier Miton Global Renewables Trust	(20.2)
Montanaro European Smaller	(11.0)
Golden Prospect Precious Metal	(10.7)
Ecofin Global Utilities & Infrastructure	(9.8)
Martin Currie Global Portfolio	(9.3)
Baillie Gifford European Growth	(9.2)
International Biotechnology	(8.4)
Edinburgh Worldwide	(8.1)
Jupiter Green	(8.0)
Bellevue Healthcare	(8.0)

Figure 28: Worst performing funds in price terms over Q3

	%
Digital 9 Infrastructure	(36.8)
Regional REIT	(36.7)
Gresham House Energy Storage	(26.0)
Syncona	(23.8)
Baker Steel Resources	(20.9)
Globalworth Real Estate Investments	(19.2)
Foresight Sustainable Forestry	(18.5)
Harmony Energy Income Trust	(18.1)
Macau Property Opportunities	(17.3)
Cordiant Digital Infrastructure	(16.2)

Source: Morningstar, Marten & Co. Note: excludes trusts with market caps below £15m at 30/09/23.

Figure 29: Money raised over Q3

	£m
JPMorgan Global Growth & Income	38.0
City of London	21.1
Ashoka India Equity Investment	13.1
Law Debenture Corporation	6.3
Odyssean Investment Trust	4.3

Figure 30: Money returned over Q3

	£m
Worldwide Healthcare	(64.4)
Personal Assets	(61.6)
Capital Gearing	(60.3)
Pershing Square Holdings	(59.1)
Smithson Investment Trust	(51.4)

Source: Morningstar, Marten & Co. Note: excludes trusts with market caps below £15m at 30/09/23.

MONTH BY MONTH NEWS

W E SUMMARISE HERE some of the most important news announcements made by investment trusts over the past 12 months. These month-by-month summaries are extracted from the excellent monthly investment trust reports prepared by the Winterflood investment trust research team and are reproduced here with their kind permission.

HIGHLIGHTS OF OCTOBER–DECEMBER 2022

DATE	FUND	TICKER	SUMMARY
Strategic reviews			
October	US Solar Fund	USF	Strategic review underway including a formal sales process
November	Chrysalis Investments	CHRY	Agreement reached on performance fee structure revision
	JPMorgan Emerging Europe, Middle East & Africa Securities (Then JPMorgan Russian Securities)	JEMA	Policy changes approved
	Majedie Investments	MAJE	Appointment of new manager and amendment to investment policy to pursue a high-conviction, long-term approach unconstrained by geography of any formal benchmark
December	Ground Rents Income Fund	GRIO	Board to consult with shareholders ahead of wind-up resolution due to be proposed by 13 Aug 2023, which would pass if any one shareholder votes in favour of wind-up
Shareholder activism			
December	VPC Specialty Lending Investments	VSL	Open letter from Metage Capital and Staude Capital requisitioning GM. Board confirms receipt of GM requisition notice
Continuation votes			
October	UK Commercial Property REIT	UKCM	EGM convened for 25 October for discount-triggered continuation vote. Continuation vote passed with 99% of votes cast in favour and c.80% turnout
November	Marble Point Loan Financing	MPLS	Continuation vote passed

DATE	FUND	TICKER	SUMMARY
Mergers and acquisitions			
October	Honeycomb Investment Trust	POLN	Merger completes
	JPMorgan Global Growth & Income	JGGI	Heads of terms signed for proposed merger with JPMorgan Elect
November	Monks	MNKS	73% of shares to roll over into from Independent Investment Trust. Merger completes
December	JPMorgan Global Growth & Income	JGGI	JPMorgan Elect listing cancelled; rollover into JPMorgan Global Growth & Income effective
Liquidations			
October	Starwood European Real Estate Finance	SWEF	Proposed orderly realisation as current discount would trigger 75% tender offer
November	Fundsmith Emerging Equities	FMEQF	Listing cancelled
	NB Global Monthly Income	NBMI	Decision to put forward wind-down proposals instead of cash exit
December	SME Credit Realisation Fund	SCRF	Completion of asset realisation strategy, fund to delist in Q1 2023
	VPC Specialty Lending Investments	VSL	Board proposing a managed wind-down, circular to be published
Discount control policies			
November	BioPharma Credit	BPCR	Changes made to discount control mechanism to free up cash
December	Aberdeen Diversified Income & Growth	ADIG	Discount control policy loosened, subject to shareholder approval
Other news			
November	Home REIT	HOME	Short seller attack, board response and delay in annual results
	Princess Private Equity	PEY	Interim dividend suspended following liquidity reduction due to hedging strategy
December	Home REIT	HOME	Additional measures announced; shareholder publishes letter to auditor; shares suspended

JANUARY 2023

DATE	FUND	TICKER	SUMMARY
Fund changes			
10-Jan	Pacific Horizon	PHI	Ben Durrant appointed deputy portfolio manager
18-Jan	JPMorgan Global Growth & Income	JGGI	James Cook joining management team, Rajesh Tanna has departed
19-Jan	Bankers	BNKR	Jeremiah Buckley succeeded Gordon Mackay as US portfolio manager
Portfolio updates			
09-Jan	Baker Steel Resources	BSRT	Caledonia Mining Corp completes acquisition of Bilboes Gold
09-Jan	Nippon Active Value	NAVF	Tender offer for Toka, lapsing on 20 February, in conjunction with other parties
12-Jan	Marwyn Value Investors	MVI	£5m of unsettled VAT claims can now be classified as receivable
13-Jan	Crystal Amber	CRS	CRS has withdrawn GM requisition for Hurricane
19-Jan	Foresight Sustainable Forestry	FSF	Funds raised in June 2022 have been fully deployed
24-Jan	JPMorgan Global Growth & Income	JGGI	C share portfolio realignment now 77% commonality with ordinary shares
25-Jan	JZ Capital Partners	JZCP	Disposal by Deflecto Holdings completed, initial proceeds of $54.3m
26-Jan	Round Hill Music Royalty Fund	RHM	Economic NAV as at 30 September was flat since 30 June
30-Jan	Augmentum Fintech	AUGM	€3m investment in cyber insurance platform Baobab
Issuance and buybacks			
09-Jan	Downing Strategic Micro-Cap	DSM	Board concluded that shareholders would benefit from buybacks
18-Jan	BH Macro	BHMG	Contemplating an equity raise
24-Jan	BH Macro	BHMG	Launched fundraising and share split
Tenders and redemptions			
06-Jan	Alternative Liquidity Fund	ALF	1.5c per share to be returned by way of redeemable B shares
09-Jan	Downing Strategic Micro-Cap	DSM	50% redemption opportunity in May 2024

DATE	FUND	TICKER	SUMMARY
Other news			
03-Jan	JZ Capital Partners	JZCP	Criminal complaints files against parties including JZCP
10-Jan	Aurora	ARR	Performance fee clawback for 0.7% of share capital
23-Jan	Downing Strategic Micro-Cap	DSM	Articles of association require technical amendment to enable buyback
25-Jan	Downing Strategic Micro-Cap	DSM	Circular published to facilitate amendment of articles of association
26-Jan	Majedie	MAJE	New investment objective and policy approved by shareholders
30-Jan	CC Japan Income & Growth	CCJI	Subscription shares may be exercised until 28 February 2023

FEBRUARY 2023

DATE	FUND	TICKER	SUMMARY
Fund changes			
13-Feb	International Biotechnology	IBT	SV Health terminates IMA; Craig and Poszepczynski willing to continue
14-Feb	Polar Capital Global Financials	PCFT	Co-manager John Yakas announces retirement
27-Feb	Mid Wynd International	MWY	Simon Edelsten and Alex Illingworth to depart, Alex Stanic joins to replace
Portfolio updates			
01-Feb	Riverstone Energy	RSE	NAV decreased by 3% over Q4 2022, stable gross MOIC
03-Feb	Augmentum Fintech	AUGM	£4m follow-up investment in Zopa
06-Feb	Riverstone Energy	RSE	$12.5m commitment in Series B funding round for Our Next Energy (ONE)
07-Feb	Syncona	SYNC	Trading update for Q4 2022, NAV TR -5.1% over the quarter
09-Feb	Third Point Investors	TPOU	Investor letter for Q4 2022, Master Fund TR +1.2% over the quarter
09-Feb	Vietnam Opportunity	VOF	Private equity investment in Chicolon Media, $38m funded by consortium
13-Feb	Mobius Investment Trust	MMIT	3 holdings in Turkey monitored following earthquakes
14-Feb	Augmentum Fintech	AUGM	NatWest agrees to acquire Cushon; +46% uplift on 30 September NAV valuation
14-Feb	RTW Venture Fund	RTW	Portfolio company Mineralys raises $192m raised through NASDAQ IPO

DATE	FUND	TICKER	SUMMARY
17-Feb	JPMorgan Global Growth & Income	JGGI	C share portfolio realignment to ordinary shares complete
24-Feb	Nippon Active Value	NAVF	Tender offer for Toka falls through
24-Feb	Third Point Investors	TPOU	Open letter voices concerns on Bath & Body Works, election contest proposed

Issuance and buybacks

DATE	FUND	TICKER	SUMMARY
02-Feb	Castelnau Group	CGL	Proposed issuance of shares for acquisition and rollover
07-Feb	BH Macro	BHMG	Shareholders approve issuance and share split proposals
08-Feb	BH Macro	BHMG	Initial issue price of 431.5p for Sterling class and $4.47 for US Dollar class
08-Feb	Menhaden Resource Efficiency	MHN	Board actively considering buybacks
13-Feb	BH Macro	BHMG	Initial placing raises gross proceeds of £315m
28-Feb	Schroder BSC Social Impact	SBSI	Buybacks commencing 28 February 2023

Tenders and redemptions

DATE	FUND	TICKER	SUMMARY
06-Feb	JPMorgan Indian	JII	Conditional tender offer for up to 25% of share capital in 2025

Other news

DATE	FUND	TICKER	SUMMARY
01-Feb	Templeton Emerging Markets	TEM	Extended undrawn RCF to January 2024, commitment fee amended
02-Feb	Conviction Life Sciences	CLSC	IPO cancelled due to challenging market conditions
09-Feb	CC Japan Income & Growth	CCJI	Subscription shares suspended from 1 March and cancelled on 15 March
13-Feb	abrdn Smaller Companies Income	ASCI	Board announces strategic review given material discount to NAV
15-Feb	JZ Capital Partners	JZCP	Completed early voluntary redemption of subordinated 6% loan notes
15-Feb	Shires Income	SHRS	Board notes ASCI's announcement regarding strategic review
20-Feb	The Investment Company	INV	Board intends to wind up the fund if no solution to liquidity issues found
24-Feb	European Opportunities	EOT	Aggregate management fees reduced from 1 June 2023

MARCH 2023

DATE	FUND	TICKER	SUMMARY
Fund changes			
01-Mar	abrdn Asian Income	AAIF	No change to management despite abrdn's proposed sale of its Jersey DFM business
01-Mar	abrdn Latin American Income	ALAI	No change to management despite abrdn's proposed sale of its Jersey DFM business
01-Mar	BlackRock Frontiers	BRFI	Sudaif Niaz joins management team
06-Mar	India Capital Growth	IGC	AssetCo acquires incumbent manager Ocean Dial, subject to approval
07-Mar	MIGO Opportunities Trust	MIGO	Board serves six months' protective notice after Nick Greenwood's resignation
29-Mar	Global Opportunities Trust	GOT	GOT to terminate IMA with Franklin Templeton after Dr Nairn's resignation
SVB updates			
13-Mar	Augmentum Fintech	AUGM	AUGM has no direct exposure to SVB
13-Mar	Syncona	SYNC	6% indirect exposure to SVB
14-Mar	RIT Capital Partners	RCP	No direct exposure to SVB
15-Mar	F&C Investment Trust	FCIT	0.09% of NAV held as shares in SVB
14-Mar	RTW Venture Fund	RTW	No direct exposure to SVB
Portfolio updates			
01-Mar	JPMorgan Global Growth & Income	JGGI	C share conversion timetable announced
02-Mar	RTW Venture Fund	RTW	New investments in Oricell Therapeutics and Cargo Therapeutics
06-Mar	Castelnau Group	CGL	Ocula receives new investment from Lloyds Banking Group
07-Mar	Nippon Active Value	NAVF	Tender offer for Ihara Science in conjunction with Michael 1925
10-Mar	Oryx International Growth	OIG	OIG reminds investors it sold WANdisco holding in May 2022
13-Mar	JPMorgan Global Growth & Income	JGGI	Conversion ratio of 2.218 ordinary shares per C class share announced
13-Mar	Vinacapital Vietnam Opportunity	VOF	2.6% decrease to NAV as result of NovaGroup revaluation adjustments

DATE	FUND	TICKER	SUMMARY
14-Mar	International Biotechnology	IBT	Acquisition of Seagen (10.2% of NAV) by Pfizer at 32.7% uplift
24-Mar	Castelnau Group	CGL	Suspension of Dignity offer timetable
27-Mar	Utilico Emerging Markets	UEM	Increased carrying value of Petalite led to c2% uplift in NAV
29-Mar	Castelnau Group	CGL	Dignity likely completion date May, further update on fundraising to follow
30-Mar	RTW Venture Fund	RTW	Milestone Pharmaceuticals (0.6% NAV) closed $125m 'strategic financing'
30-Mar	UIL Limited	UTL	Sold holdings in AssetCo and BNK Banking Corporation Limited
31-Mar	Crystal Amber	CRS	GM requisition notice to De La Rue shareholders

Issuance and buybacks

01-Mar	Jupiter Green Investment Trust	JGC	Shareholders granted right to subscribe 31 March 2023, 258.43p on 1:10 basis
16-Mar	CC Japan Income & Growth	CCJI	Subscription share listings cancelled from 15 March
16-Mar	Highbridge Tactical Credit Fund	HTCF	Redemption for 95% outstanding shares; liquidation delayed until Oct 2023

Tenders and redemptions

06-Mar	Tetragon Financial Group	TFG	Board considering $25m tender offer
09-Mar	Tetragon Financial Group	TFG	Tender offer to purchase non-voting shares for maximum of $25m
14-Mar	Weiss Korea Opportunity	WKOF	No participation in realisation opportunity by manager's employees
23-Mar	Gulf Investment Fund	GIF	Tender offer for up to 100% shares
23-Mar	BlackRock Greater Europe	BRGE	Semi-annual tender offer cancelled for May 2023
30-Mar	Highbridge Tactical Credit Fund	HTCF	£2.7m returned in partial compulsory redemption

Other news

02-Mar	Majedie	MAJE	Shareholder approval of transition to new 'liquid endowment' model
03-Mar	Murray International	MYI	Board proposes 1:5 share split following move to 3.1% premium
08-Mar	JPMorgan Emerging EMEA Securities	JEMA	Board to consult shareholders regarding recent AGM results
09-Mar	Henderson Opportunities	HOT	HOT to engage with shareholders regarding recent continuation vote
15-Mar	abrdn Latin American Income	ALAI	ALAI to be wound up

DATE	FUND	TICKER	SUMMARY
16-Mar	Rights & Issues	RIII	1:10 share split proposed by board
17-Mar	Scottish Mortgage	SMT	FT reports board dismissal of Bhidé
20-Mar	Scottish Mortgage	SMT	Bhidé remains director of fund, despite press reports
21-Mar	Scottish Mortgage	SMT	Board announced shake-up: Bhidé, McBain, Subacchi leave
22-Mar	Baillie Gifford Shin Nippon	BGS	Investment objective proposal submitted to shareholders
27-Mar	Rights & Issues	RIII	Share split proposal withdrawn
28-Mar	abrdn Smaller Companies Income	ASCI	Strategic review still ongoing; shortlisted candidates preparing proposals
29-Mar	European Assets	EAT	EMIX benchmark to be replaced with MSCI Europe ex UK SMID Cap Index
30-Mar	AVI Japan Opportunity	AJOT	Response to Japanese Ministry of Economy, Trade and Industry consultation
30-Mar	Schroder BSC Social Impact	SBSI	Move from semi-annual to quarterly NAV reporting
30-Mar	The Investment Company	INV	Board actively considering future of fund; in talks to appoint Chelverton AM

APRIL 2023

DATE	FUND	TICKER	SUMMARY
Fund changes			
03-Apr	abrdn Diversified Income & Growth	ADIG	Name change from Aberdeen Diversified Income and Growth Trust effective 31 March. Ticker, SEDOL and ISIN remain unchanged
03-Apr	abrdn New India	ANII	Name change from Aberdeen New India Investment Trust effective 31 March. Ticker, SEDOL and ISIN remain unchanged
06-Apr	Dunedin Income Growth	DIG	Limit on non-UK exposure to increase to 25% (from 20%) effective 1 May
11-Apr	Martin Currie Global Portfolio	MNP	Management fee reduced to 0.45% of net assets
21-Apr	Aurora	ARR	Underperformance 2019-2022 triggered fee clawback (+1.66p to NAV)
21-Apr	Schroder Japan Trust	SJG	Name change from Schroder Japan Growth, effective 21 April
26-Apr	Global Smaller Companies Trust	GSCT	Weightings of blended benchmark to change to 80%/20% (from 70%/30%)
27-Apr	JPMorgan China Growth & Income	JCGI	Howard Wang relocating to Taiwan, status change to advisor. Rebecca Jiang will be lead investment manager

DATE	FUND	TICKER	SUMMARY
Portfolio updates			
05-Apr	Crystal Amber	CRS	Letter to accompany De La Rue requisition notice
05-Apr	Syncona	SYNC	Led Series A for Mosaic Therapeutics, committing £16.5m
12-Apr	Crystal Amber	CRS	Hurricane Energy to be acquired by Prax. +37.4p pro-forma NAV uplift as at 31 March
13-Apr	Caledonia Investments	CLDN	Confirmed press speculation on possible acquisition
13-Apr	Marwyn Value Investors	MVI	In discussions to acquire >30% of Unbound Group, requiring waiver from Takeover Panel
13-Apr	Round Hill Music Royalty Fund	RHM	Economic NAV per share as at 31 December 2022 of $1.28, +$43m portfolio valuation over 2022. Commissioned FTI for second opinion on valuation
17-Apr	RTW Venture Fund	RTW	Top holding Prometheus Biosciences to be acquired by Merck at a 75% premium
19-Apr	Crystal Amber	CRS	Requisition notice to remove chairman of De La Rue withdrawn upon resignation
19-Apr	RIT Capital Partners	RCP	Update on portfolio, addressing discussion around private valuations
21-Apr	Caledonia Investments	CLDN	Announced acquisition of AIR-serv
21-Apr	Castelnau Group	CGL	Offer for Dignity is now unconditional
24-Apr	North Atlantic Smaller Companies	NAS	Proposed acquisition of Sureserve Group at 40% premium to share price
26-Apr	RTW Venture Fund	RTW	Participation in Series B for Abdera Therapeutics
Issuance and buybacks			
04-Apr	Geiger Counter	GCL	Reminder for 1:5 subscription rights at 51.52p
11-Apr	Ashoka WhiteOak Emerging Markets	AWEM	Intention to float, targeting £100m gross proceeds. Global Emerging Markets focus
19-Apr	Jupiter Green Investment Trust	JGC	No new shares issued as a result of annual subscription exercise
Refinancing			
03-Apr	JPMorgan Global Growth & Income	JGGI	Purchased £1,401 of £200k 4.5% perpetual debenture 'indenture stock'
06-Apr	JPMorgan Japanese	JFJ	New RCF of ¥10bn secured with the capacity to increase by a further ¥2bn
Tenders and redemptions			
06-Apr	Diverse Income Trust	DIVI	Reminder for annual voluntary redemption facility

DATE	FUND	TICKER	SUMMARY
12-Apr	Gulf Investment Fund	GIF	Tender offer closed, 0.25m shares tendered (0.6% of share capital)
12-Apr	Tetragon Financial Group	TFG	Repurchased 2.3m shares at $10.75 for aggregate $25m
17-Apr	Gulf Investment Fund	GIF	Final tender offer value $0.5m
24-Apr	Gulf Investment Fund	GIF	Tender offer completed, tendered shares cancelled
28-Apr	abrdn Asia Focus	AAS	Reminder for annual voluntary redemption facility
Other news			
03-Apr	JPMorgan Global Growth & Income	JGGI	Purchased £1.4k of £200k indenture stock. 0.06% thereof remains outstanding
06-Apr	Dunedin Income Growth	DIG	Limit on exposure to non-UK companies to increase from 20% to 25%
06-Apr	JPMorgan Japanese	JFJ	New RCF of ¥10bn with the capacity to increase by a further ¥2bn
25-Apr	Murray International	MYI	Share split 1:5 completed, new ISIN and SEDOL
28-Apr	Smithson	SSON	All resolutions passed; board to consult shareholders following chair re-election vote having less than 80% of votes cast in favour

MAY 2023

DATE	FUND	TICKER	SUMMARY
Fund changes			
18-May	abrdn Latin American Income	ALAI	Details of wind up proposals released
19-May	abrdn Japan	AJIT	Proposed merger with NAVF
25-May	Momentum Multi-Asset Value Trust	MAVT	Proposed wind up following buyback depleting fund size
Portfolio updates			
09-May	RTW Venture Fund	RTW	Portfolio company Acelyrin announces upsized $540m IPO and admission to NASDAQ
11-May	Marwyn Value Investors	MVI	No further discussions to be made regarding potential Unbound Group investment
25-May	Marwyn Value Investors	MVI	£8m investment made into Palmer Street Limited
25-May	Round Hill Music Royalty Fund	RHM	Economic NAV as at 31 March 2023 of $602.6m

DATE	FUND	TICKER	SUMMARY
Issuance and buybacks			
02-May	Ashoka WhiteOak Emerging Markets	AWEM	IPO completed; £30.5m raised vs £100m target. Dealings to commence 3 May
04-May	Troy Income & Growth	TIGT	£16.7m shares repurchased as part of zero discount control policy
05-May	Geiger Counter	GCL	Receipt of 70,655 ordinary share subscriptions not exercised
09-May	VietNam Holding	VNH	Repurchase of 31,045 shares at average price of 259p
16-May	Riverstone Energy	RSE	£11m of £46m buybacks unused; proposing further £30m buybacks at AGM
30-May	Augmentum Fintech	AUGM	Commenced irrevocable share buyback programme until publication of annual report to 31 March 2023
Tenders and redemptions			
09-May	Downing Strategic Micro-Cap	DSM	Shareholders to be offered 50% redemption opportunity in May 2024 at NAV less costs
10-May	Diverse Income Trust	DIVI	Redemption requests received for 10.5% of issued share capital
11-May	Weiss Korea Opportunity	WKOF	Redemption requests received for 0.06% of issued share capital
24-May	Weiss Korea Opportunity	WKOF	All realisation shares will be compulsorily redeemed at 15 May NAV
26-May	Third Point Investors	TPOU	Change to redemption policy; reduction in management fees
30-May	JPMorgan China Growth & Income	JCGI	Conditional tender offer not triggered due to NAV outperformance
Other news			
03-May	International Biotechnology	IBT	IBT's manager, SV Health, served notice of termination. Six potential managers shortlisted and are in the process of being reviewed
03-May	Scottish Mortgage	SMT	Board announced appointment of Sharon Flood and Vikram Kumaraswamy as NEDs with effect from 17 May
23-May	Aberforth Smaller Companies	ASL	Refinanced existing RCF in same amount of £130m for further 3 years

JUNE 2023

DATE	FUND	TICKER	SUMMARY
Fund changes			
01-Jun	JPM Global Emerging Markets Income	JEMI	Retirement of co-portfolio manager Jeffrey Roskell, effective from Q1 2024
07-Jun	Securities Trust of Scotland	STS	Changed name to STS Global Income & Growth Trust
07-Jun	STS Global Income & Growth Trust	STS	Name change from Securities Trust of Scotland
27-Jun	Invesco Perpetual UK Smaller Cos	IPU	Deputy portfolio manager promoted to co-portfolio manager
27-Jun	Mid Wynd International	MWY	Appointment of Lazard as new manager, effective September 2023
27-Jun	RTW Biotech Opportunities	RTW	Name change from RTW Venture Fund
Portfolio updates			
01-Jun	Castelnau Group	CGL	Conversion to equity of convertible loan to Silverwood Brands
02-Jun	Augmentum Fintech	AUGM	Cushion acquisition completed at +46.2% uplift to 30 September 2022 carrying value
07-Jun	AVI Japan Opportunity	AJOT	Response to NC Holding opposition to shareholder proposals
09-Jun	Syncona	SYNC	Portfolio company Quell Therapeutics agrees $2bn partnership with AstraZeneca
12-Jun	Syncona	SYNC	Led £96m Series A for Beacon Therapeutics, committing £75m
22-Jun	Augmentum Fintech	AUGM	Follow-on investment in £5.4m in Volt through $60m Series B
Borrowings			
01-Jun	Third Point Investors	TPOU	Intends to discontinue use of gearing. Repaying $150m loan
02-Jun	Murray International	MYI	Repaid maturing £60m 5Y fixed rate loan, reducing total borrowings to £140m
12-Jun	abrdn Latin American Income	ALAI	Repaid £6m RCF
26-Jun	abrdn Equity Income	AEI	Renewed £30m RCF to expire in 2026
28-Jun	AVI Global Trust	AGT	Preliminary agreement to issue 10Y ¥4.5bn fixed rate unsecured debt 1.44%

DATE	FUND	TICKER	SUMMARY
Issuance and buybacks			
08-Jun	Pershing Square Holdings	PSH	New $100m share buyback program (up to 5m shares)
Tenders and redemptions			
07-Jun	Diverse Income Trust	DIVI	Redemption requests for 38.3m shares received, redemption price 89.35p
09-Jun	Crystal Amber	CRS	Declared £20.8m dividend following £34.7m proceeds from Hurricane takeover
Other news			
01-Jun	Third Point Investors	TPOU	TPOU to discontinue use of its gearing facility, effective 2 June
01-Jun	Castelnau Group	CGL	Conversion of £1.5m convertible loan to Silverwood Brands into equity
02-Jun	Murray International	MYI	MYI repaid maturing £60m 5-year fixed-rate loan with RBS
06-Jun	abrdn Japan	AJIT	Rollover into NAVF expected in Q3 2023. Cash exit opportunity for 25% of shares
07-Jun	AVI Japan Opportunity	AJOT	AVI responds to NC Holding's opposition to shareholder proposals
08-Jun	Third Point Investors	TPOU	Significant shareholder opposition to re-appointment of COO/General Counsel
09-Jun	The Investment Company	INV	Published circular outlining proposals including new manager and amended objective
13-Jun	abrdn Latin American Income	ALAI	Wind up resolutions approved
16-Jun	Hipgnosis Songs Fund	SONG	SONG among plaintiffs in $250m civil suit against Twitter
20-Jun	abrdn Diversified Income & Growth	ADIG	Strategic review following persistent discount
27-Jun	The Investment Company	INV	Proposed changes passed with over 99% of votes cast in favour
29-Jun	abrdn New India	ANII	Proposed policy change to enable 10% of NAV investment in unquoted companies

JULY 2023

DATE	FUND	TICKER	SUMMARY
Fund changes			
13-Jul	CT UK High Income	CHI	David Moss to succeed Philip Webster as portfolio manager
21-Jul	JPMorgan European Discovery	JEDT	Management fee will be reduced from 0.85% to 0.75% of net assets p.a.

DATE	FUND	TICKER	SUMMARY
27-Jul	MIGO Opportunities Trust	MIGO	AVI appointed as AIFM and investment manager
Strategy updates			
05-Jul	RTW Biotech Opportunities	RTW	Detailed capital allocation plans following $92m Prometheus proceeds
13-Jul	Hipgnosis Songs Fund	SONG	Considering options to enhance shareholder value ahead of continuation vote
14-Jul	Hipgnosis Songs Fund	SONG	FT reports on potential strategic sale of assets to 'prove' NAV
21-Jul	Asia Dragon	DGN	Agreed terms for combination with abrdn New Dawn (ABD)
24-Jul	Momentum Multi-Asset Value Trust	MAVT	Published circular in relation to winding up, GM on 15 August
25-Jul	abrdn Diversified Income & Growth	ADIG	Update on strategic review; several proposals received
25-Jul	Boussard & Gavaudan (€)	BGHL	Board will put forward wind-down proposals
26-Jul	abrdn Smaller Companies Income	ASCI	Agreed terms for combination with Shires Income (SHRS)
26-Jul	The Investment Company	INV	Completion of tender offer, appointment of Chelverton and policy amendments
Portfolio updates			
03-Jul	RTW Biotech Opportunities	RTW	Tourmaline Bio to merge with Talaris Therapeutics, cash runway until 2026
05-Jul	AVI Japan Opportunity	AJOT	Results of shareholder proposals for NC Holdings
10-Jul	Castelnau Group	CGL	Facilitated £1.3m acquisition of 25% stake in Warlord Games by Hornby Hobbies
11-Jul	Riverstone Energy	RSE	Anuvia Plant Nutrients in liquidation, $14m write-off for RSE
13-Jul	Round Hill Music Royalty Fund	RHM	Portfolio update for Q1 2023, net revenue +94% YoY, no LFL data provided
17-Jul	RTW Biotech Opportunities	RTW	Apogee completed $300m IPO, +25% on first day of trading
18-Jul	North Atlantic Smaller Companies	NAS	Harwood Private Equity V to sell holding, £2m uplift for NAS
19-Jul	Castelnau Group	CGL	Expects to issue 7.5m shares to fund squeeze out of Dignity minorities
24-Jul	Alliance Trust	ATST	Appointed Dalton Investments as stock picker for 4% of capital

DATE	FUND	TICKER	SUMMARY
26-Jul	North Atlantic Smaller Companies	NAS	NAS responds to Nanoco plc activist shareholder
Borrowings			
14-Jul	Dunedin Income Growth	DIG	Renewed £30m RCF, option to increase to £40m
20-Jul	Impax Environmental	IEM	Issued €60m of privately placed notes, proceeds used to repay drawn debt
27-Jul	AVI Global Trust	AGT	Agreement to issue £25m fixed rate unsecured debt for 10 years at 1.44%
Issuance and buybacks			
03-Jul	Riverstone Energy	RSE	Irrevocable commitment to continue buyback programme
19-Jul	Strategic Equity Capital	SEC	Received £31m proceeds from Medica Group takeover, 50% to be used for buybacks
21-Jul	Weiss Korea Opportunity	WKOF	Significant shareholder opposition against buyback authority
27-Jul	Riverstone Energy	RSE	Repurchased 1.7m shares for £10m since May
Other news			
18-Jul	The Investment Company	SSIF	83.4% of share capital tendered under 100% tender offer
19-Jul	The Investment Company	SSIF	Tender price 337.76p per share (3% discount to NAV as at 18 July)
25-Jul	Worldwide Healthcare Trust	WWH	Shareholder approved 1:10 share split, effective 27 July

AUGUST 2023

DATE	FUND	TICKER	SUMMARY
Fund changes			
01-Aug	Scottish American	SAIN	Ross Mathison appointed deputy portfolio manager
03-Aug	International Biotechnology	IBT	Schroders appointed as manager following resignation of SV Health
10-Aug	JPMorgan Claverhouse	JCH	First tier of management fee reduced from 0.55% to 0.45% on net assets <£400m
11-Aug	Murray International	MYI	Portfolio manager Bruce Stout to retire in June 2024, co-managers to replace
Strategy updates			
11-Aug	Nippon Active Value	NAVF	NAVF and AJG announced their intention to combine

DATE	FUND	TICKER	SUMMARY
15-Aug	Momentum Multi-Asset Value Trust	MAVT	16m shares elected for rollover, 11m shares elected for cash option
24-Aug	Momentum Multi-Asset Value Trust	MAVT	Wind-up approved at GM
30-Aug	Boussard & Gavaudan (€)	BGHL	Circular published outlining managed wind-down proposals. EGM 28 September
31-Aug	Nippon Active Value	NAVF	Proposed mergers with AJIT and AJG to result in 'modest' investment policy revisions
Portfolio updates			
02-Aug	Marwyn Value Investors	MVI	AdvancedAdvT has completed acquisition of five software businesses for £33m
08-Aug	Round Hill Music Royalty Fund	RHM	Acquisition of remainder of Big Loud Shirt catalogue
15-Aug	Marwyn Value Investors	MVI	Follow-on investment for £5m into Silvercloud Holdings for Le Chameau
18-Aug	JPMorgan Emerging EMEA Securities	JEMA	Will seek to participate in tender offers in Russia, to be held in custody account
23-Aug	Riverstone Energy	RSE	Permian Resources to acquire Earthstone Energy for $4.5bn
31-Aug	Round Hill Music Royalty Fund	RHM	Economic NAV as at 30 June was $1.27 per share, FY23 dividend target confirmed
Borrowings			
01-Aug	Bankers	BNKR	To repay its £15m 8% debenture stock
Tenders and redemptions			
17-Aug	Riverstone Energy	RSE	Tender offer for up to 13.8m shares at 43.5% discount to 30 June NAV
30-Aug	Marwyn Value Investors	MVI	Received final amounts in relation to historical Praesepe VAT settlement
Other news			
01-Aug	Scottish Oriental Smaller Companies	SST	Change of benchmark index used for performance fee calculation
07-Aug	Secured Income Fund	SSIF	Listing cancelled effective 4 August

SEPTEMBER 2023

DATE	FUND	TICKER	SUMMARY
Fund changes			
01-Sep	Henderson European Focus	HEFT	John Bennett to retire in August 2024, to be replaced by Tom O'Hara

DATE	FUND	TICKER	SUMMARY
06-Sep	Gulf Investment Fund	GIF	Jubin Jose to step down as manager in December, to be replaced by Bijoy Joy
22-Sep	European Opportunities	EOT	Management fee reduction from 1 June of 0.1% for each of three tiers
27-Sep	JPMorgan Emerging Markets	JMG	Management fee reduction from 1 July, introducing tiers (formerly 0.75% flat fee)
28-Sep	BlackRock Greater Europe	BRGE	Appointed Alexandra Dangoor as co-portfolio manager from 29 September

Strategy updates

DATE	FUND	TICKER	SUMMARY
04-Sep	Nippon Active Value	NAVF	Published detailed proposals relating to rollover of AJIT and AJG into NAVF
08-Sep	Chelverton UK Dividend	SDV	Policy change to enable retaining non-material stakes in companies taken private
08-Sep	Round Hill Music Royalty Fund	RHM	Received cash offer at 67% premium to share price and 11.5% discount to NAV
12-Sep	Atlantis Japan Growth	AJG	Published circular relating to combination with NAVF, EGM scheduled for 10 October
14-Sep	Hipgnosis Songs Fund	SONG	Proposed transaction to sell 29 catalogues for $440m, proceeds to be used for buybacks and deleveraging
21-Sep	Nippon Active Value	NAVF	Shareholders approved policy changes necessary for mergers with AJIT and AJG
25-Sep	abrdn New Dawn	ABD	Published circular relating to combination with DGN, GMs scheduled for 23 October and 8 November
25-Sep	Round Hill Music Royalty Fund	RHM	Published circular for recommended cash offer, shareholder votes on 18 October
29-Sep	abrdn Japan	AJIT	Shareholders approved proposals in relation to NAVF combination, shares suspended from 10 October
29-Sep	Boussard & Gavaudan (€)	BGHL	Shareholders approved proposals in relation to wind-down for € class, £ class adjourned
29-Sep	Hipgnosis Songs Fund	SONG	Chairman to step down, proposed management agreement amendments and further continuation votes

Portfolio updates

DATE	FUND	TICKER	SUMMARY
05-Sep	Caledonia Investments	CLDN	Agreed terms of sale for 7IM majority stake, expected proceeds £255m
05-Sep	RTW Biotech Opportunities	RTW	Participated in $100m Series D for Beta Bionics
07-Sep	Impax Environmental	IEM	Issued €60m of privately placed notes, used to repay debt, and agreed new £80m RCF
11-Sep	Baker Steel Resources	BSRT	Futura completed AU$26.2m financing package, exposure increased to 28.2% of NAV
11-Sep	Syncona	SYNC	Gyroscope milestone payments to be written off, £54.5m impact

DATE	FUND	TICKER	SUMMARY
14-Sep	RTW Biotech Opportunities	RTW	Rocket share price +39% on regulatory development, completed $175m fundraise

Borrowings

DATE	FUND	TICKER	SUMMARY
07-Sep	Impax Environmental	IEM	Issued €60m private notes to funds managed by Pricao Private Capital

Issuance and buybacks

DATE	FUND	TICKER	SUMMARY
18-Sep	Brown Advisory US Smaller Companies	BASC	Policy amendment; now committed to using buybacks to reduce discount volatility and aiming to reduce discount in excess of peers
29-Sep	Syncona	SYNC	Launched £40m buyback programme, capital pool £613m as at 30 June

Tenders and redemptions

DATE	FUND	TICKER	SUMMARY
06-Sep	Ashoka India Equity	AIE	Received redemption requests for 0.5% of share capital
08-Sep	Marwyn Value Investors	MVI	Compulsory redemption of £1.05m for 2016 Realisation shares
21-Sep	BlackRock Greater Europe	BRGE	Board decided against implementing semi-annual tender in November
21-Sep	Gulf Investment Fund	GIF	100% tender offer opening at 21 September, subject to minimum size condition
25-Sep	Marwyn Value Investors	MVI	26.7% of 2016 Realisation shares to be redeemed on 5 October
28-Sep	Riverstone Energy	RSE	7% of share capital tendered at £5.78 per share, payment 6 October

Other news

DATE	FUND	TICKER	SUMMARY
14-Sep	CQS Natural Resources Growth & Income	CYN	Special interim dividend 3p per share, on receipt of non-recurring income
20-Sep	Utilico Emerging Markets	UEM	At AGM, 25.9% of votes were cast against the re-election of Mr. Stobart
29-Sep	Schroder Japan Trust	SJG	Resolution to allow investment in CFDs to be voted on at AGM

OCTOBER 2023

DATE	FUND	TICKER	SUMMARY

Fund changes

DATE	FUND	TICKER	SUMMARY
02-Oct	Mid Wynd International	MWY	Appointed Lazard as investment manager from 29 September
03-Oct	Edinburgh Investment Trust	EDIN	Manager James de Uphaugh to retire in February 2024, Imran Sattar to replace

DATE	FUND	TICKER	SUMMARY
Strategy updates			
02-Oct	Pershing Square Holdings	PSH	Received regulatory approval for SPARC structure, targeting companies aiming to raise at least $1.5bn
03-Oct	Atlantis Japan Growth	AJG	Published timetable for combination with NAVF
04-Oct	Henderson High Income	HHI	Proposed rollover of HDIV into HHI, no policy or manager change for HHI
06-Oct	Boussard & Gavaudan (€)	BGHL	Previously adjourned £ class shareholder meeting held, resolutions relating to wind-down approved
Portfolio updates			
05-Oct	Syncona	SYNC	Follow-on investment in SwanBio for $10m to support clinical trial, valued at £77.1m
Issuance and buybacks			
04-Oct	Onward Opportunities	ONWD	Raised £3.4m via subscription by new and existing investors at 1.5% premium to NAV
04-Oct	Riverstone Energy	RSE	Commitment to continue share buyback until publication of 30 September valuation
Tenders and redemptions			
02-Oct	Ashoka India Equity	AIE	Redemption completed at price of 225.34p per share, payments expected by 13 Oct
05-Oct	Miton UK MicroCap	MINI	Received redemption requests for 18.7% of share capital
Other news			
02-Oct	India Capital Growth	IGC	AssetCo acquisition of Ocean Dial Asset Management, investment team unchanged
04-Oct	Rockwood Strategic	RKW	Share split on 1:10 basis effective on 11 October

 **Invesco**

Uncovering income opportunities in the high yield bond market

BIPS invests primarily in high-yielding fixed-interest securities with the aim of providing a mix of capital growth and income to shareholders.

Portfolio managers Rhys Davies and Edward Craven, supported by their team, typically invest in a diversified portfolio of bonds issued by large and medium-sized businesses across the sectors of the economy, both corporates and financials. They are also happy, to a limited degree, to invest in bonds that have come under price pressure but where they believe the companies could turn around their businesses.

Capital at risk
The portfolio has a significant proportion of high-yielding bonds, which are of lower credit quality and may result in large fluctuations in the NAV of the product. The product may invest in contingent convertible bonds which may result in significant risk of capital loss based on certain trigger events. The product uses derivatives for efficient portfolio management which may result in increased volatility in the NAV.

The Company has a clearly defined income provision with a target dividend of

11.5 pence

per share per year, paid quarterly*

* Dividend policies and future divide payments are determined by the Board and are not guaranteed.

Scan the QR code or speak to your financial adviser to find out more.

HARD GOING

Trust expert MAX KING *reviews the performance of investment trusts in 2023.*

AFTER A DISMAL year for equity and bond markets in 2022, the outlook for 2023 seemed much better as the year kicked off. Russia's invasion of Ukraine had failed and commodity prices were retreating. An inflation peak was in sight and although interest rates clearly had further to rise, that was largely discounted. A recession was still widely expected but that again was in the price, and companies had had both time and warning to batten down the hatches.

Promise and disappointment

Equity markets had reached a low and bond yields a high in October 2022 and were steadily recovering. The average discount to net asset value across the investment trust universe had risen from 1.5% to 14.4%, resulting in terrible share price performance, but had slipped to 13.4% by year end. Better equity and bond performance in 2023 and lower discounts promised a return to investment trust outperformance.

In the event it has turned out to be much more of a struggle than expected. Equity markets have rallied, with the MSCI All Country World Index returning 7.8% in sterling in the year to 30 September; but the UK, a positive relative performer in 2022, has returned to its traditional under-performance. Although a recession has failed to materialise, inflation has been falling more or less as expected, but bond yields have risen to new 15-year peaks as real yields, too low for at least 10 years, shifted to being historically high.

Equity markets have been driven higher by a return to favour of technology-related stocks, especially the top eight names in the S&P 500: Amazon, Apple, Alphabet, Nvidia, Microsoft, Facebook, Tesla and Netflix. These companies have benefited from investor excitement about the prospects for artificial intelligence (AI), but they had also acted swiftly in 2022 to reduce costs, focus their investments and raise investor returns. Value investing has returned to the doghouse, while banks were able to shrug off a series of secondary bank collapses in the spring.

Most disappointingly for holders of investment trusts, discounts have widened again to reach 17.9%, resulting in poor performance for much of the sector. The high-yielding alternatives sector was particularly hard hit, with average discounts rising to 23% as bond yields rose. Renewable energy trusts were also affected by a growing backlash against renewable energy funds. This meant that the sector continued to underperform the broad market. The rise in the discount of conventional trusts to around 12% was more modest.

The FTSE Closed End Investments Index comprises the largest 194 investment companies but excludes 3i, which had an excellent year, and most REITs, which didn't. In terms of total return, the index fell 1.4% in sterling in the first quarter, 1.3% in the second and 0.5% in the third, compared with +3.1%, −0.5% and +1.9% for the All-Share Index. The performance was worse compared with global indices; the MSCI World Index in sterling returned 4.4% in the first quarter, 3.3% in the second and −0.6% in the third. Discount widening accounted for about 4% of the underperformance, so there was clearly asset underperformance as well.

Net outflows of capital

Inevitably, given wide discounts, new issuance was modest at only £1.2bn in the first nine months of 2023, mostly in the first quarter. It is the slowest pace of issuance since 2010. There was just one new issue – £30m for Ashoka WhiteOak Emerging Markets – the rest being secondary issues by the few trusts that continued to trade on premiums. These were led by BH Macro (£315m), 3i Infrastructure (£102m), JP Morgan Global Growth & Income (£88m) and City of London (£85m). With just 22 investment companies, 6.5% of the total, trading at premiums at the end of August, issuance is likely to be negligible in the rest of the year too.

In contrast returns of capital going into the final quarter of the year totalled £4.4bn, of which £2.8bn was in the form of buybacks, led by Worldwide Healthcare (£113m), RIT (£144m), Scottish Mortgage (£74m) and Pershing Square (£71m). Trusts with rigorous discount control mechanisms, such as Capital Gearing and Personal Assets, were as good as their word, buying back £90m in the first half and another £120m in the third quarter, while Ruffer followed suit in August, buying back for the first time in 19 years when its share price fell to a 7.5% discount.

More than £1.3bn was returned to investors as a result of the takeover of Industrials REIT (£510m), the in specie distribution of shares by Trian (£440m) and the wind-down of NB Global Monthly Income (£149m). CT Property (£194m) was acquired by LondonMetric Property in an all-shares merger. In addition, Axiom European Financial Debt (£84m) and Momentum Multi-Asset (£40m) were liquidated, as was Aberdeen Latin American Income (£36m) as part of Aberdeen's efforts to rationalise its once-ragged list of funds.

Aberdeen New Dawn announced a merger with Asia Dragon, involving a partial return of capital, and Aberdeen Smaller Companies Income with Shires Income. Aberdeen Diversified Income & Growth is "reviewing its options" while Aberdeen Japan is merging with separately managed Nippon Active Value – again with a partial return of capital. Atlantis Japan subsequently also announced a merger with Nippon Active Value.

Management changes included the decision of Mid Wynd to move from Artemis to Lazards following the retirement of its lead manager and the move of MIGO Opportunities, together with its management team, from Miton to AVI following a prolonged dispute. Having acquired 75% of Greencoat Capital, the managers of two renewable energy trusts, in 2022 Schroders increased its list of managed trusts by acquiring the management of International Biotechnology Trust from SV Health Investors.

Winners and losers

Poor asset performance in 2022 was largely explained by market weakness, but the sector continued to struggle in 2023. The relentless rise in bond yields held equity markets back and was a particular headwind for the alternative income sector. The renewables sector was further hit by a public backlash against the forced march to net zero. UK listed trusts, even those investing internationally, were affected by universal pessimism in the UK about the country's prospects.

Relatively few trusts outperformed their benchmarks in terms of investment return in the first nine months, and that contributed to widening discounts which, in turn, led to broader disillusion. Even the specialist technology trusts couldn't justify being overweight the eight mega-cap tech stocks as they rose to account for 27% of the S&P 500 Index and came to be priced at over 30 times forward earnings. Polar Capital Technology (+29%) and Allianz Technology (+25%) were among the best performers in the trust sector, but even they underperformed their benchmarks, as did the tech-focused Manchester & London (+29%).

Still, there were other winners. Private equity may have remained in the doldrums but 3i (+55%) and Literacy Capital (+29%) had outstanding years, both helped by discounts to net asset value turning to premiums. The acquisitive Nippon Active Value justified its expansion by returning 32% (and 16% in net asset value terms); the Japanese market performed exceptionally well in local currency terms, but the 11% fall in the yen against sterling trimmed those gains for UK shareholders.

A bid for Round Hill Music Royalty resulted in a 46% gain and Georgia Capital returned 35% on a 29% increase in NAV as Georgia benefited from being the back door to Russia. India Capital Growth (+24%) defied the global aversion to small and midcap companies, but the biggest winner was even more contrarian, the Russia-focused JP Morgan EMEA, up 63%, a move that represents either blind optimism or deep insight, given that all its Russian holdings were marked down to zero and remain untradeable after the invasion of Ukraine.

The losers in the first nine months were at least as contrarian as the winners. In times of economic and market uncertainty, defensive trusts with good yields might have been expected to perform best. Instead, many of the worst performers were real estate investment trusts, infrastructure funds and renewable energy. Other notable losers were the highly defensive BH Macro (−21%), biotech funds (Syncona −35%, Biotech Growth −16%), which have derived no lasting benefit from the pandemic, and Baillie Gifford's growth capital trust Schiehallion (−37%), now trading at just half its 2019 issue price and 83% below its late 2021 peak.

There were also two outright disasters, ThomasLloyd Energy Impact and Home REIT, whose shares remain suspended after uncovering serious problems that will produce an as yet unquantified permanent loss of capital. These were both relatively recent new issues, showing the risk involved in investing in untested propositions when issuance is strong. The largest shareholder in the former was the UK's Foreign and Commonwealth Office, so investors can't say they weren't warned.

Looking ahead

What will it take to cause a turnaround in the fortunes of investment trusts and issuance exceeding returns of capital? Outside the big eight mega-cap US stocks, the S&P 500 looks reasonable value, while US small and midcaps look cheap, as are nearly all markets in the rest of the world. Both interest rates and bond yields are probably at or close to peaks, and fears of a resurgence in inflation are diminishing.

The global economy has slowed with some regions experiencing mild recession, but so widely has this been expected that companies have been able to take measures to protect profits. These have turned out better than expected, a trend that is likely continue.

In the alternatives sector, investors have worried that asset values were overstated, despite repeated announcements of robust numbers. The bid in September for Round Hill Music at a 67% premium to the share price supports the valuers rather than the market; if investors do not respond by narrowing discounts, more bids can be expected.

The stuttering progress of equity markets in 2023 should broaden and become smoother in 2024, which should help investment trusts not only to generate absolute but also relative performance. This, in turn, should encourage a return of net buying by investors and a narrowing of discounts. Just because the outcome of 2023 was disappointing does not mean that it will continue to be so. Perhaps, the longer the wait, the more it will be worth waiting for.

MAX KING *was a fund manager and investment strategist at Finsbury Asset Management, J.O.Hambro and Investec Asset Management. He is now an independent writer with a regular column in MoneyWeek and an adviser with a special interest in investment companies.*

THE DARKEST HOUR?

Investment trust expert JOHN BARON *explains why he is increasing the equity exposure within the ten live portfolios managed on the website www.johnbaronportfolios.co.uk*

MY CHAPTER IN last year's *Handbook* (A New Market Regime) suggested investors recognise that the transition to higher and more volatile inflation, lower growth and higher debt, is necessitating a change in portfolio construction. A new investment landscape is upon us. Caution was also advocated, given a variety of factors.

At the time of writing, investment trust discounts are now at their widest since 1990, apart from a brief moment during the financial crisis of 2008–09, and market sentiment generally is poor relative to outlook. Having been more defensively positioned, which has compensated somewhat for the volatility, our portfolios are now pivoting toward equities and seeking to capitalise on an array of opportunities – as ever, stock selection being key.

Discount disdain

It has been a difficult year for investors in investment trusts. Discounts have widened, in some cases significantly so, as share prices have increasingly trailed net asset values (NAV) and market indices more generally. Investors have been selling and many holders are understandably nervous as to whether worse is to come.

To a certain extent, this becomes self-fulfilling – as prices weaken, more sellers appear. Sentiment has not been helped by the poor performance of some high-profile companies, particularly those pursuing an overtly growth remit such as Scottish Mortgage Trust (SMT), a FTSE 100 company.

Meanwhile, those trusts focused on smaller companies have underperformed, rising interest and discount rates have undermined many alternative assets (including infrastructure and renewable energy), while private equity investors have thrown in the towel. Markets will continue to be volatile as investors adjust to the new market regime and continuing shift in style towards 'value' investments. The transition to 'sound' money from 'free' money was never going to be smooth.

This is an inflection point, and market volatility in part acknowledges this adjustment, as do widening discounts. There are nuances regarding this issue. An evolving shareholder base perhaps suggests investment trusts are no longer the City's best kept secret. The growing presence of the retail investor at the expense of institutions is welcome, something for which many of us have campaigned.

But some investors are tempted to sell when waters are choppy and only buy when they are calm. Current discounts may in part reflect this. And at a time of consolidation within the wealth management sector, marketability becomes an issue; smaller companies are increasingly being shunned and discounts have suffered accordingly.

Another factor is cost disclosure. Because of an over-zealous interpretation of regulations and guidance by the various authorities, companies have had to roll up their corporate costs (management, financing, administrative etc.) with the fund managers' charges when declaring an overall cost figure, even though share prices reflect investors' assessment of such costs.

This double counting does not happen in other countries. The result is costs have looked high and, in an industry where more emphasis is wrongly set on cost disclosure than on performance net of fees, investment trusts have been increasingly shunned by wealth managers and investment platforms alike. Many of us are questioning those responsible and a positive dialogue is ongoing.

The need for perspective

Many company boards and stakeholders have taken up the gauntlet in trying to correct the various issues, including the discount tide. Smaller companies in particular have announced strategic reviews and combinations or mergers to ensure remits are focused on shareholders' interests and marketability is not an impediment to an otherwise positive outlook. Boards are also buying back more shares to stimulate demand and assist their NAVs.

Of course, good performance is usually the best panacea over time, but such is the malaise and poor sentiment that even good-performing companies are on wider discounts. Such factors and global uncertainties notwithstanding, experience suggests we are reaching a point where a lot of bad news is in the price. Mention it quietly but, with some exceptions, NAV performance has been sound relative to indices. Indeed there have been many notable outperformers.

Yet, courtesy of poor share price performance, the average discount has drifted out to levels not seen for 30 years, except for a brief period during the financial crisis. This widening has often been indiscriminate. Therein lies the opportunity for long-term investors willing to ride out any further volatility.

Investment trusts are particularly well-placed to capitalise on a positive shift in market sentiment when compared with their open-ended cousins, unit trusts. Because the share price is traded and not the assets, redemptions do not impact managers. Their ability to borrow and so 'gear' a portfolio also helps in rising markets.

These structural advantages largely account for investment trusts' proud track record of outperformance of unit trusts and indices. Performance can also benefit from an independent board of directors which scrutinises performance, remit and costs, and can and does remove managers as necessary.

Unusually wide discounts, these companies' inherent strengths which have stood the test of time, and poor market sentiment, in combination provide an opportunity for investors to benefit from a triple tailwind – narrowing discounts, resumed outperformance and rising markets. With apologies to Meatloaf, even two out of three isn't bad! It is usually wise to invest when sentiment trails the fundamentals, particularly when the disconnect is pronounced. There is nothing to suggest it will be different this time. Indeed, quite the contrary. But first the plague of forecasting needs to be put into perspective.

Forecasting folly

Market sentiment is unduly poor, in part because of erroneous yet influential economic forecasts from various financial institutions. J.K. Galbraith, the renowned Canadian-American economist, once said, "The only function of economic forecasting is to make astrology look respectable." This prescient insight is usually ignored, and undue importance attributed to forecasts by various economic, financial and government organisations, even though track records leave little doubt as to their worth. Yet, this folly is accepted, quoted by media outlets, and therefore often casts a long shadow, as is presently the case with the markets.

The International Monetary Fund (IMF) led the way recently on behalf of most of its peers in forecasting economic recession. As recently as the spring, their strategists were more bearish than at any point since the financial crisis of 2008–09. Yet now it has turned on a sixpence and raised its global growth forecast to 3% for 2024.

Talk of recession has vanished into thin air. Indeed, 25 of the IMF's last 28 UK growth forecasts have been too low; until only recently it was forecasting the UK would be one of the few European countries to go into recession. That is not how events have transpired, with the Office for National Statistics (ONS) recently upgrading past growth for 2020 and 2021.

This folly is also evident at home. The Office for Budgetary Responsibility (OBR) has had to significantly reduce its public sector net borrowing forecasts on several occasions. A list of 30 economic forecasts recently compiled by *The Sunday Times* showed that the OBR came third from bottom.

Meanwhile, the Bank of England's record on inflation is dire, having been long behind the curve. The defence of 'external shocks' does not wash. The period before Russia's invasion of Ukraine, the biggest 'shock' of all, saw inflation rising steeply and reaching 6.1%, yet interest rates were still at 0.5%, well below what was needed to achieve its 2% inflation target.

Ben Bernanke, the former chairman of the Federal Reserve, has since been invited to conduct a fundamental review of the Bank of England's modelling, yet many believe his record on quantitative easing (QE) does not inspire confidence. The large institutions are not alone. In the summer of last year, CEOs of large international investment houses joined the chorus in predicting an 'economic hurricane', recession, and worse.

Market pessimism

While recognising occasional significant changes in the investment landscape, the lesson for investors is always to focus on where company fundamentals are relative to sentiment, and not on economic forecasts which shift with the sand. Whisper it gently, but reality is yet again proving the consensus forecasts wrong. Economies have not slipped into recession. Budget deficits and finances generally are better than expected.

Company results have not plunged into the abyss. Corporate finances are in good shape and defaults remain low. Bond yields have not risen as far as confidently predicted. And stock markets have rallied and made steady progress. While inflation is high, and will remain stickier than hitherto, it will fall further in the short term as one-off variables fall away. We may indeed be approaching peak interest rates. This is the economic reality.

The market is certainly sensing it. It is climbing the wall of worry. Corporate earnings have been resilient because companies saw the problems ahead and tightened their belts by reducing costs and borrowing. This protected margins and profits, as is evidenced in part by the spread between corporate and government bond yields widening only fractionally. Little wonder the US market has been pleasantly surprised by strong earnings.

Anyone concerned about the 'narrowness' of the market's rise, being led by a few big tech companies, should take comfort from the 2019–21 rally which broadened once it was evident that the economy was improving. And economies are moving along. In large part, the truer litmus test as to their health is the unemployment rate, especially important given it is a social evil. Levels both in the UK and US compare favourably, with UK employment being at a record high.

Meanwhile, ironically, the forecasting folly has conditioned markets to bad news. With money supply growth now negative and budget deficits retreating, the impact of higher interest rates, as indicated by the faltering of lead indicators such as the housing market, suggest the peak is near. This should be supportive for markets.

In short, there will always be risks in investment. But now is a good time to be investing in equities, as it becomes increasingly evident that the risks are falling away. Do not wait for the forecasters to suggest it is, because by then it will probably be too late, perhaps even time to sell.

As ever, it will be prudent to retain some firepower via more defensive assets, including gold and higher cash levels for more conservative portfolios, given that volatility is the usual travelling companion on such a journey. However, while timing is important, it is usually better to be a little too early than too late. Markets can move rapidly when sentiment shifts.

Stock selection

My recent *Investors Chronicle* columns have pointed to the equity preferences of the ten live investment trust portfolios managed on the website www.johnbaronportfolios. co.uk. This has centred on the UK market and private equity. The UK looks attractive relative to many others on a variety of metrics, including yield, rating and outlook. The increased focus on value as an investment theme will also provide a modest tailwind given the market's composition. Favoured stocks have included Finsbury Growth & Income (FGT), Fidelity Special Values (FSV), The Merchants Trust (MRCH) and The Mercantile Trust (MRC).

Private equity companies look attractive given their excellent track records and the extent of their discounts. These discounts are more than compensating for expectations that NAVs will come under pressure given the wider economic scenario. Those expectations tend to downplay the often-conservative valuations attributed to investments by the managers, as seen when investments are realised. Portfolio holdings include HarbourVest Global Private Equity (HVPE), Pantheon International (PIN) and, where income is a factor, CT Private Equity Trust (CTPE) and abrdn Private Equity Opportunities (APEO).

Exposure has also been increased to other markets and sectors which we believe look good value and offer attractive opportunities. More activist shareholders in Japan and the Tokyo Stock Exchange's recent threat to delist those companies which continue to trade on a price/book value of less than one in 2026 are possible catalysts for continued market strength. The Corporate Governance Code, a lower inflation rate than most, and the recent widely publicised visit by Warren Buffett and investments by Berkshire Hathaway, all help the narrative. CC Japan Income & Growth (CCJI) is our favoured holding.

Meanwhile recent events have highlighted the importance of achieving net zero. Environmental, social and governance (ESG) themes continue however to confuse, despite some regulatory progress. The website's Green and Green ISA portfolios therefore focus on the more transparent remit of climate change and have seen a shift away from the more defensive renewable infrastructure sub-sectors toward environmental companies investing in businesses with eco-friendly products, services and technology. Impax Environmental Markets (IEM) and Jupiter Green (JGC) are examples.

More generally, we have also been increasing exposure to emerging markets given the extent that their equity markets have underperformed others over the last decade. Many countries now boast greater economic resilience and stronger growth, with deeper pools of domestic demand. JPMorgan Emerging Markets Income (JEMI), Utilico Emerging Markets (UEM) and BlackRock Frontiers Investment Trust (BRFI) are portfolio holdings. Exposure is complemented by such holdings as Murray International Trust (MYI), AVI Global Trust (AGT) and Scottish Oriental Smaller Companies (SST).

Other globally oriented holdings introduced or added to when increasing the portfolios' equity exposure have included Pershing Square Holdings (PSH), JPMorgan Global Growth & Income (JGGI) and Smithson Investment Trust (SSON). As ever, the objective is to combine good fund managers, sectors and markets offering good prospects, and attractive valuations in either the investment trust or markets, and preferably both. The current investment landscape offers such combinations in good number, for those willing to ride out short-term volatility.

JOHN BARON *is one of the UK's leading experts on investment trusts, a regular columnist and speaker at investment seminars, and author of* The Financial Times Guide to Investment Trusts. *Since 2009, he has reported on two real portfolios in his popular monthly column in the* Investors Chronicle. *The fees are donated to charity.*

His website www.johnbaronportfolios.co.uk reports in real time on the progress of ten live investment trust portfolios which achieve a range of strategies and income levels and possess good track records relative to benchmark. He also chairs the Investment Committee of Baron & Grant, a discretionary fund management company (www.baronandgrant.com).

John has used investment trusts in a private and professional capacity for more than 35 years. After university and the Army, he ran a broad range of investment portfolios as a director of both Henderson Private Clients and then Rothschild Asset Management. Since leaving the City, he has also helped charities monitor their fund managers.

VCTS: STILL GROWING

ALEX DAVIES, *founder and CEO of Wealth Club, offers his usual annual review of the progress made by Venture Capital Trusts.*

T HE UK DOMINATES the European startup and investment landscape. Globally, it ranks third for startup investment, behind only the United States and China. Since 2000, nearly 400 home-grown startups have achieved 'high growth' status, being worth more than $250m.

Part of that success is due to the increasing number of investors who every year provide vital capital to hundreds of young and entrepreneurial companies by investing in Venture Capital Trusts (VCTs). VCTs raised over £1bn in the 2022/23 tax year – the second-highest amount on record. That is despite the war in Ukraine, ongoing global supply chain issues, rising interest rates and inflation, and a looming recession.

Encouragingly, it's not just investor demand that's proven resilient. Despite a downturn in UK venture capital, VCTs have continued to fuel economic growth and job creation. In 2022, £664m was deployed across 345 investments, the Venture Capital Trust Association reports.

Meanwhile, VCT-backed companies generated total sales of £18.18bn, up 54% compared to 2021. They also exported more, with export sales totalling over £3.7bn in 2022, up 29.8% from 2021.

But can both investor appetite and growth continue? Only time will tell, but looking at the drivers behind demand might provide an indication.

Tax relief now more valuable

Taxpayers face a perfect storm. Income tax thresholds have been frozen or, in the case of the additional rate, dropped substantially from £150,000 to £125,140. At the same time, wages are rising at their fastest rate in 20 years, excluding the pandemic, and trying to keep pace with inflation. In the spring of 2023 alone, nearly two million workers experienced a 10% increase in their wages.

As a result, this year, an extra 1.6 million taxpayers will be pushed into the higher and additional rates of income tax, the Office for Budget Responsibility (OBR) predicts. That brings the total number of people who will be paying income tax at a marginal rate between 40% and 60% to 6.5 million. That number is forecast to increase further to 7.8 million by 2027/28.

Rubbing salt into the wound, the annual dividend allowance, the amount of dividends you are allowed before you have to pay tax, was halved from £2,000 to £1,000 last April. It will shrink to just £500 from 6 April 2024. Once you use the allowance, you pay tax on dividends based on your income tax band. So, if you have been pushed into a higher income tax band, you will also pay more tax on any dividends you receive.

At the same time, the capital gains tax-free annual allowance has also been halved from £12,300 to £6,000 this tax year and will be further cut to £3,000 from April 2024, taking it down to its lowest level since 1981.

VCTs offer a way to mitigate the impact of all these changes. When you invest, you can receive up to 30% income tax relief. If you use the whole VCT allowance of £200,000 per year, that would be a saving of up to £60,000 on your income tax bill, welcome news for anyone facing a higher bill.

Moreover, any growth in the value of the shares is tax free and so are the dividends most VCTs tend to pay each year. So, if a VCT pays a 5% dividend, that means you get 5p for every £1 you have invested. To match that, assuming the dividend allowance has already been used, a higher-rate taxpayer would have to receive a taxable dividend of 7.55% (8.24% for a top-rate taxpayer).

Generous dividend payments

Dividend payments by VCTs have to date been generous. We have looked at the cumulative dividends paid by VCTs over a period of three, five and 10 years, as well as in each of the last five years, and calculated the yield as a percentage of the initial NAV of each trust. There are some impressive figures – look at the Mobeus VCTs, for instance – while the average dividend yield has shown resilience.

Cumulative average dividend yield

	3 YEARS	5 YEARS	10 YEARS
Generalist VCTs			
Albion VCTs	26.4%	36.3%	68.2%
Baronsmead VCTs	25.7%	38.1%	84.3%
Blackfinch Spring VCT	–	–	–
British Smaller Companies VCTs	34.2%	47.2%	83.1%
Calculus VCT	13.8%	19.7%	–
Foresight VCTs	28.0%	34.7%	48.4%
Maven VCTs	20.0%	22.7%	73.6%
Mobeus VCTs	42.0%	65.1%	111.9%
Molten Ventures VCT	21.1%	27.1%	77.7%
Northern VCTs	25.3%	30.9%	79.8%
Octopus Apollo VCT	27.7%	33.5%	75.7%
Octopus Titan VCT	23.5%	32.9%	66.7%
Pembroke VCT	19.5%	25.7%	–
Proven VCTs	19.0%	32.5%	71.3%
Puma 13 VCT	16.4%	17.4%	–
Puma Alpha VCT	–	–	–
Seneca Growth Capital VCT	10.1%	–	–
Triple Point Venture VCT	9.6%	–	–
AIM VCTs			
Amati AIM VCT	18.2%	23.5%	69.7%
Hargreave Hale AIM VCT	25.6%	32.4%	72.4%
Octopus AIM VCTs	20.8%	27.6%	64.5%
Unicorn AIM VCT	36.8%	43.2%	91.4%
Average Generalist VCT	**22.6%**	**33.1%**	**76.4%**
Average AIM VCT	**24.4%**	**30.9%**	**72.5%**

Dividend yield in each of the last five calendar years

		H1/2023	2022	2021	2020	2019	2018
Generalist VCTs	Albion VCTs	2.5%	5.9%	11.9%	7.6%	5.5%	5.4%
	Baronsmead VCTs	4.5%	7.8%	8.3%	9.9%	9.2%	9.0%
	Blackfinch Spring VCT	—	—	—	—	—	—
	British Smaller Companies VCTs	2.4%	9.1%	13.4%	7.1%	13.5%	5.1%
	Calculus VCT	0.0%	4.7%	4.8%	4.5%	4.4%	4.6%
	Foresight VCTs	3.4%	10.0%	5.9%	4.3%	6.2%	6.0%
	Maven VCTs	3.0%	7.4%	5.1%	5.4%	2.9%	15.7%
	Mobeus VCTs	7.0%	7.7%	14.1%	15.6%	19.4%	6.1%
	Molten Ventures VCT	2.0%	7.3%	5.2%	5.4%	5.0%	2.5%
	Northern VCTs	0.0%	6.7%	11.4%	5.2%	5.3%	6.5%
	Octopus Apollo VCT	2.5%	5.0%	12.6%	5.3%	6.5%	6.2%
	Octopus Titan VCT	3.9%	4.7%	11.3%	5.3%	5.4%	5.2%
	Pembroke VCT	2.1%	4.1%	9.7%	2.7%	2.7%	3.0%
	Proven VCTs	0.0%	7.2%	5.1%	5.0%	5.2%	19.7%
	Puma 13 VCT	0.0%	8.0%	5.8%	—	—	—
	Puma Alpha VCT	—	—	—	—	—	—
	Seneca Growth Capital VCT	1.9%	3.0%	3.3%	3.2%	3.0%	—
	Triple Point Venture VCT	0.0%	2.7%	3.3%	3.0%	—	—
AIM VCTs	Amati AIM VCT	2.6%	4.1%	5.6%	5.0%	5.5%	5.2%
	Hargreave Hale AIM VCT	8.3%	4.4%	7.9%	4.5%	8.1%	3.3%
	Octopus AIM VCTs	2.0%	4.6%	6.8%	5.5%	9.8%	4.7%
	Unicorn AIM VCT	2.6%	19.0%	3.2%	3.7%	4.6%	4.0%
	Average Generalist VCT	**1.9%**	**6.3%**	**8.2%**	**6.0%**	**6.7%**	**7.3%**
	Average AIM VCT	**3.5%**	**7.3%**	**6.1%**	**4.8%**	**7.6%**	**4.4%**

Source for both tables: Morningstar. The tables show dividend yield as % of starting NAV for the period to 30/06/2023. Cells are left blank when a VCT has not paid dividends in the period or if the current share class had not yet been established.

As these tables show, not only have VCT dividends been generous over the years, but they have also remained consistent and resilient, even since 2018, when the VCT rules were changed. At that point, there were fears that the required shift in investment focus from predictable, and often interest-paying, management buyout deals to shares in early-stage businesses would mean the end of regular dividends.

Those fears appear so far unfounded, although of course this could change. Many VCTs have made the most of the healthy environment for selling companies that prevailed from 2020 to the first half of 2021 by building a war chest of distributable reserves from exit proceeds and keeping them to fund future dividends.

This could see them through the short to medium term or as long as takeover activity and realisations remain muted. Those trusts with more ambitious dividend yield targets, on the other hand, may struggle to deliver on them until the market picks up again.

Resilient long–term performance

Beyond generous dividend payments, generalist VCT long-term performance has also been strong and, importantly, resilient. In the short term, VCTs have endured a challenging environment. Higher interest rates have been the dominant theme in the last two years as central banks aggressively tighten monetary policy to try and curb inflation.

Bond yields started to rise in mid-2021 and continued to rise through 2022 and the first half of 2023. Higher bond yields tend to entice investors away from equities, given the higher risks the latter entail. In turn this tends to drive down equity valuations. 2022 was a year that saw the tide go out.

Most VCTs have felt the impact of this, albeit to varying extents. AIM VCTs were hit particularly hard, with NAV total returns down by an average 30.3% in 2022 and a further 8.3% in the first six months of 2023. Generalist VCTs with high exposure to businesses that need additional capital injections also suffered.

A notable example is used-car online supermarket Cazoo, at one point Octopus Titan VCT's largest holding. The business floated on the New York Stock Exchange in 2021 with a lofty $8bn valuation. It then sought to build a dominant position across Europe, an ambitious and cash-hungry strategy dependent on continuing access to fresh capital. However, as interest rates rose and financial conditions tightened, Cazoo was unable to tap the market for additional funding and the share price started to decline sharply.

For other earlier-stage businesses, the impact of higher interest rates has been less pronounced. VCT managers believe startups are coping with the challenges by choosing to cut costs, extend their cash runways and delay raising additional capital until conditions improve.

That said, a few managers still delivered positive performance despite the difficult environment and have produced attractive returns over three years. The Albion VCTs, for instance, posted modest positive performance in the first half of 2023. This is in part due to a large uplift in value from its largest position, Quantexa, an online fraud prevention business, which recently raised $129m at a $1.8bn valuation. This makes it Albion's first unicorn, which we define as a company whose valuation exceeds $1bn.

Cumulative NAV total returns (3 years)

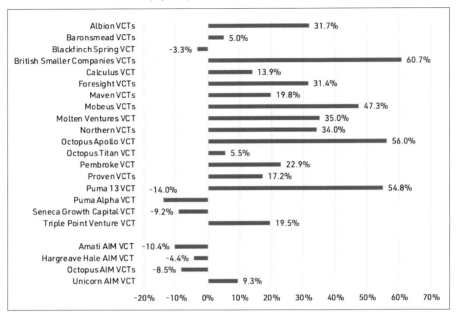

Cumulative NAV total returns (5 years)

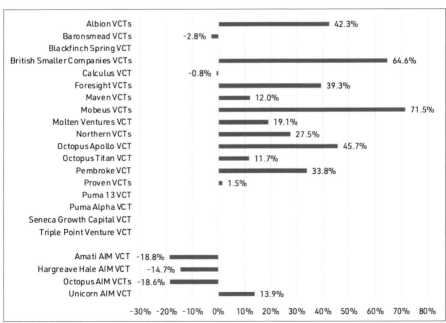

Cumulative NAV total returns (10 years)

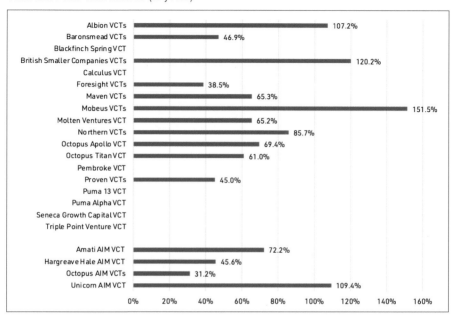

NAV total returns by calendar year

		H1/2023	2022	2021	2020	2019	2018
Generalist VCTs	Albion VCTs	6.9%	-1.0%	18.3%	1.0%	6.7%	15.8%
	Baronsmead VCTs	-2.5%	-16.1%	15.1%	6.0%	8.4%	-6.2%
	Blackfinch Spring VCT	3.3%	-2.4%	-1.1%	—	—	—
	British Smaller Companies VCTs	-3.1%	9.7%	29.9%	6.4%	7.1%	8.1%
	Calculus VCT	2.3%	3.4%	8.6%	-7.4%	-3.5%	-5.5%
	Foresight VCTs	-0.1%	4.2%	15.2%	0.9%	3.6%	2.8%
	Maven VCTs	-1.1%	0.2%	13.1%	1.9%	2.5%	2.2%
	Mobeus VCTs	1.4%	-20.4%	48.9%	21.6%	14.6%	1.4%
	Molten Ventures VCT	2.9%	-12.0%	35.8%	-7.5%	-2.5%	2.7%
	Northern VCTs	0.3%	-8.9%	17.5%	10.8%	5.4%	2.6%
	Octopus Apollo VCT	5.9%	4.2%	27.0%	10.5%	-3.8%	-0.9%
	Octopus Titan VCT	3.3%	-23.5%	20.5%	7.7%	8.0%	1.7%
	Pembroke VCT	-3.1%	0.4%	19.7%	3.8%	2.6%	14.0%
	Proven VCTs	0.0%	-8.1%	16.7%	0.7%	-7.1%	15.6%
	Puma 13 VCT	3.3%	13.9%	18.4%	23.3%	1.6%	—
	Puma Alpha VCT	-12.2%	-16.6%	12.3%	2.0%	-3.1%	—
	Seneca Growth Capital VCT	-8.9%	-15.4%	12.6%	2.0%	-3.1%	—
	Triple Point Venture VCT	-2.7%	-2.4%	23.7%	-4.0%	—	—
AIM VCTs	Amati AIM VCT	-16.0%	-26.7%	1.9%	37.2%	20.5%	-14.5%
	Hargreave Hale AIM VCT	-8.0%	-32.8%	16.1%	26.6%	7.5%	-9.5%
	Octopus AIM VCT	-7.7%	-31.6%	8.7%	23.8%	12.0%	-10.4%
	Unicorn AIM VCT	-2.5%	-28.9%	20.4%	22.4%	27.9%	-10.3%
	Average Generalist VCT	**-0.2%**	**-5.1%**	**19.6%**	**4.7%**	**2.3%**	**4.2%**
	Average AIM VCT	**-8.3%**	**-30.3%**	**11.1%**	**26.8%**	**16.0%**	**-11.0%**

Source for all charts and table: Morningstar. The charts and table show net asset value and cumulative dividends per share for the period to 30/06/2023. Cells are left blank if the current share class had not yet been established.

Still growing faster

The real picture, however, is more nuanced – and encouraging – than the averages might suggest. That becomes clear if you look at the growth of VCT-backed companies. The starting point in our research were the investments made by 21 VCT managers who together manage 38 VCTs and around 92% of the assets of all active VCTs.

We next divided their portfolio companies into three categories:

1. Companies whose revenues declined,

2. Companies with modest revenue growth of 0%–25% per annum,

3. High growth: companies with revenue growth of 25%+ per annum.

We've then applied the same categorisation to the constituents of the FTSE All-Share index, excluding investment trusts and insurance companies. You can see how they compare in the table below.

Exposure to growth: VCTs vs UK main market

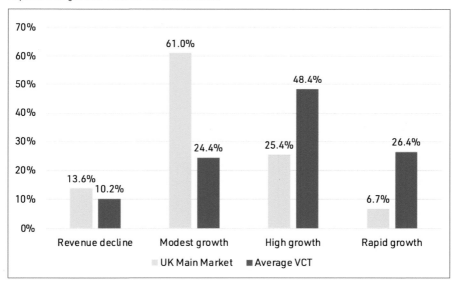

Exposure to growth: breakdown by VCT

	REVENUE DECLINE	MODEST GROWTH (REVENUE GROWTH OF 0–25%)	HIGH GROWTH (REVENUE GROWTH >25%)	RAPID GROWTH (REVENUE GROWTH >50%)
Albion VCTs	3.9%	20.4%	53.3%	44.1%
Amati AIM VCT	11.5%	23.7%	50.3%	21.3%
Baronsmead VCTs	8.1%	27.4%	28.1%	9.1%
Blackfinch VCTs	6.0%	5.1%	84.8%	46.7%
British Smaller Companies VCT	3.3%	20.6%	39.5%	10.7%
Calculus VCT	24.0%	22.1%	23.7%	14.1%
Foresight Enterprise VCT	9.4%	37.0%	43.2%	15.8%
Foresight VCT	5.2%	48.2%	40.4%	12.2%
Foresight WAE	11.1%	8.2%	36.5%	33.5%
Hargreave Hale AIM VCT	7.2%	29.1%	61.4%	32.2%
Maven VCTs	16.6%	26.3%	48.1%	23.0%
Mobeus VCTs	3.6%	32.5%	62.1%	21.8%
Northern VCTs	8.1%	27.4%	41.9%	24.2%
Octopus Apollo VCT	11.0%	36.0%	54.0%	22.0%
Octopus Titan VCT	10.1%	8.9%	35.4%	30.4%
Pembroke VCT	10.3%	28.1%	61.2%	52.9%
Proven VCTs	4.0%	27.5%	63.0%	44.8%
Puma 13 VCT	39.1%	26.6%	31.3%	3.1%
Seneca Growth VCT	7.8%	14.1%	52.1%	27.9%
Triple Point Ventures VCT	2.1%	13.1%	56.1%	46.9%
Unicorn AIM VCT	10.9%	30.3%	50.2%	18.7%
Main Market	13.6%	61.0%	25.4%	6.7%

This table shows the revenue growth exposure of 21 VCT managers as a percentage of their invested assets, compared with the revenue growth exposure of the constituents of the UK main market (FTSE All-Share excluding investment trusts and insurance companies). Revenue growth data is based on each underlying company's latest full financial year results, released in the latest 12-month period to 30 June 2023. All revenue data for public companies and AIM VCT investee companies is supplied by Morningstar.

Overall, our research shows VCTs continue to be packed full of high-growth early-stage businesses. For the 21 VCT managers featured in our research, half (48.4%) of their investments are in businesses that have grown revenues by more than 25% year on year. By contrast, only a quarter (25.4%) of the FTSE All-Share constituents, excluding investment trusts and insurance companies, have achieved that.

If we were to look at a fourth category, defined as rapid growth (companies growing revenues at over 50% a year), VCTs fare even better. 26.4% of the VCTs' portfolios are invested in companies growing revenues at 50% or more, compared with just 6.7% (by market cap) of the main market.

Pembroke VCT is a particular outlier within the VCT peer group, with rapid-growth companies representing 52.9% of its portfolio. Pembroke's largest holding, LYMA Life, the beauty and wellness brand, is an example. It ranked 11th in the *Sunday Times* Top 100 list of the UK's fastest growing companies. Triple Point Venture VCT is another outlier, with 46.9% of its portfolio in rapid-growth companies.

The numbers clearly show investors looking to gain exposure to high-growth companies are probably much better off looking at VCTs than at the main UK equity market.

Who invests in VCTs and why?

Contrary to what many may think, there is no such a thing as a typical VCT investor. The average age of our clients who invest in VCTs is just under 59. The youngest is 19, the eldest 103. The fastest-growing group of investors is those in the 30–40 age bracket. 80% are male, 20% female. In the 2022/23 tax year, they invested £36,244 on average across a number of VCTs per tax year. The average amount invested in each VCT was £11,581.

We don't record occupation, but many we speak to who invest are professionals, such as doctors, lawyers, higher earners in the City and business owners; but the list also includes head teachers and civil servants. They tend to have investments elsewhere, such as ISAs, pension and property, to which VCTs add diversification. They tend to have been affected by tax rises and pension restrictions.

What prompted them to start investing in VCTs? We asked investors in a recent survey. 71.7% of respondents cited tax as a reason that prompted them to start investing in VCTs. The exposure to high-growth-potential investments, with commensurate high risks somewhat mitigated by the tax reliefs, the diversification VCTs can add to one's portfolio and the opportunity to support UK entrepreneurship were all mentioned.

Over 94% believe investing in VCTs helps back the next generation of UK entrepreneurs. All those reasons are independent of what the economy does or where the next crisis is going to come from. That is why, if you have sufficient assets elsewhere and a certain level of financial sophistication, VCTs may well be a worthwhile option for you to consider, after using your pension and ISA allowances. As a rule of thumb, VCTs should account for no more than 10% of your total portfolio.

When you invest in a VCT, your money will typically be spread over 30 to 100 companies, which provides an important degree of underlying diversification. In addition, it may be prudent to spread your annual investment over several VCTs, preferably with different investment strategies, to further diversify your risk. Don't forget you also have a 30% cushion in the form of tax relief, should things go wrong.

Clearly, for someone who doesn't have sufficient assets or earnings, and doesn't fully understand the risks, VCTs are not a suitable investment. Young, small companies are more likely to fail than older and larger ones. If something goes badly wrong for a small company, it is much harder for it to recover than it is for a large and well-established company. Small companies are also a lot more illiquid, as are VCTs themselves – meaning it may be difficult to buy and sell the shares.

This year's VCT season

The VCT season has only just started this year. The world looks very different from what it did 12 months ago, and investor sentiment has certainly taken a hit. But taxes are still at a record high this tax year. Pensions, whilst slightly improved, remain non-viable for many. And if you are after growth, the VCT investment case is just as compelling as it ever was.

The total funds raised may or may not surpass last year. However, if we've learnt anything from the past, it's that the most popular offers always sell out. It is a reminder to investors that if they spot a VCT they like, they should act quickly whilst there is still capacity available.

ALEX DAVIES *is the founder and CEO of Wealth Club, the largest broker of VCTs and tax-efficient investments for experienced investors.*

Historic VCT fundraising (£m)

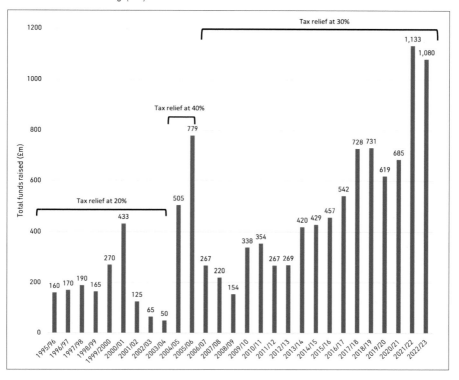

Reliable, informative, relevant.

Instant investment and market insights. Never miss a beat.

Doceo has been working with over 40 investment companies for two years developing watchable, engaging, and informative content for active investors seeking updates directly from decision makers. A selection of the very best articles, podcasts, interviews, and webinars explore trends and set out how top investment thinkers are navigating the current market environment. Join the Doceo community for high quality insights or find our content on one of our partner platforms.

Get the App

Stay Connected

doceo.tv

INTO THE HEADWIND

JAMES CARTHEW, *a director of the research firm QuotedData, reviews a tough year for the alternative asset trusts.*

The boom is over

I N THE YEARS following the global financial crisis, the investment companies industry boomed as investors in search of income poured money into alternative assets. Not everything worked. Aircraft leasing and reinsurance funds proved to be notable problem areas, for example. However, the sector had a hugely positive impact in other areas such as infrastructure and renewable energy.

The investment company structure provides access to a wide range of asset classes for all types of investors and is ideally suited to these kinds of investments. Most alternative assets cannot be turned into cash in a hurry. Redemptions from open-ended funds holding these assets would no doubt have been suspended long ago. Holders of investment companies can, with a few unfortunate exceptions (discussed later), always cash in their investment. However, the price for liquidity is often accepting that you may have to sell at a discount to the underlying net asset value.

It is clear now that higher interest rates were needed to choke off inflation and, for the first time in a very long time, investors can now earn meaningful income from cash deposits and bond funds. With these other options now available, they have been selling alternative income investments to fund these purchases.

As a result, share price discounts to NAV have been widening across the investment companies sector. As the following chart shows, while discounts on funds investing in equities have generally held up fairly well, alternative income funds have been hit much harder. The universe of alternative income funds shown in the chart encompasses debt, infrastructure, insurance, leasing, property, renewable energy and royalties.

Median discounts for investment companies

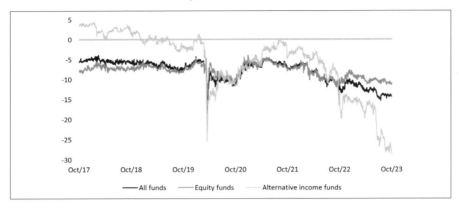

Source: Morningstar, QuotedData.

The problem is not just weak share prices. There has also been downward pressure on NAVs. Most of these funds are valued by calculating the net present value of their future cash flows using a discount rate. This discount rate is made up of a 'risk-free' rate – usually the yield on a government bond of equivalent maturity – plus a risk premium. As risk-free rates have risen, so too should these discount rates. However, in practice, risk premiums appear to have been squeezed. For some investors, that calls into question the accuracy of the NAV and they are looking for transactional evidence that the NAVs are realistic.[1]

10-year UK government bond yields

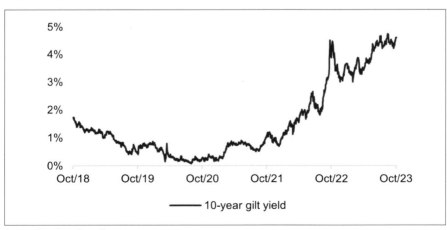

Source: Bloomberg, QuotedData.

---

[1] See P241 for further insights into how alternative asset NAVs are calculated.

Inflation and interest rates

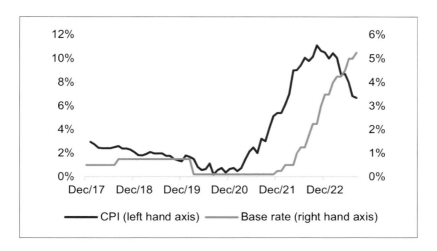

Source: ONS, QuotedData.

The great derating

With hindsight, it should have been obvious that a return to more normal levels of interest rates would dull demand for alternative assets. However, I am not sure anyone would have predicted how far the pendulum would swing against this part of the market. Nor can we be sure whether the pendulum has swung too far, but it feels to me as though there may now be bargains to be had from share prices that have been marked down excessively.

Of 103 alternative income funds that existed at the start of 2023, only 14 have seen a narrowing of their share price discount to NAV over the course of 2023 year to date. Those included Civitas Social Housing (CSH) and Round Hill Music (RHM), which were bid for, and Ediston Property (EPIC), which is selling its portfolio in advance of a return of capital to shareholders.

As share price discounts widen, yields are rising. Incredibly, there are now 48 alternative income funds that have a dividend yield of more than 8%. The big question, as always, is: are these yields sustainable?

There are pressures on some of these funds that need to be factored in. Clearly the cost of debt has risen. Fortunately, most seem to have fixed their interest payments, some at very advantageous rates. For example, Triple Point Social Housing (SOHO) has fixed-rate debt that matures between 2028 and 2036 and comes with an interest rate as low as 2.4% and none more than 3.2%. However, there are a few funds that are either paying down, or have plans to pay down, their floating-rate debt, with HICL Infrastructure (HICL) being an example.

Another major concern that investors have is the possibility of recession. Growth is fairly anaemic already, but high interest rates could tip us into recession. There are large parts of the alternative income universe that would not be much affected by that – renewables and infrastructure, for example. However, there are obvious concerns about debt funds and the likelihood that more borrowers will default on their loans. There are also some worries about tenant failures for property companies, and demand for the assets held by leasing funds.

Misleading charges disclosures are also unhelpful. This is an industry-wide problem for the investment companies sector, and one that has sparked a war of words with the Financial Conduct Authority, which never seems in a hurry to lend a sympathetic ear or act quickly when it comes to investment trust issues.

All of this is happening against a backdrop of consolidation within the wealth manager industry. Unfortunately for their clients, many of these wealth managers are now too big to hold smaller funds and so they are becoming net sellers, regardless of the return opportunity that their clients are ultimately forgoing.

A challenge for boards

The widening discounts present directors of alternative income funds with a difficult challenge. However, as already highlighted, it is not easy to turn assets held by these funds into cash to fund share buybacks, and funding them with additional debt is not an attractive option either. In addition, shrinking funds through buybacks risks alienating the big wealth managers, so there are also calls for funds to merge.

In the circumstances, some boards have decided to throw in the towel. This seems to be particularly true in the debt sectors where funds such as Blackstone Loan Financing, ICG Longbow Senior Secured UK Property Debt, NB Global Monthly Income, RM Infrastructure Income, Starwood European Real Estate Finance, and VPC Speciality Lending, are all now in wind-up mode. I am sure a case could have been made for persevering with at least a couple of these.

In addition, having failed to convince investors of the merits of a merger with GCP Infrastructure Income (GCP), GCP Asset Backed Income (GABI), another fund managed by Gravis Capital, will face a continuation vote in 2024. Henderson Diversified Income (HDIV) meanwhile is planning another in-house merger that would involve it folding into Henderson High Income (HII).

Amongst renewable energy funds, Aquila Energy Efficiency (AEET) had disappointed shareholders with the pace of investment of its IPO proceeds. It was too small, and its discount had become entrenched. It was not a great surprise, therefore, when it said it would look to sell its portfolio and return the proceeds to investors.

More peculiar was the decision of US Solar Fund to initiate a strategic review towards the end of 2022. On the face of it, the company appeared to be making good progress. Unsurprisingly perhaps, faced with this apparent loss of confidence, members of the management team then left in search of new opportunities following the announcement.

In the end, having failed to find a buyer, the company has appointed a new manager. Its closest peer, Ecofin US Renewables, has also now announced a strategic review, hinting that it plans to sell its portfolio. We have been told that the two funds explored a merger some time ago and it might be time to think about this again.

Some alternative income funds have been buying back stock for a while, but it has to be acknowledged that – as yet – this does not seem to have had much of an impact.

Of the leasing funds, Tufton Oceanic has been able to sell some vessels and it has now repurchased over 13.5m shares, but its discount is almost as wide as it has ever been, meaning it yields over 8.5%. In the infrastructure sector, Pantheon Infrastructure announced on 31 March 2023 that it would buy back up to £10m worth of its shares, using cash that would otherwise have been deployed on new investments.

A clutch of funds has been buying back shares in the renewable energy sector. For example, Aquila European Renewables (AERI) announced a €20m share buyback programme in February 2023 and it has now repurchased almost 29m shares. The board and the investment adviser bought shares too. Unfortunately, while this had some initial success, over the summer the discount widened again. We could point to many other similar situations.

Given that many of these funds have mature portfolios of assets with 25–30+ year lives, money for buybacks would have to come from asset sales. For example, NextEnergy Solar is planning to sell a portfolio of solar farms and JLEN Environmental Assets says that it continues to assess disposal opportunities to recycle capital from lower-returning parts of its portfolio. We think these sales will be at prices that will underpin the validity of their NAVs.

Alternative solutions

Not everyone is convinced that these buybacks make sense. The commercial property sector, which is a notable holdout, has been through downturns like this before. High frictional costs of buying and selling assets and the dangers of buying high and selling cheap mean that it is easy to destroy value with short-term thinking. Instead, there is considerable upside to be had from conserving cash to buy assets at the bottom of the cycle from distressed sellers such as open-ended property funds.

It was perhaps inevitable that opportunistic buyers would emerge for some of these assets. Back in 2021, as the economy began to recover from the effects of Covid-19, we saw bids for Drum Income Plus REIT, GCP Student Living, RDI REIT, Sigma Capital and Yew Grove REIT. Then in 2022 Secure Income REIT was absorbed into LXI REIT.

In May 2023 Civitas Social Housing was trading close to a 50% discount to NAV. A shareholder in the company's investment adviser bid 80p per share for the company, at a 26.7% discount. That looked absurdly low to me. Bizarrely, the board admitted that the offer undervalued the company but recommended it anyway. I assumed that the large shareholders would push back on this and demand a higher price. In the event, they caved in, handing the bidder a quick gain of about £175m.

The ease with which the bidder gained control of Civitas and the amount of money that it made must surely give encouragement to other large investors running a slide rule over alternative income funds. In the case of Round Hill Music, the bid price from its American purchaser was much closer to NAV (an 11.5% discount). To give you an idea of the degree of the disconnect between the value that shareholders were putting on the company and what the bidder thought it was worth, the shares jumped by 64% when the bid was announced. The bidder should still get a $58m uplift (assuming that the NAV is correct and ignoring the often sizeable fees associated with doing these kinds of deals).

Continuation votes and redemption opportunities are uncommon in the alternative income sectors, but shareholders may become more vocal about demanding them in 2024.

Hard cases

In the midst of the general malaise, two funds attracted headlines for all the wrong reasons. ThomasLloyd Energy Impact, with its focus on Asian renewable energy, was a promising new addition to the sector in December 2021. At the time, it made headlines for being backed by the Foreign & Commonwealth Office.

For much of 2023, the headlines were all about a falling out between the board and the investment adviser. This reached a head in April when the board, unable to finalise the company's first set of annual accounts, decided it had no choice but to suspend the shares. The board persuaded investors to vote against the continuation of the company, as the investment adviser had proposed, and appointed a new manager on a temporary basis. More recently it said it had decided to go ahead with the big solar project in India that has caused most of its difficulties, but only on the grounds that going ahead would lose less money than stopping it.

Far worse than the saga at ThomasLloyd, has been the situation with Home REIT. Backed by many investors, including me, the fund was supposed to help tackle the scourge of homelessness by providing accommodation funded by central government through local authorities. Again, it was unable to finalise its accounts and the shares have been suspended since the beginning of 2023.

The litany of failures here is a long one. Unable to collect the majority of its rents and with many of its tenants in liquidation, the company appears to have been reduced to selling property at bargain prices to cover its outgoings. At least we now have a new manager and soon a new board. Home REIT has done incalculable damage to the reputation of our industry and my hope is that all those responsible will be brought to account.

Another trust which has spent more time in the headlines than is probably good for it is Hipgnosis Songs Fund (SONG), Round Hill Music's larger peer in the music royalties business. Confronted with demands from its larger shareholders to do something to reduce its near 50% discount, the board upset them instead when it announced a plan to sell about a fifth of its portfolio to a fund that its manager also has an interest in.

At the suggested purchase price, investors would have been handing about $93m to the buyer. Unsurprisingly, investors rejected this and were sufficiently riled to eject the chairman and vote against the continuation of the fund. What remains of the board has six months to decide on the best course of action.

What next?

So, what does 2024 hold for alternative income? The main hope is that we are quite close to, or even at, the peak in interest rates. If that turns out to be the case, that should help to ease the downward pressure on NAVs and may suffice to help rebuild confidence in these sectors. It seems likely that we will see more takeover bids. It seems reasonable that Triple Point Social Housing, which is a near-identical fund to Civitas Social Housing, would be a target, for example.

In time, as the outlook for interest rates becomes clearer, many of these funds should be rerated, but in the meantime, there is an opportunity for investors to build a diversified portfolio of funds with fairly solid, long-term and often growing income streams at an attractively discounted price. The onus though is on the boards and managers to demonstrate that the NAVs are really as good as they appear.

JAMES CARTHEW, a former investment trust manager, has been a director of QuotedData, the investment trust research firm, since it was founded in 2013. He is a regular contributor to the Money Makers investment trust podcast.

THE REVOLVING DOOR

ANDREW McHATTIE, *editor of* Investment Trust Newsletter, *explains how and why the investment trust sector is moving into a consolidation phase.*

Nothing new here

WHILST IT IS fun to focus on IPOs and the newest shiny offerings in the investment trust sector, there has always been a two-way flow of trusts both in and out of the sector. Some dusty old trusts that no longer suit the purpose for which they were created reach the end of their lives and head for the exit door – or one of several exit doors that tend to gape open more widely in bear markets.

Tough market periods when discounts are widening, and many shareholders become unhappy with their returns, do tend to focus more attention on the trusts that are struggling in some way. When the tide goes out it exposes the low-lying debris scattered along the shoreline. Trusts that are sub-scale, or underperforming, or with specific structural problems, or failing continuation votes, became 'fair game' to be part of what is often kindly termed 'industry consolidation' or 'rationalisation'.

Those with a harsher vocabulary might call it a cull or 'cutting out the dead wood'. Whatever term is used, this periodic refreshing of the industry is usually considered a good thing, a Darwinian quality control mechanism that keeps investment trusts relevant and attractive. On that basis the last 12 months have been quite invigorating.

Some new market vocabulary has been introduced too. When responding to shareholder concerns, boards will often now launch a 'strategic review' to consider their options. These have become quite commonplace as a prelude to various sorts of corporate developments, though there is never a guarantee of any action.

Triggers for action

In 2022–23 there were five common reasons why boards felt the need to instigate strategic reviews, or to call time on their trusts more directly. First, a number of trusts, including abrdn Latin American Income (around £33m market capitalisation), abrdn Smaller Companies Income Trust (£60m), The Investment Company (£15m), and Momentum Multi Asset Value Trust (£40m) have admitted they were simply too small to remain viable.

After a period of consolidation in the wealth management industry there was a lot of discussion about the lack of liquidity in smaller trusts and the need for trusts to have a minimum market capitalisation of £300m+ to attract demand from this key group of buyers. Sub-scale trusts have difficulty marketing successfully to find new shareholders, and this is literally an existential question for some boards.

For trusts that own mainly publicly listed equities, it is a comparatively straightforward process to sell those in the market, liquidate the company, and return the cash to shareholders. For trusts with less liquid assets the task becomes much more complex, and in any event this may not be the best exit for shareholders. In some cases for investors with tax issues a roll-over option is a good alternative to a cash exit or simply preferring to continue in a similar trust. This can reduce the costs. Over the last year there have been some clear beneficiaries as a result, in the form of trusts that have been able to claim some of these assets that might otherwise have left the industry.

In the case of JPMorgan Global Growth & Income it effected a merger with JPMorgan Elect in late 2022, following an earlier similar deal to absorb the much larger Scottish Investment Trust, propelling it towards the £2bn market capitalisation mark. More recently Nippon Active Value Fund has announced plans to absorb both abrdn Japan and Atlantis Japan Growth to form a decent-sized trust with around £325m of assets.

Similarly, Henderson High Income is taking in the smaller Henderson Diversified Income. Trusts that have consolidated in this way have greater scale and a firmer footprint in the modern investment trust industry. Pulling off the transactions is not always straightforward, however, as evidenced by the failure of some talks to come to a successful fruition, leaving boards to looks for alternative solutions. Completing a merger with a trust managed by the same fund management stable is easier than doing to with a rival entity.

Persistent discounts

The second obvious trigger for corporate action, linked somewhat to the first, is the existence of a persistently wide discount. Smaller trusts often cannot see how they will attract sufficient demand to close a wide discount, and other trusts that have perhaps tried numerous strategies to close stubborn discounts also face pressure from disgruntled shareholders to realise this latent value with a winding-up or other radical manoeuvre. This has been the stated reason for a number of corporate actions, including VPC Specialty Lending and Blackstone Loan Financing, both of which have entered run-off mode whereby they will cease making new investments and return capital to shareholders as it becomes available.

Third, sub-par performance that has failed to live up to expectations and is more deeply rooted than a change of personnel can lead to closure. This is the market acting as a meritocracy and ensuring the survival of the fittest. In the case of Fundsmith Emerging Equities Trust, Terry Smith, the chief executive of the management company, was typically forthright in declaring "whilst FEET has made a positive return since launch in 2014 it has fallen below our expectations", whilst in other cases it is an unspoken factor, the elephant in the room.

The fourth spur for corporate action is when the impetus comes explicitly from shareholders who fail to support a continuation vote or vote positively for discontinuation. This was the case for Aquila Energy Efficiency Trust in February 2023, and it has become more common for trust boards to canvass the opinions of major shareholders ahead of such votes. Atlantis Japan Growth Fund, for example, announced its proposals to merge with Nippon Active Value Fund ahead of an impending continuation vote. There are several more forthcoming dates for continuation votes that look like pinch points for other vulnerable trusts. They concentrate the mind of boards.

Fifth, there are trusts with other structural issues, which may be sector-related. Over the last 12 months there has been a slug of activity in the real estate sector, which is probably the most sensitive of all areas to changes in interest rates. The sharp increases in interest rates that marked the end of the near-zero interest rate era since the global financial crisis has led to some severe dislocations in values and in pricing in the sector, and some corporate activity has followed as a fairly direct result.

This is the primary area in which we have seen traditional-style takeover bids, which are rare for more mainstream investment trusts (although Round Hill Music Royalty Fund did attract a bid). Industrials REIT was bought by Blackstone for 168p per share, at a small discount to its net tangible assets; CT Property Income Trust was acquired by LondonMetric Property through an all-share merger at a 6.3% discount to its net tangible asset value; and Civitas Social Housing was bought by a Hong Kong-based property and infrastructure investor called CK Asset Holdings for 80p a share in a contentious deal in June 2023.

The Civitas Social Housing takeover was unusual because it was effected at a big discount of 26.7% to net asset value. CK Assets paid £485m against net assets of £662m, and whilst many commentators came out against what looked like an opportunistic bid, shareholders decided to accept and draw a line under what had been a tough period for a trust under fire. The trust had previously suffered multiple bouts of negative publicity, a short-sellers' note, and ongoing issues with the new Regulator of Social Housing.

Civitas Social Housing was undoubtedly a special situation, but it has still created an uncomfortable precedent for a trust to be acquired at a large discount to asset value, and there is a risk this may encourage future buyers targeting illiquid assets to make speculative bids at low prices. In the same sector, Ediston Property Investment Company initially sought a merger partner, but then announced that it had agreed to sell its entire portfolio to a US real estate investor.

The revolving door can be sticky

Once the battle is won with a takeover, the conclusion is generally clean and quick. Accepting shareholders get paid and move on. With many corporate actions in the investment trust sector though, it can be a much slower and trickier process. The revolving door can be sticky and slow to turn a full cycle.

Let's come back to those trusts with illiquid assets. It is well known that the closed-end structure can be well suited to illiquid assets, such as property, infrastructure, private companies and structured loans, but selling them off in the case of a voluntary liquidation is not so easy. This leads to trusts entering 'run-off' or 'managed wind-down' whereby the managers avoid a fire sale but realise the assets over time, returning the cash gradually to shareholders.

A number of trusts have recently joined this category, including Aquila Energy Efficiency Trust, Blackstone Loan Financing, Crystal Amber Fund, NB Global Monthly Income, RM Infrastructure Income, Starwood European Real Estate Finance, and VPC Specialty Lending. The run-off times can be long – Blackstone Loan Financing has indicated at least seven years – so patience can be required for those choosing to remain.

So what have we learnt from this recent burst of corporate activity? One key lesson is that although many trust combinations are labelled as 'mergers', the two sets of shareholders do not benefit equally. Typically it is the smaller trust being absorbed that contributes to an uplift in value, and this is where the gain accrues. Not only is there a boost from a narrowing of the typically wide discount to net asset value, but frequently a partial cash exit option as well, at close to NAV.

There is no equivalent for shareholders in the larger trust, who benefit only in more nebulous terms from greater liquidity and lower costs going forward. Thus, when the £300m abrdn New Dawn (ABD) trust merged into the £500m Asia Dragon Trust (DGN), removing some significant portfolio overlap to create a stronger single entity with lower costs per share and a more compelling proposition for wealth managers and others needing more liquidity, ABD shareholders stood to gain much more from the deal than DGN shareholders.

Boards and managers

Whilst managers are often asked about these matters, the structure of investment trusts means that all such decisions are board decisions. That does not mean they are free of influence from the managers though, particularly if those managers have indicated they would prefer not to continue. Abrdn does seem to have been particularly proactive in rationalising its portfolio of investment trusts.

It has already closed abrdn Japan, abrdn Latin American, abrdn New Dawn, and abrdn Smaller Companies Income while abrdn Diversified Income & Growth is in the midst of a strategic review that the board has already indicated means an exit is likely. Abrdn is trading some short-term loss of fees to strengthen its core long-term position at the heart of the industry and deserves some credit for leading the way in this latest burst of corporate activity.

Investors may be tempted to buy on the first news of a strategic review, but of course there is no promise of definite action or of an uplift in value. The process sometimes stalls. US Solar Fund, for example, tried to throw in the towel, but found no willing buyers at the right price for its portfolio, so it eventually switched managers instead, by which time the share price had drifted lower.

That said, it remains good sport to try to spot the next trusts likely to be subject to corporate action. Some analysts expect more activity in the renewables infrastructure sector, which is entering a new phase after the rush of capital-raising initially drew in many new managers with plans and investment pipelines that have not all proved to be of the highest quality. Investors can also look ahead to trusts with planned continuation votes. Amongst that group, some names that have been mentioned as vulnerable include Downing Strategic Micro Cap, Jupiter Green Investment Trust, Premier Miton Global Renewables, Riverstone Credit Opportunities, and Palace Capital in the REIT sector.

On a larger scale, there have been some rumblings about the manager of the FTSE 100 constituent Pershing Square Holdings being unhappy with its persistently wide discount. For as long as discounts across the sector remain at wide levels there will be scope to unlock value through corporate activity, and at the time of writing it certainly looks as though there will be more to come. In previous cycles we have seen arbitrageurs or vulture funds enter the market to act as agitators and facilitators, and it is possible they will still have a part to play as the exit door keeps spinning.

ANDREW McHATTIE *is the editor of the* Investment Trust Newsletter, *which has been published monthly since November 1996. Details can be found at www. tipsheets.co.uk.*

Investing in the engine room of India

The Indian economy has been in the limelight as one of the few bright spots in an uncertain world. Some are even calling it 'India's decade' and with India's population exceeding China's and its imminent promotion to the world's third largest economy, we believe it's justified. Reforms, digitalisation and improving infrastructure all contribute to the positive story and when India moves, it moves fast, making it near impossible to chase.

That is why we believe it is worth investing in small and medium sized companies - the Engine room of India.

With specialist investment managers based on the ground in Mumbai and London, the team can seek out innovative opportunities, identifying companies with sustainable growth at an attractive price. Using a bottom up approach the team meet the companie they invest in, undertake proprietary research and truly understand the business model enabling them to invest with conviction.

India Capital
GROWTH FUND

www.indiacapitalgrowth.cor

PROFESSIONAL PERSPECTIVES

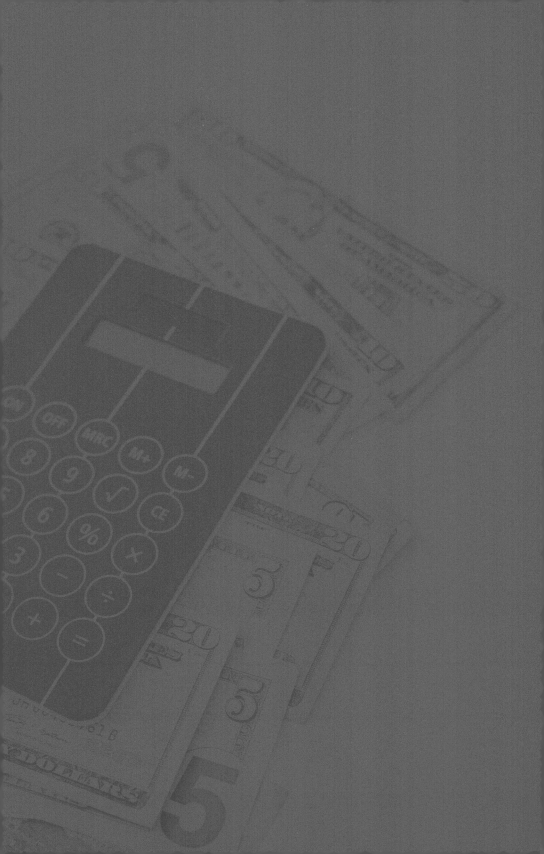

INVESTOR FORUM

We asked some of the most experienced professional investment trust investors we know to give their answers to some topical questions.

Who's who?

Alan Brierley is the director of investment company research at Investec and has covered the sector since the early 1990s.

Richard Curling is an investment director at Jupiter Fund Management and manages the Jupiter Fund of Investment Trusts and the Jupiter Monthly Alternative Income Fund.

Nick Greenwood has been the manager of Miton Global Opportunities (MGO), which invests only in other investment trusts, since its launch in 2004.

Peter Hewitt has been managing CT Global Managed Portfolio, a fund of investment trusts, since 2008.

Alastair Laing is CEO of Capital Gearing Asset Management and a co-manager of Capital Gearing Trust since 2011.

Anthony Leatham has been head of investment trust research at broking firm Peel Hunt since 2015.

Which trusts have been the most creditable performers over the past 12 months?

Alan Brierley: This is a difficult question in what has been a difficult year, but Edinburgh Investment Trust and Pershing Square stand out. We don't tend to obsess about short-term performance but in these two cases the past year has further enhanced impressive longer-term performance records. Somewhat counterintuitively, in our view, attractive fundamental investment cases are compounded by wide discounts.

Richard Curling: European equity trusts have provided some of the strongest performance, but the prize must surely go to 3i, which is, of course, not officially an investment trust. It has produced a remarkable return. Within the alternatives group the best performance has been amongst the credit group, with the CLO funds such as Fair Oaks (FAIR) standing out.

Nick Greenwood: Aurora has had a good year and is a good example of a manager using the closed-end structure to build conviction in their portfolio. Temple Bar has bounced back with new managers after the loss of a long-standing and well-regarded manager. Rockwood Strategic (RKW) made decent returns despite being in a sub-sector suffering a bear market. Nippon Active Value (NAVF) made money and seems to have pulled off a difficult three-way merger, which will make it more attractive to the wealth management community.

Peter Hewitt: The technology trusts Allianz Technology (ATT) and Polar Capital Technology (PCT) have surprisingly performed strongly, particularly from February and March onwards.

Alastair Laing: Finsbury Growth & Income Trust (FGT), Smithson Investment Trust (SSON) and European Opportunities Trust (EOT) are all examples of trusts with high-profile managers and strong retail followings that were significantly derated in the 2022 bear market. From those lows last year, they have benefited from firmer performance and discount tightening. That cycle keeps on turning!

Anthony Leatham: In a year of unusual market gyrations, it is perhaps surprising to point to a Japanese equity trust as being a standout performer, but we have seen some exciting returns from this region. CC Japan Income & Growth (CCJI) was the first dedicated equity income trust to join the peer group in December 2015 and has outperformed the index and peers.

And which have been the most disappointing performers?

Alan Brierley: It is really difficult to look beyond Home REIT (HOME), which remains suspended. Digital 9 Infrastructure (DGI9) arguably comes a dishonourable second.

Richard Curling: This has been a year with a lot of disappointments, nearly all of them connected in one way or another to the rise in interest rates. The growth capital trusts, such as Schiehallion (MNTN), have continued to underperform and sectors that were expected to recover with favourable tailwinds, such as healthcare and biotech, have not. Perhaps most disappointing has been the share prices of the infrastructure and renewables group, which have moved to surprisingly large discounts.

Nick Greenwood: Phoenix Spree Deutschland (PSDL) has seen its shares fall sharply despite owning a portfolio of Berlin residential properties during a housing shortage. The Chinese slowdown has been painful for a number of emerging market trusts. Baillie Gifford funds are now at the bottom of the one-year performance tables, and JP Morgan Core Real Assets (JARA) has lost 20% since launch – not what investors were expecting, given the mandate.

Peter Hewitt: Renewables, core infrastructure, property and private equity have all been disappointing, with share prices declining a lot faster than asset values.

Alastair Laing: Digital 9 Infrastructure (DGI9) is a good example of a trust that pushed far too hard, gathering assets at the top of the market, resulting in real vulnerability when the cycle turned. The principal issue was not asset quality. It was self-inflicted overreach.

Anthony Leatham: In the context of a very tough period for property portfolios, it has been particularly unfortunate to witness the troubles faced by the social housing sector. The series of negative announcements has detracted from investment strategies that were designed to have a positive social impact, the worst offender being Home REIT (HOME).

Is the continued movement in discounts understandable or overdone?

Alan Brierley: I think it is understandable. We have moved from a period of great moderation to a new regime of higher inflation/volatility and lower growth. Meanwhile a flawed cost disclosure regime has created a perfect storm, exacerbating the sell-off and contributing to much higher volatility. The infrastructure sector has been very exposed to this; having consistently traded on healthy premia for more than a decade, it has moved to very wide discounts.

Richard Curling: Understandable in many ways. With an entirely new interest rate environment it was necessary to reset share prices so that the returns on offer reflected a reasonable risk premium over bonds. This is especially true in the alternatives group, although it is worth noting that whilst share prices have moved considerably, NAVs and cash flows of the underlying assets are largely unchanged. Within equity trusts, the growth style of investing has been penalised. As so often in markets I suspect these moves have been overdone.

Nick Greenwood: It simply reflects the imbalance between supply and demand, especially within alternative asset classes. Many of these funds were created to offer yield at a time when deposit rates were effectively zero. Now that gilts yield around 5%, demand for these has evaporated. Following the new issue boom some weaker funds have failed to attract a following. We have been buying Aquilla European Renewables (AERS), which is doing a decent job at portfolio level but is too small for the wealth management community to use. Even if a buyer paid net asset value for the portfolio, it would still represent a cheap bolt-on acquisition.

Peter Hewitt: The extent of the correlation between interest rates and the effect on share prices of the alternative trusts was not fully appreciated, but as with many things it has probably been overdone, especially in private equity trusts.

Alastair Laing: Both! When picking through the wreckage of the investment trust market the excesses of the 2021 'everything bubble' are clear. 2021 was a huge year of trust fundraising, including IPOs of specialised funds focusing on space, shipping and hydrogen. It seems unlikely some of these immature propositions will ever reattain their ratings or reach critical mass amongst retail investors. That said, the discount widening has been near universal and indiscriminate. The stark difference between valuations in the private and listed markets verges on revulsion in certain cases. The recent private bids at significant uplifts for Civitas Social Housing (CSH), Round Hill Music Royalty (RHM) and Ediston Property (EPIC) show how overdone certain discounts have become.

Anthony Leatham: We consider the initial phase of derating, whether in response to equity market volatility, weak investor sentiment or a rebasing of yield expectations, to be understandable. Given the composition of many shareholder registers, it is also understandable that many trusts fell too far as selling pressure and risk aversion took hold. The longer-term history of investment trusts helps to put this discount widening into context however. It is now at a statistically significant low ebb. Take HarbourVest Global Private Equity (HVPE) as an example. In 2023 this private equity fund-of-funds dropped to a discount level only seen on six occasions in its 23-year history. Buying in at these low levels can be rewarding.

Where do you think that the market has got ratings most wrong?

Alan Brierley: Round Hill Music Royalty Fund. The market didn't understand the relative exit dynamics between this company and Hipgnosis Songs Fund (SONG).

Richard Curling: In the equity group some of the growth-biased companies, such as Scottish Mortgage (SMT) on a 20% discount, now look cheap. Private equity to me continues to stand out as being on too high a discount, although the catalyst to change this is unclear. The infrastructure and renewables group also looks to be priced too pessimistically, given the relatively stable nature of businesses such as Greencoat UK Wind (UKW) on a 16% discount.

Nick Greenwood: I don't think it's a case of the market getting it wrong, it's just a case of some selling and not a lot of buyers. Expectations for interest rates are now headed lower, which should make asset classes such as infrastructure, renewables and shipping attractive again given the yields on offer.

Peter Hewitt: The ratings of private equity trusts have moved far too far and offer attractive value. I would also highlight UK equity trusts, especially those that are specialists in, or have large exposure to, UK small and midcap companies.

Alastair Laing: Core and renewables infrastructure such as Greencoat UK Wind. Unlike private equity, gearing levels are lower, debt is largely fixed rate and falling in real terms. There is explicit inflation linkage on roughly half of the revenues which are government-backed, with the balance exposed to resurgent power prices to varying degrees. The energy levy has ended a period of supernormal profits, but long-term risk-adjusted returns remain attractive. The government's failure to attract any offshore wind developers in the latest auction is supportive of longer-term power prices and could encourage a more sympathetic policy environment in the next political cycle.

Anthony Leatham: Private equity in all its forms has struggled in the face of an increased perception of risk. This reflects a number of external factors, including the listed market read-across, growth-to-value style rotation, concerns around valuations, debt multiples and opaque and infrequently valued NAVs. 'Sell first and ask questions later' has left a number of strategies stranded on wider-than-average discounts. Investors need increased transparency to assess risk in the portfolios and identify potential NAV drivers.

Is more consolidation on the way? Which trusts are most vulnerable?

Alan Brierley: Yes. We have said for more than 10 years that the industry needs to address what we regard as zombie companies, those that lack critical mass, have poor liquidity and indifferent track records. The latest 'perfect storm' has been a catalyst for this process to gather momentum.

Richard Curling: Yes. In the equity group I expect trusts with a similar mandate to be merged, as we have seen with some of the abrdn-managed trusts this year. In alternatives many sub-scale trusts now cannot grow because of the change in interest rates and need to merge or wind up. I think every trust under £100m needs to have a plan. As ever it is difficult to persuade boards to be as proactive as investors would like, but we should keep up the pressure. Liquidity is becoming ever more important.

Nick Greenwood: Consolidation is healthy. In addition to newer funds from the issue boom, simple long-only equity funds are at risk. Unless they properly use the closed-end structure, they are only adding illiquidity and discount volatility to the equation compared to open-ended funds. This makes it difficult for them to justify their existence.

Peter Hewitt: Almost certainly. The investment company sector has a wonderful way of reinventing itself and correcting things. There are too many small trusts with mandates that are no longer attractive to private investors.

Alastair Laing: I certainly hope so! Calls to consolidate have gone unheeded in the boardroom for years, but it's only really in periods of stress that change becomes more feasible. The listed credit sector has seen some activity already and any trust under £400m that is trading at a discount should be seriously considering its future. The number of small infrastructure trusts needs to reduce and there are a number of UK smaller companies trusts that would benefit from greater scale.

Anthony Leatham: Yes. We now have a number of activists in the market looking to take advantage of wide discounts and potentially agitate for change. Several trusts face continuation votes or will trigger discount controls which they did not expect. Scale matters, particularly in a world of large, centralised wealth management firms, and those trusts with limited size and relatively poor liquidity will need to think carefully about how to future-proof their strategies.

What has been your biggest regret this year? What were you most pleased by?

Alan Brierley: The end of a most benign environment and transition to a new macro-regime was always going to be incredibly challenging, but in too many cases this has been compounded by board/manager incompetence. Having been critical of listed private equity trusts for allowing discounts to become embedded, we welcome the new capital allocation policy of Pantheon International (PIN). This throws down the gauntlet to the rest of the sector.

Richard Curling: My biggest regret this year has been failing to appreciate quite how high interest rates would go and as a result not being as active as I should have been in reducing interest-rate-exposed stocks. I have been most pleased by my exposure to the activist Japanese plays AVI Global (AGT) and Nippon Active Value (NAVF).

Nick Greenwood: My biggest regret is being too early buying into UK microcap trusts, as they have continued to decline. It has been very pleasing however to see Geiger Counter (GCL) and Yellowcake (YCA) doing so well. Nothing fundamental has really changed, but other investors have now spotted that uranium is going to be in very short supply for some time.

Peter Hewitt: My biggest regret is that widening discounts in most sectors, particularly in alternatives, has produced poor relative performance against mainstream equity indices. I have been most pleased that dividends have come through strongly, so although capital performance has been disappointing, this has been partially offset by strong dividend growth, often from a decent level of starting yield.

Alastair Laing: Moving too slowly to reduce our property exposure ahead of the Truss and Kwarteng debacle and the associated 'giltmageddon'. Our thesis that inflation-linked rents would grow at record rates proved correct. However the value put on these rental streams collapsed as investors turned to higher yielding government bonds. On a positive note, and for the second year running, our large holdings in the energy market delivered very strong returns.

Anthony Leatham: I was expecting discounts to bounce back more quickly and relied too heavily on the historic precedents in forming my view that there would be a V-shaped recovery, instead of what now looks like an elongated U-shape. The dominance of macro-factors has had a part to play. We did though get the value versus growth call right. In an environment of low growth and compressing bond yields, it is reasonable for successful secular growth companies to trade at a premium.

What trust would you nominate as your trust of the year?

Alan Brierley: Pantheon International, for the reasons already given. I would also nominate the new chairman of Round Hill Music Royalty who looked after investors and produced a win-win for everyone.

Richard Curling: Literacy Capital (BOOK) for outright performance or Pantheon International for finally doing the right thing in terms of capital allocation. A special mention too for Greencoat UK Wind for continuing to increase its dividend in line with inflation, which most other renewables companies have failed to do.

Nick Greenwood: Georgia Capital (CGEO), which you might think an unusual choice given it trades on a 50% plus discount. However, they have always done what they said they would do and have executed well. It has been a profitable experience for investors. Looking forward there is still plenty of scope for the discount to narrow, allowing further strength in the shares.

Peter Hewitt: I like Law Debenture (LWDP) a lot. It has a unique structure with the investment portfolio sitting alongside its corporate services business, which is now up to 21% of assets. That underpins the dividend going forward and allows James Henderson, the fund manager, a lot of flexibility with his investment selections. It is one of the best in the important UK equity income sector and ideal for retail investors with its combination of capital and income growth.

Alastair Laing: During a tough year those boards that showed dogged commitment to protecting their shareholders by preventing a material discount from emerging deserve particular praise. Personal Assets Trust (PNL) is an example to the whole sector.

Anthony Leatham: Octopus Renewables Infrastructure Trust (ORIT). The messaging is clear and the management team is highly experienced and risk aware. Total returns have been consistent, dividends have been fully covered with good levels of inflation linkage and dividend growth has been one of the strongest in the sector.

What changes would you most like to see in the investment trust world?

Alan Brierley: A successful resolution of the current cost disclosure debacle. Boards should remember who actually owns the company and put shareholders first.

Richard Curling: I too would like to see the playing field levelled on cost disclosure, which I hope is underway, as well as more boards being proactive in realising value for shareholders and facing up to the changed interest rate environment, which in some cases now means their business model is no longer viable. More 'strategic reviews' are needed.

Nick Greenwood: An end to the sector being caught in the crossfire of misguided regulation. The closed-end fund structure allows managers to build conviction in the absence of daily inflows and outflows, which is why trusts usually outperform, but they are different to most investment products and are hurt in the drive for standardisation.

Peter Hewitt: The playing field needs to be levelled regarding cost disclosures for investment companies, as it is misleading and actively puts off the retail audience. Regulation needs to be changed. Board behaviour is gradually improving with regards to mergers, buybacks etc. More trusts, especially in the alternative sectors, need to grasp the nettle and improve returns for shareholders, as Pantheon International has done with its significant buyback initiative.

Alastair Laing: Fairer PRIIPS rules, honest conversations on responsible investing and better liquidity.

Anthony Leatham: A level playing field. Cost disclosures are a millstone around the investment trust industry's neck and ultimately will have unintended consequences that end up with investors receiving worse, not better, consumer outcomes.

Are you optimistic or worried about the future of investment trusts?

Alan Brierley: This is a critical period for the industry. While many current headwinds will prove cyclical, the structural issues do need addressing. Perhaps it's time for a serious reset. Best practice must be locked down. Effective capital allocation policies are critical in this new environment. Strong corporate governance should be a core and differentiating feature. We would welcome greater accountability from boards, managers and brokers.

Richard Curling: So long as participants continue to focus on the benefits of investment trusts and offer clearly differentiated products, there will be a future. Big discounts can be seen as big opportunities! The real advantage of investment trusts is enabling investors to access illiquid assets, which they cannot do in any other way, and which previously were only available to institutions, such as renewable energy. In that way they are democratising investment.

Nick Greenwood: Historically the trust movement has evolved, frequently finding new audiences as the landscape changes. The law of natural selection remains alive and well within the sector. The relentless consolidation of the wealth management chains is spawning new smaller investment-led firms where the principals want to advise clients rather than becoming client liaison officers. Self-directed investors are becoming a greater presence on trust registers, a trend that will continue.

Peter Hewitt: The cost disclosure issue needs to be addressed, as investment companies are exactly what retail investors should be putting their savings into. Just as many commentators appear to be giving up on the sector, I am more optimistic. Trusts are good at evolving and changing and at present offer very attractive value for investors.

Alastair Laing: Whilst the economic outlook is precarious, we are excited about the long-term returns outlook. The historical record suggests that trusts starting from a point of wide discounts will outperform most other retail investment options.

Anthony Leatham: I hope that the investment trust universe finds its footing, discounts narrow and we return to growth mode. Investment trusts have stood the test of time and been through periods of oversupply, consolidation, reinvention and growth. Given the ever-present need for patient, permanent capital, investment trusts will continue to fulfil a role. I am resolutely 'glass half full' and look forward to investors making outsized returns when the recovery takes hold.

Are investment boards doing enough/the right thing? Which aren't?

Alan Brierley: A mixed bag, with a marked polarisation. In our view, too many boards are falling short of the traditional high standards.

Richard Curling: They could and must do more. There have been some good examples this year of positive board action such as Pantheon International's new capital allocation policy (buying back shares at a big discount) and RM Infrastructure Income's (RMII) decision to wind up rather than merge with another trust. I would urge boards to ensure proper challenge of their manager, focus more on capital allocation and to consult more with their shareholders.

Nick Greenwood: We don't talk to boards that often, and then its usually because something has gone wrong. When we do, we often find them helpful and resolve whatever issue we have. It has been frustrating that the listed private equity trusts have resisted buybacks given the oversupply situation within the sector. Hopefully others will follow Pantheon's lead. That would allow discounts to return to more typical levels.

Peter Hewitt: They can always do more, but it would be churlish not to say the direction of travel is good. In the ThomasLloyd Energy Impact (TLEI) trust fiasco, the board has done the right thing while the manager has not.

Alastair Laing: Over the last year we have pressed trusts on buybacks, gearing, capital allocation policy and fees. Some boards have shown real backbone, but many seem reticent to grasp the nettle. Infrastructure trusts like Gore Street Energy Storage (GSF) and Cordiant Digital Infrastructure (CORD) need to show capital allocation discipline. There is no excuse for any fund with liquid underlying holdings to trade on a material discount. In the words of the late investment trust guru Robin Angus, all discounts are voluntary.

Anthony Leatham: Governance continues to improve year on year, in terms of the composition of boards, the introduction of complementary skillsets and the diversity of backgrounds and genders. Responsibilities for oversight are taken seriously, but there is always more that can be done. Boards need to address wide discounts, stay close to shareholders, hold the manager to account and address the potential for consolidation. I have faith in boards to do the right thing and look out for shareholders' interests.

WE NEED TO TALK

BEN CONWAY, head of fund management at the wealth management firm Hawksmoor Investment Management, challenged the investment trust world this year to face up to some critical issues. This is a summary of the firm's arguments, which I reproduce here to encourage further debate.

Why we need reform

THE RECOMMENDATIONS THAT follow might be construed as being overly critical and we must make clear that we do not believe we have a monopoly on wisdom. This is not our intention. We care deeply about the investment trust sector, as closed-ended funds have always formed an important part of our portfolios and been a major driver of our long-term outperformance.

Whilst it is true that some of the recent travails faced by investment trusts are cyclical in nature, we think there are also some deeper structural issues at play. We hope that our series of articles, *We Need to Talk About Investment Trusts*, will help stimulate engagement between trusts and their investors and ensure that the sector continues to grow and flourish in the future.

Reforming the IPO process

Investors should receive £1 of assets for a £1 investment at Initial Public Offering. The brokers, who play a crucial role in the process, alongside solicitors, the London Stock Exchange and so on, should have their costs, typically around 2% of the amount raised, paid for by the investment adviser. The latter clearly benefits hugely from the launch of the fund through the future stream of management fees received from a fixed pool of capital.

Where portfolios are sold at IPO, as opposed to investment advisers being given cash shells, there should be greater involvement of investors in first-day pricing, as there is with normal operating companies' equity IPOs. The price paid for the assets at IPO should ultimately be determined by investors.

Some consideration should be given to incentivising and rewarding first-day shareholders, such as stakes or revenue shares in the management company of the investment adviser. Greater use of subscription shares might also be appropriate. The investment adviser is too often the largest beneficiary of the launch of a fund.

The risk-adjusted rewards to the shareholders of the investment adviser are too large relative to those of first-day shareholders.

In addition, most often with new launches in alternative asset classes, there is a clear asymmetry of information between the adviser and the shareholders. The latter cannot possibly do the due diligence required to understand the asset class as well as the adviser, and this leaves shareholders vulnerable.

Sometimes cash shells are unavoidable, for example where a pipeline of assets is ready to be acquired once the IPO has happened, but in such instances no fees should be charged on uninvested cash. Penalties on the investment adviser, such as earlier continuation votes, should be considered if cash is not invested in line with the execution timetable given at IPO.

Board selection should ensure independence. We worry that boards chosen after the appointment of the broker and investment adviser result in those boards being too close to the investment adviser. Non-executive boards are there to look after the interests of shareholders. Too much proximity to the adviser risks undermining this principle.

More care needs to be taken in the book-build process with greater consideration on how this might impact secondary market trading. Exhausting all investor demand for shares at an IPO can result in poor secondary market trading immediately after IPO, as any selling from the IPO investors can quickly push the company to a discount to NAV.

Too often funds only launch at a sub-scale size with the barest minimum of assets under management at launch, in the hope of raising more capital and improving liquidity later on. Early backers can end up stuck in very illiquid vehicles, even if they are managed successfully, with the only exit option being a wind-up, which can take years to facilitate (e.g., if private debt is involved).

All IPOs should be accompanied with rock solid longer-term protections in the form of continuation votes or return of capital provisions.

Promoting alignment of interest

The investment adviser's fees should be calculated as a percentage of market capitalisation, not NAV. This is not the norm, but it should be. Alternatively, consideration should be given to lower base fees with remuneration arrangements that create greater alignment with shareholders, such as rewards linked to NAV per share growth.

Directors' fees should include an explicit element of alignment with the interests of shareholders. An example would be stipulating that 50% of a director's fee is paid in shares, and/or long term incentives based on growth in NAV per share. We always like to see directors with 'skin in the game', meaning a significant shareholding, and believe this should be encouraged.

While the investment trust is a fantastic vehicle for accessing less liquid assets, it is not perfect, and the IPO process should ensure that structural weaknesses and alignment issues are addressed at the outset, not left to later. Once a discount has become entrenched, it becomes harder to shift investors' perception that a premium is possible.

Towards better capital allocation

Best practice guidelines concerning share buybacks should be formulated. The onus should always be on the board to justify why buybacks are not taking place, or, if illiquid assets are held, why they are not being sold to prove the NAV and fund share buybacks or the repayment of outstanding debt. When an investment company trades at a discount to NAV, and it has liquid resources available, any new investment should always be justified by comparing it to the potential growth in NAV per share from alternative uses of the capital, including buybacks.

If discounts persist, there should be mechanisms that guarantee a return of capital to shareholders, whether that takes the form of redemption facilities, tenders, continuation votes, liquidation and so on. While all new IPOs should come with these provisions in place, we think that existing trusts should also incorporate them as a matter of course.

In general boards and brokers should be more open to mergers and consolidation, and winding up trusts that have persistent discounts or concerns about their continued relevance.

Staying relevant and communicating better

The boards of trusts which trade on persistently wide discounts must ask themselves whether the company remains relevant. This is particularly true of trusts that are sub-scale and have poor liquidity. Provisions like those just discussed need to be in place to guard against the risk of becoming irrelevant.

The stock market exists to provide access to growth capital. When an investment company trades at a discount to net asset value, it is effectively barred from accessing further growth capital. A persistently wide discount should have boards questioning whether it is appropriate for the company's assets to remain listed.

Transparency and disclosure of information need to be improved, particularly in the case of less mature alternative assets. NAV calculations are too often opaque. Companies with similar assets frequently use different valuation methods and assumptions. These make NAV-to-NAV comparisons between different companies in the same asset class nigh-on impossible.

All shareholders must be motivated to engage, and for those at risk of being disenfranchised, such as retail investors, boards and advisers should make concerted efforts to engage with them. We urge brokers to encourage communication among shareholders and more creative destruction in their dialogues with boards.

Ongoing structural change in the wealth management industry, where continued consolidation results in ever-larger asset management firms, is clearly a headwind for the sector. The minimum liquidity requirements set by these managers mean they can only invest in the very largest and most liquid trusts that can be invested in. Boards need to recognise the challenges this development poses. It clearly reduces the likelihood of smaller trusts trading on discounts ever being able to grow.

Finally, all stakeholders who care about the investment trust sector should engage with industry bodies and boards on the issue of misleading cost disclosure. The use of aggregated portfolio ongoing cost factors is arbitrary and unfair and has created damaging unintended consequences. The requirement to report fees as a percentage of NAV, when investors buy and sell at the share price, has no logical rationale.

A fuller description of the issues raised in this article, written by the team of Ben Conway, Daniel Lockyer, Ben Mackie and Dan Cartridge can be found on the 'Funds Crescendo' blog section of the Hawksmoor Investment Management Limited website www.hawksmoorim.co.uk.

EYE OF THE STORM

RICHARD STONE, *chief executive of the Association of Investment Companies, sums up the challenges facing the industry and discusses which reforms are most needed.*

Hard going this year

THE RELENTLESS RISE in interest rates has created headwinds for many assets, and it has not spared investment companies. The average industry discount is moored in the mid-teens, similar to levels briefly seen when Covid-19 hit the UK and in the global financial crisis.

The impact has been felt unevenly by different investment company sectors. In particular, income-producing alternatives, many launched during a period of near-zero interest rates, have been derated. The discounts of the property, infrastructure and direct lending sectors all exceed the industry average.

This all adds up to a challenging time for the boards of investment trusts. They have responded by implementing share buybacks at record levels, cutting fees and proposing mergers and even wind-ups. We expect there is more of this to come.

We are focused on supporting our members through this difficult time. This includes providing guidance on areas such as ESG reporting and bringing directors together to discuss issues such as private asset valuations. We have also kept up our initiatives to promote the sector, driven by our mission that investment companies should be understood and considered by every investor.

This year that has included the Investment Company Showcase in October, a large-scale event for private investors, and the launch of the 'Investment Companies Made Simple' guide for pension trustees in association with the Pensions and Lifetime Savings Association (PLSA). Meanwhile we have worked hard to improve our website and ensure our profile remains high.

To give just one example, we expanded our investment company AGM calendar this year to include shareholder presentations, so that shareholders can easily see which meetings are coming up on a single webpage. On the same page, investment professionals can view upcoming analyst presentations and capital markets days. We are also expanding the third-party research on investment companies available on our website.

We also remain committed to educating financial advisers and wealth managers about the sector. The launch of our Investment Company Accreditation in February provided a way for advisers to develop and demonstrate their knowledge. The rapid take-up has indicated strong demand for this both among users and non-users of investment companies.

Grit in the system

Another branch of our work is focused on removing 'grit in the system'. By that we mean regulatory, legal or tax obstacles that unfairly disadvantage investment companies or get in the way of their wider use. We are delighted that the Treasury has decided to abolish the PRIIPs regulatory regime and with it Key Information Documents (KIDs). The AIC has been campaigning on this since before KIDs were introduced in 2018, highlighting the dangers of the documents' misleading risk indicators and unrealistic performance scenarios. We look forward to seeing the back of them.

More work needs to be done on retail disclosures, however, and on cost disclosures in particular. The current regime results in perverse incentives for some investors to seek low-cost investments at the expense of other considerations. The aggregation of investment company costs into fund-of-fund and other product charges has also had unintended consequences.

We are pushing for an acceleration of the FCA's work on an overall cost disclosure framework which will provide a long-term solution. We are also leading work with the FCA and policymakers, urging more immediate action to remove investment company costs from the aggregated single-figure disclosure of products that use investment companies.

We are very supportive of the government's efforts to reinvigorate the London public markets, and not just because investment companies make up more than a quarter of the FTSE 250. A healthy stock market is a cornerstone of innovation and economic growth, as well as a way for ordinary savers to claim a stake in the country's success.

IPO drought

The lack of initial public offerings (IPOs) is mostly due to unfavourable market conditions. Indeed, there is a drought across all companies and sectors, not just for investment company IPOs. However, we believe more could be done to ease the path for new issues. The Treasury has placed this within the bailiwick of the FCA and we are contributing to the ongoing discussions. We believe that there is scope to reduce red tape without sacrificing investor protections.

We have also campaigned for the abolition of stamp duty on investment company shares. This levy is unfair for two reasons. It biases the market in favour of open-ended funds, whose investors do not pay stamp duty; and in the case of investment companies that invest in UK shares, it is a form of double taxation, as the investment companies themselves pay stamp duty when they buy shares for their portfolio. We have therefore recommended that stamp duty is abolished on the shares of UK investment trusts, UK REITs and VCTs.

These are challenging times for government, not least because of budget constraints, and our advocacy work must always acknowledge this. Nonetheless, we have taken every opportunity to highlight that investment companies have the potential to support many of the government's ambitions, boosting investment in infrastructure, renewable energy and other less liquid assets that underpin sustainable economic growth. It has been encouraging to see several parliamentarians taking up the cause of investment companies this year and arguing for a more level playing field.

We have also seen strong support from the government on VCTs, and in particular a recognition of the need to extend or abolish the 'sunset clause' that will otherwise bring an automatic end to VCT income tax relief in 2025. VCTs provide funding to high-potential UK companies that would not otherwise be able to access it. Many of the businesses they back fulfil worthwhile social or environmental aims as well as driving economic growth. Putting the scheme on a permanent footing is crucial to maintaining the confidence of advisers and investors.

Encouraging engagement

While we will always seek the best regulatory, tax and legal environment for investment companies, it is shareholders who are central to all that our members do. Engagement between investment companies and their shareholders enables directors to ensure that shareholders' interests are being served. Facilitating this engagement remains a high priority for our member boards.

Platforms have a key role to play here, helping their customers vote their shares and attend the AGMs of investment companies they own. Shareholder engagement hasn't always been a priority for the platform industry in the past, principally because of the costs of delivering services such as digital voting which do not come with any immediate revenue benefit. This is changing as investors are becoming more engaged, have higher expectations and platforms see customer service and engagement as important differentiators now that the core services of custody and trading have become commoditised.

To help raise the prominence of this issue, we launched the Shareholder Engagement Award in 2021, recognising platforms that do the most to enfranchise and empower investment company shareholders. The award has been won for three years by interactive investor, indicating their long-standing and undoubted commitment to this area. However, it has been encouraging to see other platforms also improving their offerings, especially in terms of digital voting. We look forward to further progress.

Engagement is not always a comfortable process. A report from Quilter Cheviot about the wealth manager's engagement initiative with 41 equity-based investment companies highlighted concerns around board composition, board effectiveness and responsible investment disclosures. The lessons from this valuable exercise will be closely studied by boards and shareholders. Engagement is a two-way street: our member directors are telling us that they want to engage more with shareholders, and this is an area we will be continuing to work on.

Enduring advantages

Neither market conditions nor regulatory impediments do anything to alter the fundamental advantages of the investment company structure. Unchanged in its essentials since 1868, the structure provides a firm foundation for truly long-term investing.

Permanent capital means that market volatility has little effect on the underlying portfolios of investment companies. Discounts take the strain, giving impatient investors the opportunity to exit without damaging the long-term prospects of the more patient.

This creates the right conditions for strong long-term returns. Over the past ten years, the average investment company has returned 158%, equivalent to an annualised return of 9.9%. These attractive returns have been assisted by the ability to gear during a period when interest rates have been historically low.

Investment companies also have considerable advantages for income investors. This year, we saw the number of Dividend Heroes increase to 20. These are investment companies that have increased their annual dividends for at least 20 years; remarkably, nine of them can boast 50 years of dividend increases.

Investment companies are also the best (and only proven) vehicle for giving investors access to private capital and real assets. It is these assets that are the driving force behind the government's agenda on infrastructure investment and transitioning to net zero. Hence the critical role we believe the sector can play in delivering these ambitions if given the freedom and ability to do so.

To work in the investment company industry is to work with people who are passionate about the advantages of the structure and want to make our companies work even better for shareholders. We will continue to campaign to remove the grit from the system and promote the sector to all investors. This will position it as well as possible for when the current economic headwinds turn, which they eventually will. We remain optimistic that investment companies, with their enduring advantages, will continue to deliver for long-term investors.

RICHARD STONE has been the CEO of the Association of Investment Companies, the industry trade body, since September 2021.

WHY INVESTMENT TRUSTS?

The well-known investment trust analyst ROBIN ANGUS *was a longstanding advocate of investment trusts and in this extract from an anthology of his commentaries for Personal Assets Trust, where he was Executive Director for many years, he makes the case for private investors using investment trusts to manage their finances.*

This extract from A Shared Journey *by Robin Angus, an anthology of his quarterly commentaries for Personal Assets Trust, is reproduced here with permission. The 180-page anthology is readily available online. Robin Angus died in May 2022 and his lucid prose and investment insights are sorely missed.*

Private investors

WHAT FOLLOWS IS not a report of an actual conversation, but it could have easily have been so. It is an imaginary dialogue between a shareholder and myself, an amalgam of conversations and correspondence I have had over the last six months.

What's the problem? There are lots of well-recognised ways for private investors to invest their money in the stock market.

Our Chairman, Bobby White, (who is not only himself a retired stockbroker but also someone who gave his name to a large and well-respected private client broking firm) has a favourite saying:

"A stockbroker is someone who invests your money until it's all gone."

Ian Rushbrook claims that this could be extended to investment managers as well. The common thread? Always too much pressure to 'do something', resulting in too much buying and selling.

Perhaps the simplest fact of life for a private investor is that buying and selling can (literally) cost you a fortune. It makes no difference whether you manage your portfolio yourself or pay an adviser to do it on your behalf. Active portfolio management always means buying and selling. Thanks especially to Capital Gains Tax (and despite the steep market falls of the last three years, most long-established portfolios are still heavily pregnant with capital gains), this costs the private investor money.

There are lots of good independent financial advisers (or wealth managers, or whatever you want to call them) in the market place, as well as some bad ones. All of them, however, will involve you in doing what buying and holding a range of generalist investment trusts never will – paying CGT year after year. This guarantees that active management, whether by yourself or by an adviser, will be cost-ineffective.

It's better to spend your money on a lawyer or accountant who will find the best tax structure for your finances as a whole, than on paying tax that (if you invested through investment trusts and held on to them) you wouldn't have to pay.

You don't seem to be very keen on people having their money managed directly for them by professional financial advisers.

I wouldn't want to put it quite like that. It would be far too sweeping. The trouble is, however, that entrusting your money even to the best-known and most prestigious of personal financial advisers can be a gamble – and I've tended to meet the losers.

Here's a horror story for you. Ian Rushbrook and I know an expatriate couple who at their retirement some years ago had around US$50m of capital to invest. On the recommendation of friends prominent in the financial world, they arranged for their money to be managed by a leading Swiss bank. It was not a success. Over a period during which markets in general rose, their $50m fell in value to $25m.

Understandably dissatisfied, during the second half of 1999 (just as equity markets worldwide were on the verge of peaking) the couple interviewed some of the most highly respected private client fund managers in the UK and abroad and grilled them about their views. Needless to say, they got the same enthusiastic advice from all of them:

"Now is an excellent time to buy equities!"

The only dissenting voice was Ian's (they had contacted him through friends they had in common). Ian told them he thought markets were hugely expensive and riding for a fall. However, Ian was not pitching for their business – and anyway, what was one voice among so many, all urging them to buy equities?

So they transferred their remaining $25m to an international bank specialising in managing money for wealthy individuals. Despite this bank's excellent reputation and impressive presentation skills, however, they found that their affairs were in the hands of an eager 25-year-old lad who soon started churning their portfolio aggressively. Before long, it was underperforming again – whereupon the eager lad (contrary to the couple's instructions) began investing their money heavily in US over-the-counter technology stocks.

By now it was the middle of the year 2000, so readers will not be surprised to learn that many of these technology stocks quickly joined the '90% club' of companies which had lost 90% of their market value from their peak at the start of 2000. All in all, by this year the couple's $25m had halved again to around $12.5m.

This is an appalling story, all the more so because the couple did not fall into the hands of sharks or scoundrels but had their money managed by blue-chip names of the highest reputation. Of course, pretty well anyone who invested in equities at the start of 2000 would have lost money by 2003. But the damage done to the couple's wealth by these high-powered, prestigious private client fund managers was far worse than would have resulted from investing in a few 'boring' diversified trusts.

Despite such hard cases, surely it's better to get a personal service tailored to your own requirements than to be just one investment trust shareholder among thousands?

Why? After all, what are your requirements? Surely, to protect and increase the value of your capital over the long term. Endless costly buying and selling and paying Capital Gains Tax won't achieve that, irrespective of how bright the managers are. And why should placing your £100,000, £1m or even £10m with a wealth manager buy you a better service than a £1,000m investment trust will get from its own dedicated team of professional managers?

In my experience, people often feel that having their money managed by a wealth manager is the proper and expected next step up from holding investment trusts or other pooled investment vehicles. They think that the only appropriate kind of investment management for people in their position is something with a designer label. But it shouldn't be a matter of what sounds best at the golf club. It is a paradox that the richer you are, the less logical it is (because of the impact of CGT) to use discretionary fund management and the more advantageous it is to invest through investment trusts.

You talk a lot about 'generalist' trusts. But depending on your definition, the term could cover anything from well over a hundred trusts to a mere dozen or so.

This question has already cropped up several times in my postbag, so I'll quote from what I recently wrote to one shareholder.

"To put it in a nutshell, the kind of trust I mean has probably been around for the best part of a century, will have a market capitalisation of at least a quarter of a billion and may well be managed in Scotland or at least have Scottish links. But I don't want to make exclusive claims for such trusts. I invest in trusts of that kind because of the kind of person I am, the kind of place I live, the kind of training I've had and the kind of people I know… I suppose ultimately one feels happiest investing in what one personally knows, likes and trusts."

I must stress that there are trusts I would happily buy that don't meet all these criteria. There are many trusts which would be at home in an individual investor's portfolio like my own – notably our fellow independently managed trusts Alliance and Second Alliance, the Dundee-based standard-bearers of the private investor market.

Can't you get the same effect from holding a range of geographical specialists as from holding some diversified trusts?

Yes, but it's a lot more work. You have to be a fund manager yourself, deciding what markets and currencies to be in. Then you must monitor the portfolio carefully, making sure it reflects your preferred mix of markets and currencies at any given time. Even though I've spent my entire working life in the investment business, I still don't feel competent to do that for myself singlehandedly. I'm sure that this feeling is shared by many private investors who know just enough about investment to be conscious of how little they actually *do* know!

How can you guarantee that the boards and managers of general trusts will behave sensibly and not, for instance, get gearing or liquidity badly wrong?

You can't. All you can reasonably expect is that, while they may get it badly wrong, they don't get it so disastrously wrong that the trust is crippled for the future. The only way to hedge the risk (and it's very far from perfect, since investment managers always tend to hunt as a pack) is to spread your investment over several trusts. This is why I always speak of investing in half a dozen, rather than just one or two.

Please note, however, how much greater the risk is from gearing and liquidity than it is from individual stocks. Individual stocks are eye-catching but usually irrelevant. To take the worst possible case, occasionally a major company does go bust. If this happens, an investment trust which holds the stock may lose 2% or 3% of its assets. Even if a trust's top holding goes bust, a loss of 5% or so would be regrettable but hardly catastrophic.

You and others endlessly talk about 'investing for the long term'. But I never know what is meant by long-term investment.

How long is 'long term'? How long is a piece of string?! It's an expression that can easily be used as a cop-out in the investment management world. As the Red Queen in *Alice in Wonderland* said, it can mean "what I want it to mean, nothing more, nothing less". The trouble is that 'long term' genuinely does mean different things to different people in different situations. For instance, a market-maker might think of it as 48 hours. On the other hand, when asked for his opinion of the effect of the French Revolution, Chou En-lai (the Chinese Premier under Mao Tse-tung) famously remarked: "It is too soon to tell."

You should therefore decide what 'long term' means to you and choose managers who employ the same timescale.

How important are management and other costs?

Not very. Not enough for management costs to be the main factor in making your investment decisions, anyway. There are lots of commentators on the investment trust industry who get very uptight about management fees. However, it seems to me that they often allow a kind of moral outrage to overcome their investment judgement. Sometimes this moral outrage is unjustified; sometimes it is simply irrelevant. Look, for example, at Jean-Pierre Garnier's much-criticised £5m a year and possible £22m severance package at GlaxoSmithKline. In the context of Glaxo SmithKline's £80bn market capitalisation it is of no economic importance to shareholders. But if M. Garnier really is the best value-adding manager for the job and they lose him as a result of quibbling over his pay, shareholders will have done themselves economic damage.

As with the boardroom 'fat cats' who today evoke so much indiscriminate sneering, some apparently high fee rates may be worth every penny while some cheaper-looking ones would still be dear at half the price. ("The labourer is worthy of his hire." Luke 10.7) What is important is value for money, and that (rather than fees and expenses in absolute) is what I look for in an investment trust.

You would sing the praises of investment trusts, though, wouldn't you? You work for one yourself.

Yes, I do indeed work for an investment trust. But I don't praise investment trusts just because I work for one. I work for one because I have deliberately chosen to do so in preference to any other area of the investment world. This is because I think investment trusts are the best. Of course, in practice they can fall short of the best; and however excellent the investment trust structure may be in theory, this is no guarantee against failure or misuse. But we think that well-run investment trusts are still unbeatable as investment vehicles for private investors.

OK. Summarise the case for us.

*   Investment trusts offer private investors the benefit of full-time, professional portfolio management, while the direct relationship between the shareholders and the board of directors they elect ensures maximum accountability.

- Investors managing their portfolios directly or through an adviser can't offset any of their investment management, administration or interest costs against tax. Investment trusts can offset all such costs against tax.

- Higher-rate taxpayers are currently taxed at 40% on all realised capital gains in excess of £7,900 per annum. Such investors managing their portfolio themselves or through professional advisers will therefore find themselves either paying CGT or being forced to make unsuitable, tax-driven investment decisions. Investment trusts are wholly free of CGT on gains realised within their portfolios and so can buy and sell shares on investment grounds alone.

Ever heard of Victor Kiam? No, I hadn't, either – but then I haven't shaved for over 30 years, so it's understandable. An American entrepreneur, he was famous for his TV advertising slogan for Remington Razors, of which he was chairman and part owner: "I liked the shaver so much, I bought the company."

Ian Rushbrook liked the story because this is what he did too. He liked investment trusts so much, he decided to manage a major part of his own money through Personal Assets, the trust he and I together created.

Both Ian and I love investment trusts. Neither of us would ever want to do anything else. Indeed, such are our feelings that for words to express them we can only turn to Sir Winston Churchill himself: "My tastes are simple. I am easily satisfied by the best."

Quarterly No. 29 (May 2003)

LOOKING BACK

SIMON EDELSTEN, *manager of Mid Wynd International, retired in 2023. He looks back on his near 40-year career as an investment trust specialist and fund manager.*

A long perspective

MY FIRST JOB in the City was in 1985 at the stockbroking firm of Grenfell & Colegrave. They had an early computer – black screen, green symbols – and using some guidebook I programmed it to work out the redemption yields on investment trust debt. Some years later I was told that my boss had used this to arbitrage bonds against the jobbers' prices for 20 years after I had left and made a pretty packet. Good luck to him! I realised then that investment trusts required a little specialist knowledge, some arithmetic and some common sense. That sounded good to me.

After a period at Phillips & Drew I joined BZW, the wannabe investment bank, and was asked to help manage their trust-broking business after the previous team had left. That team had been energetic in issuing zero coupon debt for various trusts and we acted for a number of trusts with what had become very complex structures. Two of them, British Assets and Investors' Capital, aimed to merge.

We built a model of how the combined company net asset value would change given various assumptions and found that the Intel 386 processors struggled to drive the models, so we crashed the computer. It is easy to forget how radical the development of computing power has been in making analysis easier. When Pentium processors were released, modelling the numerous zero-preference shares and debentures together finally became feasible. If I remember correctly, the combined company had over a dozen bonds attached. I learnt the lesson that no amount of financial engineering saves an investment trust. It all depends on good stock-picking in the end.

At the end of the 1990s bull market, it seemed a good time to move into fund management. One of my best clients was Nils Taube, who had set up the independent fund management company THS Partners, mainly managing global equity funds for St James's Place, but also managing the quoted equities of RIT Capital Partners.

In the early days, we were vigorously selling our telecoms, technology and media stocks, as we felt the TMT bubble was sure to burst. However, we noted that the valuations of unlisted investments in the same sectors fell much more slowly, as the auditors tended to look backwards for valuation points – maybe that is a portent for private equity today?

Nils was one of the Great Men of the City, previously senior partner of Kitcat & Aitken and on the board of George Soros' first Quantum Fund. I had spoken to him as a broking client for a decade, but to invest alongside him for six years was a further education. He had been on many investment trust boards, most recently the Electric & General fund, although he had retired from that role when THS won the mandate from Hendersons in 2004. The best lesson I learnt from Nils is that it's for the fund manager to make the investment decisions. Boards and shareholders often have interesting and important views and recommendations, but fund managers should not take those views to limit their responsibility to manage the portfolio or select stocks.

Many Henderson directors were shareholders in the trust (I believe shares had been used to pay bonuses in a tax-efficient manner), which made the project a bit spicy. We halved the number of stocks, made the trust rather less like the index, did a bit of marketing and managed to cheer up the shareholders.

The 2008 financial crisis caused the trust to fall sharply in value, albeit not by more than the index as a whole. Unfortunately, this prompted some board members to become quite unhelpful in their comments and withhold their support when as managers we wanted to take more risk at the market lows.

Some time later, after I had left THS, the trust ended up being turned into an OEIC, a sad end for a trust with a successful hundred-year history. Boards of trusts tend to emphasise calming managers down when they are overexcited. However, encouraging them when things are going badly is perhaps a more valuable input.

After THS I joined up with Alex Illingworth and Rosanna Burcheri to form a new global equity team at Artemis. A couple of years later, in similar circumstances, we were asked to pitch for the Mid Wynd Investment Trust, then managed by Baillie Gifford. Winning a trust off such a successful fund management house seemed a long shot, but the Mid Wynd board backed our plan.

The importance of sound principles

Our pitch was built around the view that shareholders were likely to get the best returns if they stayed invested for long periods of time, ideally a decade or more, a belief that I still hold. This meant that we should try to make the shareholders' ride as steady as possible, especially when market conditions became stressful.

Drawing on my previous experience, this suggested five strands to our policy:

- First-class performance driven by stock selection (while minimising the impact from currencies and hoping to avoid valuation bubbles).

- A dividend which grows in real terms, even when inflation flips higher (providing the reassuring sight of steadily rising dividend cheques).

- A share price which trades in a small range around the net asset value (to reduce share price volatility).

- Using debt only in a modest way to take advantage of tactical opportunities (since debt increases asset price volatility).

- Communicating with shareholders and laying out clearly the risks being taken in the fund (so that errors, when they inevitably occur, were not surprises).

I also thought that it was important for the manager to have a significant personal investment in the trust and for the trust to be managed by an independent investment house whose name was not in the name of the trust. Anything that limits the freedom of the board to oversee – or be seen to oversee – the trust independently is undesirable.

Clearly it is not possible to achieve all the above ambitions all the time, but they are somewhat mutually supportive. In my view it is critical to appreciate that a discount management policy is of little use without performance and good performance will reduce the discount more effectively if accompanied by clear shareholder communication.

At the same time the board and the fund manager tend to be wholly aligned on what they are trying to achieve. The board's role is to represent the shareholders in this, which is tricky as they tend to meet them rather less often than the fund manager does.

In the trusts I have managed, I think there was a clear shared objective, to increase real wealth over time. There were moments when boards did a good job in cooling us down as fund managers when we had got lucky, but there were fewer occasions when boards encouraged us to take more risk at market lows – a shame, as this should be a strength of the trust structure and an advantage over unit trusts.

What about my biggest triumphs and mistakes? I think I would nominate LVMH, the French luxury goods business, as my greatest success. Although the rating of the company has hardly changed in eight years, the share price rise has come from cash flow growth through high margins and good management decisions.

My biggest mistake has to have been owning a small amount of Siemens Energy after Siemens bought the Gamesa wind turbine manufacturing business a year ago, believing that the company's problems were ending. However I should have remembered Warren Buffett's maxim: "When a management with a reputation for brilliance tackles a business with a reputation for poor fundamental economics, it is the reputation of the business that remains intact".

The industry today

Looking at the trust industry today, I think there are clear opportunities for trusts to stand out from the crowd by following the above principles. Many trusts have had indifferent performance in recent years, which is a disappointment, but not unknown over the centuries of trust investment history. Discounts have therefore become wider, and some trusts have bought in significant numbers of shares as a result.

As I have mentioned, one cannot expect this wave to end until performance improves. Before that happens, however, trusts should still review and revise what they are trying to achieve, to understand what they do differently from other trusts and how this might affect investment returns, and finally make sure that they communicate these matters clearly to their shareholders.

Even for someone who is ever so slightly obsessed with trusts, I do not see from many trust websites clear statements of what they are trying to achieve. Sometimes they seem to be trying to achieve eight things at once, of which half seem irrelevant to the most critical one, which is performance.

Putting money to work

My last day at Artemis was towards the end of October, and by the time *The Investment Trusts Handbook* is published I will have been busy scouring the sector to assess the attractive-looking discounts on offer in both conventional and infrastructure trusts. My holdings in investment trusts have given me excellent returns over the last 20 years, and I expect they will continue to do so in the years to come.

Equity markets are getting used to persistent inflation and interest rates around 5%, which although they may appear startling to more recent investors are only around the average I have faced over my career. Valuations are a bit higher in the US than Europe, again as they have been for most of my career. I see my main task as being to find good stock-picking fund managers, preferably at boutique fund managers, and entrust my savings with them for the next decade or so.

*SIMON EDELSTEN has been the manager of Mid Wynd International since 2014.
Following the announcement of his retirement, the board has decided to move the
mandate from Artemis to Lazard Investment Management.*

A FRESH PERSPECTIVE

SIMON ELLIOTT, *former head of investment trust research at Winterflood Securities, weighs up the outlook for the sector from his new – very different – vantage point as a client director at J.P. Morgan Asset Management.*

C HANGING JOBS AFTER 20 years is not for the fainthearted. Those of us blessed with good memories may have distant recollections of a first day at a new school. The nervousness, the uncertainty, the sneaked backward glance at a loved one, all hopefully to a backdrop of a September sun. Some things change over the years, others don't. The disorientation that comes from being part of a new organisation is very real. In my case, it took an entire day to work out how to make a cup of tea.

After 20 years as an analyst covering the investment companies sector at Winterflood Securities, I moved to J.P. Morgan Asset Management (JPMAM) in September 2022 to be a client director helping to look after the firm's investment trust stable. This is a completely different role. As a friend observed recently, I had gone from being a restaurant critic for over two decades to joining a successful restaurant, thinking I knew something about the business. JPMAM manages 19 investment trusts with aggregate assets of £13bn as of 31 August 2023.

The role of the client director is to act as a liaison between the independent boards of these trusts and JPMAM, including portfolio managers, company secretaries and the operation teams. It is, in my opinion, a fascinating role, which provides huge insight both into the workings of an investment trust business and some of the issues facing investors and boards. When I was approached with the opportunity to move from the sellside to the buyside it was this that attracted me. That and the chance to help shape the fortunes of the second-largest trust provider in the UK market.

So how has it gone? Well, the first thing to observe is that the year has sped by. Every job has its own natural rhythm. With an analyst, the focus is often on company results and announcements, which are usually announced at 7am, followed by regular meetings with investors and portfolio managers. Early starts and late finishes are not uncommon.

A client director's focus is on board meetings, of which there tend to be between four and six per trust a year. A huge amount of work goes into each of these meetings, and invariably a long list of action points ensues. Boards are understandably focused on the actions of the portfolio managers and their performance, understanding the decisions that have been made and the key factors in driving the fortunes of their respective trusts.

However, an even greater amount of time is spent on addressing regulatory and compliance related matters. In the last 12 months, boards have had to grapple with issues such as: the reporting obligations on Consumer Duty standards; Treating Customers Fairly disclosures; UK Sanctions requirements; and the Parker Review, which is focused on the ethnic diversity of UK boards. As public listed companies and regulated entities, these are important elements to get right.

A lot of time is also spent by boards considering developments across the investment companies sector and how they may impact their trust. As I'm sure has been well documented elsewhere in this handbook, it has been a year of turmoil for the sector. While the JPMAM stable trades on a narrower discount than the overall sector, it has not been immune from the derating of investment trusts.

According to Winterflood, the sector average discount in 2023 has been as wide as 18%, a level that has more in common with the aftermath of the global financial crisis in 2009 than in more recent years. In addition, the wave of issuance that had revitalised the sector over the last decade has ceased, with IPOs few and far between and regular tap issuance limited to a handful of the remaining premium-rated investment companies. Unsurprisingly, there is an air of despondency across the investment companies sector at present, with some voices suggesting we are seeing the beginning of the end of the sector.

I would take a different view, reflecting my experience over the last 21 years. On my first day at Winterflood in 2002, a City grandee took me to one side to wish me the very best in my new role, albeit with the qualification that he did not believe that the sector had a future. Fortunately, he has been proved wrong, but this view was not uncommon at that time, given the turmoil created by the split capital scandal. The ensuing years saw considerable contraction as investment trusts were wound up or repurposed, with arbitrageurs hunting wide discounts acting as the catalyst.

By 2008 the sector was back on firmer ground, with narrower discounts and a number of successful launches. However, the global financial crisis of that year presented another challenge, with the discounts of funds invested in less liquid assets, such as private equity, hit particularly hard. This resulted in a round of rescue financing, managed wind-downs and takeovers, although it took a number of years for this to work through.

There is a lot to be learned from these two periods. Firstly, after 155 years, predictions of the sector's imminent demise may be overstated. Secondly, there is a cyclical element to the sector's fortunes that of course reflect the realities of the day. The unprecedented rise in interest rates since 2021 (in terms of speed) has had a dramatic effect on the entire investment industry. Investment companies generating yields from alternative assets had previously benefited from the demand for bond proxies. However, with the repricing of bonds, these vehicles, regardless of the merits of their respective asset class, no longer look so attractive.

In my opinion, this offers a considerable opportunity for investors willing to do their homework. We have already seen bids come for whole portfolios at significant premiums to share prices, while a wave of managed wind-downs has also been announced.

One of the key talking points amongst investment trust boards is the challenge presented by their respective shareholder bases. The last ten years has seen a huge increase in the level of ownership by retail (i.e., private) shareholders, who have used investment platforms to access investment trusts. To generalise, this segment of the market is increasingly well-informed and engaged, using sources such as Citywire and podcasts such as *Money Maker*s to keep tabs on developments and identify opportunities.

However, a real concern for boards is their tendency not to exercise their right to vote at AGMs or other public meetings. Low shareholder turnout is a growing trend and opens the risk of unintended and unforeseen outcomes. This should not be confused with apathy from private investors. Historically, it has been more difficult than it should be for them to exercise their rights, although there are signs that this is changing, with the investment platforms recognising the importance of this element of shareholder rights.

It should also be noted that one of the positives during this period of retrenchment for the sector is that there is no evidence of retail investors selling up and moving on. If anything, many seem determined to take advantage of the widening discounts.

Investment trust boards are also concerned about the impact of developments in the wealth management industry. Wealth managers have historically been significant investors in investment trusts, reflecting both their heritage as private client stockbrokers and the willingness to access more esoteric asset classes. However, the growing adoption of buylists and the increasing importance of centralised research teams have led to a focus on a narrower cohort of investment trusts.

This has been exacerbated by the ongoing consolidation in the wealth management industry. Not that long ago, an investment trust would have to have a minimum market cap of £100m – for liquidity reasons – before a wealth manager would consider investment. Today, that level is more like £400m for many, with a greater focus on the liquidity the secondary market can provide.

Investment trust boards are very conscious of this, and it has been one of the drivers behind a wave of consolidation across the sector. Despite the oft-heard claim that boards are averse to consolidation for the same reason that turkeys don't vote for Christmas, in my opinion, in general this is no longer the case. Boards are increasingly mindful of the importance of size and potential advantages of merger opportunities. However, they are also focused on how any corporate activity would benefit their existing shareholders. They are not in the business of growing assets at any price.

There has to be some demonstrable benefit for their investors to justify the cost and potential disruption of consolidation. Mergers of investment trusts are still relatively infrequent, largely reflecting the complexities and costs involved. However, it is a trend that I would expect to continue, particularly during this period of retrenchment for the industry.

Looking three years down the track, I believe that the investment companies sector will look markedly different. Assuming relatively benign market conditions, I would imagine that discounts would narrow in aggregate as a function of the consolidation and retrenchment process that has already started. A number of managed wind-downs will take some years to complete, and many will still be with us in three years' time. However, there will be fewer investment companies, particularly in sectors where there is an oversupply. I would expect to see far fewer funds providing access to specialist sectors and a reduction in the number of investment companies with assets of £200m or less.

Some well-known portfolio managers across the sector will have hung up their boots in that time too. While it is always sad to say farewell to talented investors, retirement often paves the way for the next generation of investment talent to come to the fore. In future, I would also expect to see a more diversified slate of professional investors, a trend that is already gathering pace, albeit slowly.

Another characteristic of the investment companies sector in three years' time will likely be an increase in the level of retail ownership to even greater levels. This will be driven by the recognition of the benefit of the closed-ended fund structure for long-term investors and facilitated by the prominence of retail platforms.

This will reinforce what is already a huge priority for investment trust boards: the necessity to attract, educate and inform private investors. Investment trusts have an important role to play in ensuring adequate levels of retirement provision for UK investors. Despite the undoubted challenges that the sector currently faces, there remains a huge opportunity.

TRUST
PROFILES

PANTHEON'S PROGRESS

by JONATHAN DAVIS

With alternative trusts at the heart of the sell off prompted by higher interest rates, I look at how two large trusts managed by Pantheon are rising to the challenge of reducing their discounts.

The discount challenge

T HE TWO INVESTMENT trusts that Pantheon manages have contrasting histories. The origins of Pantheon International (PIN) as an investment trust go back to 1987, when it was first listed, meaning that it has notched up 37 years as a listed private equity vehicle. By contrast Pantheon Infrastructure (PINT), which as its name suggests invests in a broad range of infrastructure assets, came to the market just two years ago, in November 2021.

Unsurprisingly therefore it is still much smaller in size, with an asset base that is around a fifth of Pantheon International's £2.4bn. The latter is the third largest trust in the listed private equity sector on that measure, behind only 3i (III) and HarbourVest (HVPE), while PINT is the smallest of the ten generalist infrastructure trusts, albeit with a still not inconsiderable £485m of assets (as at 1 October 2023). Both trusts in turn are part of Pantheon's much larger global private markets business, which runs or advises on more than $90bn around the world, but they play an important role that goes beyond their respective shares of the business.

Because the two trusts are listed, they are the most visible of the many funds that Pantheon manages and therefore are seen within the firm as a shop window for its broader private markets business. Both trusts, one can note in passing, are no strangers to launching into difficult markets. PIN's IPO took place in September 1987, just a month before the infamous stock market crash of October 1987, while PINT was launched only months before a combination of the Russian invasion of Ukraine and surging inflation prompted the big investment trust rerating of the last two years.

In common with the great majority of other trusts, both trusts have subsequently found themselves trading on significant discounts. In the case of PIN the discount at one point, in October 2022, widened to almost 50%, which is well above its long-term average, while shares in PINT have moved from a premium to a discount. It reached 25% at one point this year, in line with the sector average.

A difference between the two is that while the majority of private markets trusts have consistently traded at a discount for over a decade, although not at these wide levels, infrastructure trusts have rarely done so since they first appeared on the London market. In both cases therefore, given the higher profile that a listing gives them, the derating poses an important challenge for everyone involved – boards, shareholders and managers alike.

In the case of PINT, with hindsight launching in 2021 may not have been ideal timing, but the trust did complete its IPO before the market for new issues closed. It followed that up with a successful subscription share issue in the summer of 2022, which increased its share count by 20%. The idea behind the trust's IPO, says Richard Sem, the head of Pantheon's European infrastructure and real assets business, was to offer investors a general broader exposure to infrastructure as an asset class, in contrast to other trusts which concentrate on specific sub-sectors, such as renewable energy or public sector projects like roads and airports. The best example of this diversified approach is 3i infrastructure, which I think can be safely described as the proven leader in the field, and has the best performance track record since its launch in 2007.

For Pantheon International, using new shares has rarely been on the cards, given the longstanding discount on which it and most of its peers have habitually traded, but the challenge has been how far the discount has widened, rather than the discount itself. Although the discount did briefly exceed 50% during the global financial crisis, when many private equity funds were caught going into the crisis with too much debt, a more normal level of discount for PIN over the past decade has been in a range between 15% and 25%.

Making waves

The board of PIN has stood out this year by seizing the investment opportunity that has been provided by the wide discount. Having announced a modest initial buyback programme in 2022, which appeared to have only a modest impact, more recently it has stepped up the pace. In September 2023 it announced a £200m buyback programme and shortly afterwards gave shareholders the option of a tender offer as an alternative. This allowed a maximum of £150m of shares to be sold back to the company by shareholders in a form of competitive auction.

The board will no doubt be pleased to see that this more active approach has begun to bear fruit, with the discount coming in by more than 10% over the course of a few weeks and the shares rising some 25% since its earlier lows. The chairman of the trust, John Singer, won plaudits from observers (myself amongst them) by coming up with a strong statement in the latest annual report about the need to take the discount issue more seriously. In his words: "I believe that the listed private equity sector has not kept up with the changing needs of shareholders and that there is a real opportunity now to do more to put shareholders' interests first".

More specifically he argued that buying back the shares at such a wide discount was clearly a good use of the trust's money: "By using buybacks we are effectively committing capital to a portfolio that we know well and in whose asset value we have faith. At high discount levels… the resulting improvement in NAV per share is significant and immediate". In addition to the £200m buyback/tender offer programme, which is equivalent to some 15% of the trust's market capitalisation, the board said it would in future commit to dedicating a proportion of any net cash proceeds realised by asset disposals to share buybacks, the exact proportion to be determined by the extent of the prevailing discount.

Changing perceptions

By proceeding in this way, Pantheon is clearly trying to counter a common perspective that private equity managers have historically been reluctant to scale back the size of a trust, which would – coincidentally or not – directly reduce their already potentially significant management and performance fees. At the same time the trust has also decided to beef up its marketing and communication efforts, the better to persuade retail investors of the merits of listed private equity as an asset class.

Mr Singer made the point that, just as the first investment trusts in the Victorian age gave private investors access to a diversified portfolio of investments they could not easily make themselves, so listed private equity trusts today are a gateway to an 'invitation only' asset class that has become a staple element of the most successful professional investor portfolios in recent years, but is not one that private investors can readily invest in directly, other than through listed investment trusts.

Having started life as a fund of funds private equity house, investing in funds on either a primary or secondary basis, Pantheon International has steadily over the years switched its focus towards direct and co-investment opportunities. They now account for just over half the value of Pantheon International's total portfolio. Among other advantages this makes it easier to directly control what the trust is investing in, and to provide more insight into the underlying companies, a key element in explaining the intricacies of what has long been seen as a somewhat opaque and misunderstood asset class.

Helen Steers, the Pantheon partner responsible for the trust, lists several reasons why she thinks private equity is not as well understood as it should be. Some people confuse what it does with venture capital, for example, when in fact high-risk early-stage companies make up just 3% of Pantheon International's portfolio. Nor are mega-buyouts, the multi-billion dollar leveraged acquisitions made famous in movies like *Wall Street* and books like *Barbarians at the Gate*, what it mostly does. Its bread-and-butter businesses are small and midcap buyouts, investing in growing entrepreneurial businesses that have exciting potential, but may need capital and private equity expertise to help them reach the next stage.

PIN's NAV has been marked down from a high of 492p per share (as at 30 September 2022) to 470.8p (as at 30 September 2023), largely due to adverse foreign exchange movements (around 77% of its portfolio is denominated in USD), but the share price has begun to move in the opposite direction. Even after a difficult year in 2022, Steers says, the average five-year rate of revenue growth across Pantheon's portfolio was 18% per annum and the average earnings growth rate 20% per annum. Contrary to myth, most investments aren't loaded up with debt and then sold to gullible stock market investors through IPOs, but typically end in sales to corporate acquirers.

The average gain on realising investments over the last decade in Pantheon International's case has been 31%, which gives the lie, she says, to the idea that the valuations of private equity trusts are out of date and overstated. This is another of the common explanations you will hear for why the discounts of most private equity trusts have widened so dramatically over the last two years.

What about the idea that private equity firms load too much debt onto the companies they invest in, making them vulnerable to the sharp rise in interest costs that we have also seen? "We don't believe that", Steers says. Concerns about debt are "overblown". There has been no rush of rescue refinancings, for example, in the portfolio, and many companies Pantheon International invests in don't need to refinance their debt for a few years yet.

The obvious next question then is why, if everything is so rosy in the garden, have the discounts widened so much? Have the markets just got it completely wrong, always a dangerous assumption to make? Her response to that is not only that the realisations in the portfolio have been consistently at prices above the most recent NAV, but that it is actually in the interests of the private equity managers to be conservative in their assessment of portfolio company valuations.

One reason is that they like to give investors pleasant surprises rather than bad ones. Another is that unlike hedge funds, private equity managers don't get fees on unrealised gains, only on the amount of capital that investors have committed. They earn their carried interest (or 'performance fee'), which is potentially the greater part of their reward, only when an asset is turned into cash, and even then it has to be offset against any losses made on other invested companies.

There is one exception however, she concedes, which is when less successful private equity funds are out fundraising and struggling to find investors, there can be a temptation to use or stick with higher valuation marks in order to get more capital. But that is not Pantheon's situation: "If you've got top-quartile private equity fund managers in your portfolio, they're not incentivised to do that. Because if they pump up their valuations, people commit to a new fund, and then it's all a disaster six months later, that's actually not going to help their reputation. It's a bit of a desperate tactic".

Turning to Pantheon Infrastructure, Richard Sem gives two main reasons when asked to explain the existence of his trust's discount. "Historically, infrastructure has had a tremendous ability to pass through inflation, either through contracted inflation or through some form of regulatory underpinning. Ninety percent of our assets have that underpinning in one form or another. Investors have typically looked to infrastructure in bad times as well as good because it gives them that inflation hedge. I don't personally think the market is properly appreciating the extent of that inflation protection at the moment".

Secondly, he thinks, they may not be looking closely enough at the nature of the assets which PINT is invested in. "These are all growth-oriented assets. We're looking to back management teams that have living and breathing operational businesses. Our 13 assets all have growth paths". In addition, they also have long-term funding and hedging programmes in place so that they are not greatly exposed to changes in interest rates. Maybe the market is getting the message, as the shares here too have been rallying since the lows of August, with the discount narrowing by 5% while the published NAV has increased slightly to above the original issue price.

Valuations in the spotlight

In terms of valuations, the discount rate PINT uses to value its holdings is around 14% on average, notably higher than some of the older more established infrastructure trusts, which are using discount rates of 7%–8%. (Sem himself worked for several years for InfraRed Partners, the managers of HICL, one of the older core infrastructure trusts.) That, he says, reflects the greater delivery risk in the portfolio or – if you want to view it from the other side of the camera – the greater upside potential. Overall risk is also mitigated by the portfolio being diversified across North America, Europe and the UK.

It is a mistake however, Sem says, just to look at the discount rate in isolation when assessing the valuations in infrastructure. The important thing is to look in detail at the expected cash flows; when valuing those cash flows infrastructure firms have already made adjustments to allow for changes in the macro-environment. Summing up the factors that investors have been worrying unduly about, he says, "If I look at the portfolio today I would say inflation is net positive, debt mildly negative, and discount rates probably very mildly negative". The key point, he adds, is that "the underlying assets are doing exactly what they should be doing. I believe the NAVs are correct".

In his view the discount problem is all about a shortage of investor demand, rather than a problem with valuations. In order to stimulate new demand PINT is also making conscious efforts to make its portfolio more transparent. "We provide a case study on every asset investment thesis, so that people can really understand what they're investing in. Not everybody understands why the digital infrastructure space, for instance, is an attractive place or the differences between data centres, mobile towers and fibre to the home ('FTTH') infrastructure. Investors should be able to really understand each of the individual assets we own".

For her part Steers says that increased disclosure, greater transparency and more information is good for all investors, not just private investors. "We get feedback from our institutional investors as well saying that they want more of everything. They want more data, they want more disclosure, they want more ESG. It is actually very important to private equity because there has been this reputation in the past that it there hasn't been enough transparency". The main problem is having to sign confidentiality agreements with many of the trust's fund partners, which limits the amount of detail that can be published.

Towards the future

The initial response to Pantheon International's £200m buyback and tender offer programme looks positive and will be closely watched by its peers to see if it provides a template for others to follow. The discount has certainly narrowed more than that of other private equity trusts, even those that are doing buybacks. In the case of PINT, which announced a more modest £10m buyback programme in March, the impact has been positive but so far been less marked. Its latest interim results, showing a small gain in reported net asset value, were however well received in September.

Discounts are of course not ultimately what will determine the popularity of the two trusts. There has to be good NAV performance as well, while the cost of investing in private markets remains a big topic of discussion. It is clear that private equity as a business is experiencing a downturn in terms of fundraising and deal activity, while the pressure on discount rates as bond yields rise continues to put infrastructure valuations under pressure. While they see mitigating factors for their own trusts, both Steers and Sem are at pains not to underplay the potential impact of macro-factors and in particular the risk of an economic slowdown.

"I think the recessionary risk is very real and the greatest concern that we are all very focused on" says Sem. While interest rates may be close to peaking, there is no sign yet of them starting to fall. He takes comfort in the portfolio's inflation linkage and the fact that only one of its 12 assets is particularly sensitive to changes in GDP. Steers adds that PIN's portfolio is currently tilted towards defensive businesses in information technology and healthcare, and points out that the best private equity trusts tend to outperform public markets even more in bear markets than in bull markets.

It remains to be seen how this all plays out. The economic environment will be what it is. For the moment, the revenue and profit growth of the trusts' portfolio businesses continue to show resilience. The boards of the two trusts are signalling that they are taking heed of shareholders' discount concerns and opting for self-help measures where they can. If Pantheon International's blunderbuss approach to tackling its discount continues to prove successful, you can be sure that other trusts across the alternative asset sectors will be forced to sit up and take note – while their shareholders may be wondering why such a robust approach has not been attempted earlier.

MURRAY INTERNATIONAL

STUART WATSON explores Murray International (MYI), the second-largest fund in the Global Equity Income sector. After 20 years at the helm, Bruce Stout plans to retire in June 2024, handing over management of the portfolio to two of his long-time colleagues: Martin Connaghan and Samantha Fitzpatrick.

URRAY INTERNATIONAL WAS founded in 1907 and was originally known as The Scottish Western Investment Company, reflecting its Glasgow roots. Like many trusts of that vintage, it initially focused on bonds before shifting more towards equities during the 1930s and 1940s.

The company used its accountants as its investment managers in its early days. When this practice became frowned upon in the 1960s, the firm of Murray Johnstone was created to take on the portfolio management business. The name of the trust became Murray Western in 1979 and then finally Murray International in 1984.

Murray Johnstone was swallowed up by Aberdeen Asset Management in 2000, now of course known as abrdn after its merger a few years back with Standard Life. Murray International is currently the largest of 19 trusts run by abrdn and has total assets of £1.7bn. The wider abrdn business looks after around £500bn of assets, so Murray International makes up a relatively small but high-profile part of its overall operation.

Although the trust's objective has been tweaked over the years, a high level of income from a globally diversified portfolio of equities has been a consistent theme. The current objective is "to achieve an above average dividend yield, with long-term growth in dividends and capital ahead of inflation, by investing principally in global equities".

There is also a history of long-tenured managers and promotions from within the wider investment team. David Briggs managed Murray International from 1988 to 2004. Bruce Stout began working with Briggs in 1992 and served as deputy on the trust for a while before being made its lead manager in 2004.

In June 2024, Stout intends to retire, and the portfolio will then be managed by Martin Connaghan and Samantha Fitzpatrick, currently co-managers of the trust, both of whom have worked with Stout since the early 2000s.

Under Stout, Murray International shares have returned around 625%, a little ahead of global markets, and the dividend per share has been increased every year from a split-adjusted 3.3p to 11.2p with an average year-end yield of roughly 4%.

Stout is famous for his clear and consistent criticism of the way Western economies have managed their affairs in recent years, and that has led to Murray International's portfolio looking distinctly different to the typical global trust with around a quarter of its assets in each of North America, Europe, and Asia and a sizeable weighting towards Latin America. One example of the contrarian nature of the trust's approach is that for many years now one of its largest holdings has been Aeroporto del Sureste, a Mexican airport owner.

The portfolio is concentrated for a trust of its size, with around 50 equity positions and around a dozen fixed-income holdings. However, no one position tends to exceed 5%, so it's a flatter-looking portfolio than most, with most holdings having a weighting of between 1% and 3%. Portfolio turnover has tended to be extremely low, often less than 10%. Even in 2020, when there was considerable volatility and Stout was more active in the market than usual, turnover was just 17%.

The look of the portfolio has changed quite a lot since Stout took over from Briggs. Back in 2004, there were well over 100 equity positions and a few dozen fixed-income holdings. Around 40% of the portfolio was in UK companies or bonds but now it is just 4%.

The trust's high yield has made Murray International very popular with retail investors, and it has often traded at a premium to NAV as a result. Its emphasis on capital preservation can also be seen in its average monthly returns. Figures from abrdn for the 20 years to December 2022 (reproduced in a recent Edison research report) showed that the trust outperformed by an average of 0.79 percentage points in 85 months of down markets and underperformed by 0.24 percentage points in the other 155 up months.

Given that Connaghan and Fitzpatrick have been working with Stout for over two decades, no major style changes are expected; but it will be interesting to see what changes they do make to the portfolio. I suspect one change we will notice is far less of the strident macro commentary that has made Stout such a quotable figure.

Key stats for Murray International

- Founded: 1907
- Domicile: UK
- Management firm: abrdn
- Managers: Bruce Stout (since June 2004 and retiring June 2024), Martin Connaghan and Samantha Fitzpatrick (since Jan 2020 and ongoing)
- Ticker: MYI
- AIC Sector: global equity income
- NAV return over the last 10 years: 7.5% annualised (6th out of 7)
- Comparator: FTSE All-World
- Recent price: 240p
- Market cap: £1.5bn
- NAV per share: 257p
- NAV update frequency: daily
- Discount to NAV: 7%
- Five-year average discount: 2%
- Charges: 0.52% OCF and 0.9% KID
- Management fee: 0.5% of net assets up to £0.5bn and 0.4% thereafter
- Performance fee: no
- Discount control policy: may issue or buy back shares if they trade at a "persistent significant discount or premium"
- Continuation vote: no, unlimited life
- Net gearing: 8%
- Number of holdings: 64 (50 equity and 14 fixed-income)
- Top 10 positions: 33%
- Year-end: 31 December
- Results released: March (finals) and August (interims)
- Dividend and historical yield: 11.2p for 2022 and 4.7%
- Dividends paid: August, November, February, May (final)

Price and related data as at August 2023.

Investment style and policies

Murray International uses a conservative, quality-based, and bottom-up approach to portfolio construction, so despite Stout's strong macro views the distinctive geographic mix of its holdings is primarily driven by the companies it believes have the best long-term sustainable prospects.

According to its annual report, holdings are evaluated using five key factors:

* the durability of the business model and moat,

* the attractiveness of the industry,

* the strength of the financials,

* the capability of management, and

* an assessment of the company's ESG credentials.

In terms of company valuation, there is a focus on "earnings yields, free cashflow yields and dividend yields, set against expected long-term growth rates for those elements". The managers target "a double-digit implied annual return".

A global coverage list of 2,000 stocks is whittled down to between 40 and 60 positions plus a further watch list of around 8–10 potential holdings that might be added to the portfolio when they are deemed to offer a more attractive rate of expected risk-adjusted returns.

New equity positions tend to be 1% to 1.5% but any position that ends up exceeding 5% will usually be sold down within 30 days, hence the flat nature of the overall portfolio.

Fixed-income positions tend to be smaller, typically 1% or less. Stout says there have essentially been two times during his time in charge when the portfolio shifted significantly towards fixed income.

The first was in the summer of 2007, when gilts and US treasuries looked very attractive and the weighting towards fixed income went as high as 28%. Although Stout expected to hold these positions for several years, they were mostly sold within 18 months in favour of cheap-looking equities in the wake of the global financial crisis. The second occasion was 2014–15 when emerging market debt looked attractive and 15% of the portfolio was fixed income. These positions were still unwinding in the summer of 2023 when the weighting to fixed income was in the region of 7%. When the Covid-19 pandemic struck in early 2020, they provided a useful source of funding to buy cheap equities, just as the fixed-income holdings had done in early 2009.

There is little in the way of formal investment restrictions with no geographical, sector, or industry constraints. Instead, there is a risk-based approach to ensuring the portfolio has a sufficient level of diversification on various metrics. The official maximum position size is 15%, but in practice, and as already mentioned, holdings are trimmed should they go over 5%.

Murray International has the authority to own a wide range of securities such as convertibles, preference shares, and unlisted investments; but it seems to be rare for there to be any significant exposure to these instruments. Although it is predominantly a non-sterling portfolio and there is structural gearing in the form of sterling-based debt, there's no currency hedging.

Performance

This table summarises Murray International's last 20 years. All the per-share figures adjusted for a 5-for-1 share split that took place in April 2023:

YEAR TO 31 DEC	NAV (£M)	SHARE PRICE (P)	DISCOUNT	SHARE COUNT (M)	DIVIDEND (P)	DIVIDEND COVER (X)	GEARING
2003	371	78	−8.5%	438	3.3	0.80	17%
2004	413	87	−7.5%	438	3.3	0.96	18%
2005	524	112	−5.9%	438	3.5	1.01	12%
2006	579	124	−6.5%	438	3.8	1.03	12%
2007	646	132	−10.2%	439	4.2	1.00	15%
2008	569	118	−5.9%	454	4.6	1.06	11%
2009	742	153	−1%	480	5.4	1.08	15%
2010	968	188	1.1%	520	6.9	1.11	16%
2011	999	183	2.7%	560	7.4	1.18	14%
2012	1,192	210	7.4%	611	8.1	0.98	10%
2013	1,237	210	7.2%	630	8.6	1.02	15%
2014	1,241	205	6.1%	642	9.0	0.91	14%
2015	1,091	166	−2.3%	643	9.3	0.98	17%
2016	1,448	238	4.6%	637	9.5	1.08	13%
2017	1,599	254	1.3%	639	10.0	1.04	11%
2018	1,420	226	2.2%	641	10.3	0.96	13%
2019	1,539	252	5.9%	647	10.7	1.01	11%
2020	1,462	226	−0.7%	642	10.9	0.86	13%
2021	1,561	231	−6.8%	629	11.0	0.94	12%
2022	1,617	267	3.1%	625	11.2	1.07	11%

Murray International uses the FTSE All-World Index as a comparator rather than a formal benchmark. Up until April 2020, it used a blended index of 40% UK and 60% world-ex-UK indices. When Stout took over in 2004, the portfolio was around 40% weighted towards the UK, so the blended index made sense. But the UK weighting was reduced pretty quickly, so the eventual move to a purely global index was long overdue.

That said, Stout has long put more emphasis on both income and capital growth and paid little heed to any short-term differences relative to global indices. Indeed, it's rare to see the trust and global markets have a similar year in performance terms. Typically, the two will diverge by at least several percentage points and there have been several years under Stout's watch where the difference has been between 10 and 20 percentage points. Not everyone may agree with Stout's view of the markets, but his trust could never be accused of being a closet tracker!

Now that Stout's 20-year tenure is almost complete, the trust's returns since June 2004 give us a good idea of his overall legacy. It's undoubtedly impressive although the first half, when conditions very much favoured his style of investing, was much stronger than the second.

In broad terms, the share price total return is around 650% versus around 550% for the FTSE World Index and 270% for the FTSE All-Share. On an annualised basis, that's about 11%, 10% and 7% respectively. It's worth highlighting that the trust has been geared throughout this period, at an average of around 13%, and that has been beneficial for returns in most years.

From 2004 to 2012, Murray International returned nearly 16% a year while global markets produced around 7%. From 2013 to 2022, the period when US markets have outshone just about everything else, is almost the reverse, with Murray International at around 7% a year and global markets at roughly 12%.

On a capital preservation basis, Murray International has an excellent record under Stout with NAV losses in just three of the last 19 years: −12% in 2008 and −8% in both 2015 and 2018. Technically, there was a −0.1% loss in 2011, but I'm more than happy to give Stout a pass on that one given that global markets were down some 7%.

Recent returns provide another illustration of how the trust's performance often diverges from world indices. In the heady markets of 2021, the NAV rose 14%, but world markets raced ahead with a 20% gain. In the much more sober environment of 2022, Murray International rose 9% but world markets fell 7%. Investor enthusiasm returned in the first half of 2023, with the trust's NAV rising 2% but world markets up 8%.

The trust has a strong retail following, partly thanks to its income focus. This has meant that it's been strongly rated for most of the time that Stout has been the lead manager. The average year-end discount has been 1% and the trust has often traded at a premium and been able to issue new shares.

The share count went from 439m at the end of 2007 to 630m at the end of 2013, an increase of 44%, coinciding with the trust's best period of returns. There have been periods of both issuance and buybacks over the last decade, and the share count is little changed since 2013 at 625m.

There is no fixed discount control policy, but the latest period of buybacks began in July 2023 when the discount hit around 5%. The trust also bought back its shares in 2016, 2020, 2021, and 2022. There are no other discount control policies in place, such as continuation votes, conditional tender offers, or regular redemption opportunities.

Historically, the trust also had B shares as well as ordinary shares. The B shares came into existence in the 1960s as a response to regulation change, allowing dividends to be issued in the form of new shares rather than being paid out in cash. Their usage dwindled over time, and the last of them were converted into ordinary shares back in 2016.

As this is primarily an income trust, dividends are a key component of overall returns. Murray International has increased its dividend every year since 2004, so it has an 18-year record of a rising payout and should enter the AIC's Dividend Heroes list when it publishes its 2024 results.

There have been several years since 2004 when the dividend hasn't been covered by earnings, but the average dividend cover over the last 20 years has been 1.0 times. The directors are happy to add to revenue reserves when times are good and draw them down in leaner years.

In 2020, when many companies cut or ditched their dividends, Murray International's revenue return declined a relatively mild 14%, demonstrating the financial strength of its underlying holdings. The dividend was fully covered in 2022 with revenue return per share 11% higher than it was in 2019, before the pandemic struck. Revenue reserves were £69m at the end of 2022, identical to what Murray International paid out in dividends that year.

Comparing the recent performance of Murray International against the rest of the Global Equity Income sector paints an unflattering picture. The trust's 7.5% 10-year annualised NAV return puts it sixth out of seven trusts behind JPMorgan Global Growth & Income (13%), Scottish American (12%), Invest Select Global (11%), Henderson International Income (9%), and STS Global Income & Growth (8%). Only the tiny British & American comes in lower (7%).

Most global trusts have also outperformed Murray International over the last decade, with the bulk of them falling between 9% and 12% on an annualised basis. But if we were to look back to 2004, Murray International's returns are similar or better than most of its rivals.

Periods of relative underperformance are always a risk with a highly distinctive approach, and it's next to impossible to know when the tide will turn in Murray International's favour once again. However, if US markets continue to prosper for the next several years, the trust could once again struggle to keep up.

Portfolio

Currently, 93% of Murray International's portfolio is in equities and 7% is in fixed income. Within equities, North America is the largest regional weighting at 26% with both Europe-ex-UK and Asia-Pacific-ex-Japan at 25%. Latin America is 13% with the UK at 3% and Africa at 1%. Asia-Pacific-ex-Japan and Latin America plus other emerging markets make up around 5% of the 7% in fixed income.

The absence of any Japanese holdings strikes me as unusual given this market's lowish valuation multiple. And there are just three Chinese positions totalling 3%. Indian exposure is even lower at 1% via two fixed-income positions. The two African positions are both in South Africa (MTN and a government bond).

Taiwan accounts for 9%, with TSMC making up nearly half of that. Korea, Singapore and Indonesia account for most of the other Asia-Pacific holdings. Brazil, Mexico and Chile account for the Latin America positions. The US holdings include Broadcom, Philip Morris, AbbVie, CME, Bristol-Myers Squibb, Cisco, Johnson & Johnson, Merck, and Verizon – all of which are relatively gently valued compared to most other US stocks. The European positions cover similar sectors and are almost exclusively in Northern Europe, with Italy's Enel being the lone exception.

You can tell that sector weightings aren't considered that important as they don't feature in either the trust's interim reports or its monthly factsheets. The annual report mentions them in passing with the end of 2022 weightings being financials (14%), technology (13%), telecoms (12%), health care (12%), consumer staples (11%), industrials (9%), energy (9%), and basic materials (6%). Consumer discretionary is the most notable absentee, although sector weighting can be a somewhat crude way to look at overall exposure given the way many companies can straddle several industries, depending on how you view their operations.

Directors and major shareholders

Murray International currently has seven directors. David Hardie was appointed to the board in 2014 and took over as chair in 2021 when the previous chair, Simon Fraser, sadly passed away after a short illness just a few months after taking on the role. The other directors were appointed in 2016, 2018, 2021, 2022, 2023 and 2023. Hardie is set to retire from the board at the end of 2023 with Virginia Holmes, who joined the board in 2022, taking on the role of chair in January 2024.

Total share ownership by the directors is around 140,000 (£0.33m) as at August 2023, quite low for a large global trust, with more than half of those shares being held by the soon-to-retire Hardie. All of the directors are independent of the manager, and they have a wide range of experience in the financial industry and the trust sector.

Bruce Stout's holding in the trust isn't disclosed, but he has said in the past that it is substantial. In a video interview with interactive investor, he characteristically quipped "Like any Scotsman, as soon as it goes to a discount I'm always very interested".

The list of major shareholders as of March 2023 shows a strong retail following, with the three major platforms plus abrdn's retail plans accounting for nearly a third of the overall register:

- Hargreaves Lansdown: 10.5%
- Rathbones: 10.1%
- interactive investor: 9.9%
- abrdn Retail Plans: 8.3%
- Evelyn Partners: 5.8%
- Charles Stanley: 5.5%
- Investec Wealth & Management: 4%
- AJ Bell: 3.5%

Charges

There's been a pleasing downward trend in the charges levied in recent years. When Stout took over in 2004, the basic fee was 0.5% of total assets (i.e., excluding any long-term borrowing) plus a performance fee.

At the start of 2016, the performance fee was removed and a tiered fee structure from 0.575% to 0.425% was introduced but on net assets rather than total assets.

Reductions to the tiered fee structure were made in 2019 and 2022 and the basic fee is now 0.5% up to £500m of net assets and 0.4% above £500m. With net assets of around £1.6bn, the majority of the fee is charged at the lower rate of 0.4%.

That gives Murray International an ongoing charge of 0.52%, fractionally lower than JPMorgan Global Growth & Income's 0.56% and Scottish American's 0.59%, the two closest in terms of size within the global equity income sector. Murray International is also pretty competitive against the global sector with only Scottish Mortgage and Monks having lower ongoing charges.

The Key Information Document for the trust puts charges at 0.93%. Within this, a figure of just 0.07% is ascribed to portfolio transaction costs, which is not surprising given the low level of portfolio turnover, and the remaining difference is most likely due to the inclusion of interest costs (which aren't included in the standard ongoing charges calculation).

Gearing

Murray International hasn't altered its level of gearing much in the last 20 years. Recently it has been carrying around £200m in structural gearing and a small amount of cash, so variations in its net gearing level largely arose from changes in the valuation of its portfolio rather than any active decision to increase or lower the level of borrowing.

The average level of year-end gearing since 2003 has been 13%, meaning that Murray International has traditionally been one of the most highly geared trusts across the global and global equity income sectors.

The structural gearing used to consist of a number of fixed-rate bank loans that were refinanced every four or five years on a rolling basis. In 2021, the trust decided to issue loan notes instead, agreeing a £200m shelf facility to do so. The first loan rate using the shelf facility was for £50m at a fixed rate of 2.24% and it runs for 10 years to May 2031. A further £60m was issued for 15 years to May 2027 at a slightly higher rate of 2.84%.

A bank loan for £60m matured in May 2023, but no new loan note was issued in its place as the directors decided the rates available in the market were not competitive enough. The final bank loan for £30m matures in May 2024, and we'll have to wait and see whether a new loan note will be issued to replace it.

That means that Murray International currently has total borrowings of £140m and net gearing of 8%, its lowest level since 2007. The average rate for all the trust's borrowing is a fixed rate of 2.5%. If Murray International does decide to take out further loan notes, that average rate could be somewhat higher.

Closing thoughts

Stout will undoubtedly be a tough act to follow, but as both Connaghan and Fitzpatrick have been working with him since before he became the lead manager of Murray International, there should be no one that is better placed to do so. The pair have had an increased profile promoting the trust in the last couple of years, so the timing of Stout's retirement isn't a particular surprise, and it's good to see that shareholders were given almost a year's notice of the change.

Nevertheless, it seems likely that both the portfolio and the overall strategy might evolve a little bit, so portfolio turnover will be a useful area to monitor for those who want to gauge the extent of any changes made.

Rather than the change of manager, the bigger question for many investors is how long the trust's distinctive style might remain out of favour, which is an issue facing many value- or income-focused funds. In the last decade, Murray International outperformed its reference index only in 2016, 2017, and 2022. Of course, shareholders have been rewarded with a steadily rising income and rarely suffered any prolonged and significant drawdowns. Nevertheless, those nervous about the way US stocks dominate global indices may also find Murray International a useful diversifier.

A unique investment philosophy

AGT
AVI GLOBAL TRUST

Nearly four decades of bottom-up fundamental investing.

Asset Value Investors (AVI) has managed the c.£1.2bn* AVI Global Trust since 1985. Our strategy has remained consistent for this period: buying quality companies held through unconventional structures, trading at discounts. The strategy is global, bottom-up, benchmark agonistic and research driven.

AVI's robust investment philosophy guides investment decisions. Emphasis is placed on three factors: (1) companies with attractive assets, where there is potential for growth in value; (2) a sum-of-the-parts discount to a fair net asset value; and (3) identifiable catalysts for value realisation. **A concentrated high conviction core portfolio of c. 30± investments allows for detailed research which forms the cornerstone of our approach.**

AGT's long-term track record bears witness to the success of this approach, with a NAV total return well in excess of its benchmark. We believe that this strategy remains as appealing as ever and continue to find plenty of exciting opportunities in which to deploy the trust's capital.

Discover AGT at www.aviglobal.co.uk

Past performance should not be seen as an indication of future performance. The value of your investment may go down as well as up and you may not get back the full amount invested. Issued by Asset Value Investors Ltd who are authorised and regulated by the Financial Conduct Authority.

*Gross Assets at 31 August 2023
±As at 31 August 2023, holdings >1% of NAV

AVI
Asset Value Investors

FIDELITY EMERGING MARKETS LIMITED

JONATHAN DAVIS *talks to Fidelity Emerging Markets Limited about the upside potential in emerging markets.*

FOLLOWING A STRONG period of performance in the years before and after the global financial crisis, recent emerging market returns have been lacklustre, with dollar strength one of several headwinds. The MSCI Emerging Markets Index has returned just over 5% per annum (in sterling terms) over the last 10 years, nearly 6.0% less than the MSCI All Country World Index and trailing the S&P 500 Index by even more. With valuations below historic levels, a revival in this asset class is now overdue.

Fidelity Emerging Markets Limited (FEML) offers investment company shareholders a differentiated way to invest in this asset class. The mandate for running this company, formerly known as Genesis Emerging Markets, was handed to Fidelity in October 2021 when the board and the larger shareholders of GEM saw greater upside potential in moving the mandate to Fidelity, the family-run global fund management group, whose FAST Emerging Markets strategy had produced some good results in its open-ended form since its launch in October 2011. By the end of September 2021, the fund had delivered a 7.7% annualised return since launch (net of fees, A-ACC-USD share class) relative to the benchmark index which had returned 4.8% over this period.

The Genesis/Fidelity deal was completed in the autumn of 2021. After a difficult start when Russia's invasion of Ukraine meant the company had to mark down its Russian holdings to zero, the board and managers, led by Nick Price, believe that as market conditions improve their distinctive strategy is well placed to return to its past form.

Heather Manners, a former fund manager with more than 30 years of experience investing in Asia and emerging markets, took over chairing the company's board at the end of 2022 and is certainly bullish about its prospects. Although she was not involved in the original decision to choose Fidelity, she says that despite the Russian setback she is more than happy with it. "Nick Price and his team have a phenomenal reputation and an excellent track record. Fidelity offers an incredibly deep resource of really good-quality research, as well as teams that have been together for a long time, and they have this demonstrable track record over a long period".

"In my mind the current situation gives investors a really great opportunity to come in and buy a great team at a massive discount with a lot of value in the company. And that's how people should be looking at it. The past 18 months", she continues, "have been spent repositioning the portfolio after the shock of the war in Ukraine, talking to shareholders, reviewing all our service providers and reconstituting the board, and that process is now largely complete".

More ways to deliver

The time is ripe therefore, she believes, for the company to start delivering on its promise of superior performance and getting the message out to potential investors about the upside potential. Market conditions are favourable for both the asset class and the managers' go-anywhere, quality-growth approach. More demand will come once the performance starts improving, as there are signs that it may have started to do more recently.

In the 12 months to 30 September, during which the emerging markets index eked out a small positive gain (in sterling terms), the company delivered a net asset value total return of 3.2%, although the discount, at 15%, remained wider than the sector average. "I believe", Manners says, "we have to trust that the team really know what they're doing and they're going to produce excellent numbers. Our job is to do everything else around that in that belief, so that everything comes together at the same time".

While a maximum 25% of the shares held by investors were tendered under the terms of the deal that switched the mandate from Genesis, suggesting a possible overhang of stock, she doubts that it is still there. In any case, she says, share buybacks at the present time would have been unhelpful in the past year. While buybacks are "on our agenda at every board meeting, we are not yet doing them. We have first focused on areas we believe will be much more supportive to keeping a sustained narrower discount in the future".

The value of an enhanced toolkit

The broad long-short approach of the Fidelity team, unique in the emerging markets investment trust sector, may well be one of the keys to finding new demand for the shares, as Chris Tennant, co-manager of the company with Nick Price, explains. He lists several reasons why having the ability to both go short (to bet that share prices will fall) and make use of options is an attractive approach for the portfolio and for emerging market investment companies more broadly.

First of all, Fidelity's large team of analysts around the world are trained to look in depth at companies in their sector. This includes not just the successful ones, but those that they deem are failing as well. This generates plenty of good shorting ideas. The research process, unlike those of long-only rivals, is specifically designed to throw up these opportunities.

At the same time emerging markets are a "fertile hunting ground" for shorting, he points out. "Shorting in emerging markets is particularly attractive in a high-interest-rate environment, with many emerging economies particularly proactive in raising rates to bring inflation under control. When a company has a broken balance sheet, [these higher rates] will often result in huge interest burdens that they are unable to afford".

Another reason why this approach can work is that emerging equity markets are generally less efficient. "Badly run emerging market state-owned enterprises are ignored by a lot of market participants, and I think that leads to a lot more inefficiencies in pricing. What we're really looking for are companies that are in structural decline or have a number of red flags around their business. That can be red flags around the balance sheet. It could be bad corporate governance, bad management, companies that are hiding debt off balance sheet and so on".

It should be pointed out that trusts that take short positions have to pay particular attention to liquidity, including the possibility of being trapped in losing positions they cannot easily sell. To reduce the risk, individual short positions are kept to a maximum of 100bps of the value of the portfolio. The average position size is around 40bps.

Overall Fidelity's long-short strategy involves running a gross exposure of up to 165% but keeping net exposure around 100%. In simple language, it is looking to add value from its stock-picking abilities, not from trying to time the market. It uses CFDs (contracts for differences) rather than borrowing to implement the strategy.

A second way that the company uses derivatives to manage the portfolio involves using options to hedge the company and generate additional income and control risk. This includes both selling call options when the shares of a company the portfolio managers are bullish on is nearing its target price, and also selling put options against short positions. That is a way of hedging the exposure of the individual stock positions, and serves to reduce the volatility of the portfolio and provide a useful source of income.

The results to date of both the shorting strategy and the options book have been encouraging. As of the end of September 2023 the short positions (including both individual shorts on stocks and the short index positions) had added over 3.3% to the company's relative performance since the start of the year, while the options book had also contributed positively. It is logical to expect that the short book's contribution could increase as interest rates rise, Tennant says, because many of the companies he and his colleagues are shorting are the ones with broken balance sheets, making them especially vulnerable.

Towards a new cycle

The traditional arguments for investing in emerging markets are that they offer access to countries with faster-growing economies, an expanding class of consumers and lower stock market valuations, together with attractive diversification potential. Those arguments still apply, notably so in terms of valuations, which are below their historical average.

Why then has the performance of emerging markets been relatively poor recently? Tennant offers two main reasons. One is the impact that the Russian invasion has had on sentiment towards emerging markets. The second is developments in China, including the hit to growth from the country's lengthy Covid lockdown and the question marks hanging over its over indebted property sector. China accounts for such a large part of the emerging market index, at around 30%, that it has a disproportionate impact on the performance of emerging markets as an asset class.

When the emerging market cycle turns, as it likely will in due course, the investment company structure and the extra dimensions of Fidelity's strategy will both be helpful. "What is really exciting", he says, "is the ability to invest much further down the market cap spectrum. We are able to invest in a lot more exciting midcap ideas, companies that are poorly covered by the sell side and are less commonly owned by other funds". Whereas open-ended funds have to sell positions to fund redemptions from their investors, the investment company structure enables the managers to take a more long-term view.

Drawing on her three decades of experience, Manners points out that there are still many good reasons for believing that emerging markets are in a good position to weather a weaker macroeconomic environment. Valuations of the quality growth businesses that Fidelity looks to own in its long portfolio are at attractive levels.

"I am generalising here, but many emerging market countries have much lower inflation than we are struggling with in the West and they don't in general have the deficits that a lot of Western countries have. They also have a huge amount of natural resources, which is going to be massively in demand as time goes by and bodes well for quite a lot of these countries. Many of them are more self-sufficient in food than Western countries and they are still only starting on their trajectory towards creating new generations of middle-class consumers, which creates extraordinary investment opportunities, as we have seen in China and India".

"Speaking now with my old fund manager hat on, I used to work on the basis that people roughly have five-year memories at best, and if something has prevailed for five years, or certainly 10, it is then usually seen as the norm that would just continue. But usually when people start to think like that, actually everything changes. I think we may be on the cusp of one of those points where the prevailing trends have been there for too long and the writing is on the wall for them".

This could be emerging markets' turn to shine, in other words. "You can see that in terms of the narrowness of what's leading markets up in America, for example. Quite honestly, looking at the American market today, I think there's way more value and diversification to be had from putting money to work in emerging markets. At this point, we're still messengers of that change, rather than proof of that, but I am confident that idea will be borne out in time".

There are a couple of other sectors, she adds, in which there are companies which have the ability to take short positions, and they are not only doing well against their peers, but also tend to trade at a much narrower discount. The room that having shorting as an option creates to move away from the benchmark could be especially valuable from here. It allows the company to benefit from investing in disruptors and make money by shorting the disrupted.

"Take the example of AI" she says. "AI will be a very disruptive thing. There will be companies that will do brilliantly by using AI or by supplying the 'picks and shovels' that make it happen. But there will be many companies which will be horribly disrupted by it to the point of death. Being able to invest and make money from both sides of that disruption is a really valuable proposition, and it's not something that other investment companies can do".

"What you've got to remember is that this company hasn't really started on its journey yet. We are really only now starting to settle down to proper business and showing what this strategy can do. Certainly if the managers are able to produce the numbers that the strategy has done in the past, or anything close to it, then my guess is that this company could easily trade at a premium because it will be able to offer differentiated performance in a differentiated way and do so at a cost less than its peers".

Fidelity Emerging Markets Limited (FEML) took over the management of the Genesis Emerging Markets trust in October 2021. At 30 September 2023, it had a market capitalisation of £539 million, making it the third-largest company in the sector.

Cut through with conviction

Available in an ISA

FIDELITY INVESTMENT TRUSTS

Truly global and award-winning, the range is supported by expert portfolio managers, regional research teams and on-the-ground professionals with local connections.

With 400 investment professionals across the globe, we believe this gives us stronger insights across the markets in which we invest. This is key in helping each trust identify local trends and invest with the conviction needed to generate long-term outperformance.

Fidelity's range of investment trusts:

- Fidelity Asian Values PLC
- Fidelity China Special Situations PLC
- Fidelity Emerging Markets Limited
- Fidelity European Trust PLC
- Fidelity Japan Trust PLC
- Fidelity Special Values PLC

The value of investments can go down as well as up and you may not get back the amount you invested. Overseas investments are subject to currency fluctuations. The shares in the investment trust are listed on the London Stock Exchange and their price is affected by supply and demand.

The investment trusts can gain additional exposure to the market known as gearing, potentially increasing volatility. Investments in emerging markets can more volatile that other more developed markets. Tax treatment depends on individual circumstances and all tax rules may change in the future.

To find out more, scan the QR code, go to fidelity.co.uk/its or speak to your adviser.

F&C INVESTMENT TRUST

STUART WATSON *takes a look at F&C Investment Trust (FCIT), the first investment company to be launched back in 1868 and now a widely diversified global equity trust with around 400 positions.*

WITH A HISTORY that spans over 150 years, F&C is believed to be the oldest investment company. It was set up in 1868, a time when security frauds and scams were rife, and the aim was to give investors access to a diversified portfolio of overseas government securities. As the 1990 annual report describes, "British Government securities were then yielding about 3% while overseas bonds offered a much better return".

The initial portfolio consisted of £1m invested in 18 government securities from various countries with yields ranging from 5% to 14%. The idea of a collective investment scheme took a while to catch on, but it soon proved the benefits of diversification. A Spanish government bond was the sole defaulter from the initial portfolio, missing a payment in 1875.

In 1891 the trust branched out into railway and industrial debentures. Equities entered the mix in the 1920s, again with a heavy overseas tilt, and this asset class has dominated the portfolio for many decades now.

The oldest accounts available via Companies House are from 1975 and show a portfolio of over 300 companies with 40% invested in the UK and net assets of £110m. The overweight toward UK equities persisted until 2013 when the trust's benchmark was switched to the FTSE All-World index. Today, the number of holdings is around 400 with around 10% in UK companies, and net assets are around £5bn.

Remarkably, F&C has had just 11 investment managers over its entire 155-year history, and it has only had three managers over the last 55 years. Michael Hart ran the show from 1969 to 1997; F&C's share price rose twentyfold to 160p over that period, and he is also credited with the invention of the savings scheme, which F&C introduced in 1984.

Hart was said to have fans that included Warren Buffett and Tony Blair, and his 'low-risk, nibble away' approach resulted in 500 shareholders attending F&C's AGMs at the height of his popularity. Citywire quotes Hart describing how he cashed in when prices plunged a few years after he took charge:

In 1974 stocks fell so far and so fast that everyone lost hope. But panic creates great opportunities and towards the end of the decline, I presented a list of stocks I wanted to buy to the board. They were blue-chip stocks at bargain basement prices, so we agreed I would borrow some money and take a big bet on them.

Jeremy Tigue was the lead manager of F&C from 1997 to 2014, although his involvement with the trust dates back to the early 1980s. Over 17 years, he produced a share price return of 220% compared to 170% for the FTSE All-World index.

Tigue introduced many changes to the way the trust is managed that are still used today. For example, a 5% allocation to private equity was introduced in 2003, starting long-term relationships with Pantheon and HarbourVest. The allocation was raised to 10% in 2006, and it was around 12% in the summer of 2023.

In 2005 Tigue outsourced the management of some of F&C's US portfolio to external managers. One of the original three firms chosen, Barrow Hanley, is still used today while another, T. Rowe Price, was only dropped from the portfolio in early 2023.

Since July 2014 F&C has been managed by Paul Niven. As I write this, F&C has returned around 150% in the nine years he has been in charge, pretty much in line with the FTSE All-World Index. Niven was previously head of multi-asset investment at F&C and chair of its asset allocation committee. He joined the trust's management company straight from university in 1996, suggesting he is around 50 years of age.

In 2014, F&C Asset Management, the trust's original management firm, was acquired by BMO. A few years later in 2018, the trust opted to ditch the Foreign & Colonial name and it became known simply as F&C Investment Trust. BMO sold its EMEA investment business to Columbia Threadneedle in 2021. Columbia Threadneedle manages around $600bn with 2,500 staff including more than 650 investment specialists. So, despite being the fourth largest investment trust on the London market, F&C makes up just 1% of Columbia Threadneedle's overall business.

Key stats

- Launched: 1868

- Domicile: UK

- Management firm: Columbia Threadneedle

- Manager: Paul Niven (since July 2014)

- Ticker: FCIT

- AIC Sector: global

- NAV return over the last 10 years: 11% annualised (4th in sector out of 13)

- Benchmark: FTSE All-World

- Market cap: £4.4bn

- Discount to NAV: 11%

- Five-year average discount: 5%

- Charges: 0.5% OCF and 1% KID

- Management fee: 0.3% up to a market cap of £4bn and 0.25% thereafter

- Performance fee: no

- Discount control policy: regular buybacks to achieve a "long-held aspiration of the shares trading at or close to NAV per share" and to dampen discount volatility

- Continuation vote: no, unlimited life

- Net gearing: 4%

- Number of holdings: 433

- Top 10 positions: 13%

- Year-end: 31 December

- Results released: March (finals) and July (interims)

- Historical dividend and yield: 13.5p for 2022 and 1.6%

- Dividends paid: August, November, February, May

Data as at August 2023.

Investment style and policies

F&C's official objective is "to achieve long-term growth in capital and income through a policy of investing primarily in an internationally diversified portfolio of publicly listed equities, as well as unlisted securities and private equity, combined with the use of gearing". Its approach "benefits from a range of individually concentrated global and regional portfolios alongside the diversification benefits of lower risk and lower volatility achieved by managing these portfolios in combination".

Under oversight from F&C's board of directors, Niven takes overall responsibility for asset allocation, gearing, stock and sector selection, and risk management. Although he has responsibility for overall portfolio composition, he delegates stock selection decisions and has the flexibility to use other fund managers both within Columbia Threadneedle and externally to manage parts of the portfolio.

F&C has arguably only been a truly global trust for the last decade, having maintained a high weighting towards UK equities prior to 2013. The timing proved prescient as the UK market has mostly lagged behind global equities since that point. Many other global trusts had high UK weightings until relatively recently as well, so F&C is not atypical in this regard.

While F&C invests primarily in listed equities, it can invest in other types of securities or assets. It has no geographic or sector exposure limits and up to 5% can be invested in unlisted securities in addition to its private equity holdings. Shareholder approval would be sought if the long-term exposure to private equity looked likely to exceed 20% of the portfolio (it has ranged from 7% to 17% over the last decade). No single investment should exceed 10% at the time of acquisition.

Borrowing should typically be in the range of 0% to 20% although it rarely exceeds 10%. F&C has done some currency hedging recently, which is relatively unusual for a mainstream global equity trust. In 2020, the trust bought £300m of sterling as a "strategic, partial hedge on our overseas currency exposure". This was reduced to £200m in 2021 and to £20m by the end of 2022. The trust made a profit on this decision in 2021 but a similar-sized loss in 2022 so it seems to have had relatively little impact on overall returns.

Portfolio

With roughly 400 positions at any one time, F&C has an extremely well-diversified portfolio. Typically, the largest equity position will be around 2% followed by half a dozen other positions between 1% and 2%. By the time you get to the hundredth-largest position you are down to 0.3%, so there is a very long tail. There is one private equity fund that accounts for around 4% but this, of course, consists of many underlying investments.

A lot of portfolio commentary relates to high-level allocation decisions between regions and underlying strategies rather than individual company buy and sell decisions. The following table shows the high-level weightings in June 2023 with the global and private equity investments reallocated to show how F&C differs from its benchmark global index:

CORE STRATEGIES	STRATEGY WEIGHTING	WEIGHTING REALLOCATING GLOBAL AND PE	BENCHMARK
North America	38%	54%	63%
Europe including UK	13%	27%	16%
Japan	5%	7%	6%
Emerging markets	7%	9%	10%
Developed Pacific	-	3%	4%
Global strategies	26%	-	-
Private equity	12%	-	-

After reallocating, we can see there's a higher weighting to Europe including the UK at the expense of North America, similar to many other mainstream global trusts.

The North American weighting primarily consists of US value and US growth strategies, managed externally by Barrow Hanley and JPMorgan respectively, and a smaller, internally managed US core set of positions that use a 'growth at a reasonable price' approach. The Japan strategy is managed by another team within Columbia Threadneedle.

With global strategies, there are three sub-strategies: income, sustainable opportunities, and quality value. Two of these are delegated to other parts of Columbia Threadneedle. There was previously a fourth global strategy for global smaller companies, but this was exited in 2022.

The private equity strategy has shifted focus somewhat under Niven's watch. Legacy fund-of-funds positions run by Pantheon and HarbourVest are now just a couple of percent of total assets. The majority of the private equity allocation now consists of direct investments made alongside Columbia Threadneedle and Pantheon. Some positions in other investment trusts, such as Schiehallion and Syncona, are included within this total as well.

F&C has made commitments to invest in various private equity funds which will be drawn down over the next few years. These came to £482m at the end of 2022, a big increase from £187m at the end of 2021, but still fairly manageable in the context of around £5bn in net assets. However, it looks like the weighting towards private equity could increase over the next few years, perhaps back up to the high teens once again.

One useful table in the F&C annual report breaks down the medium-term returns by strategy:

Returns from 2018 to 2022

STRATEGY	FCIT	INDEX
North America	67%	70%
Europe including UK	21%	23%
Japan	8%	13%
Emerging markets	0%	5%
Global strategies	38%	46%
Private equity	83%	n/a

F&C has lagged the indices a little in all regions over this period, but private equity has boosted its returns to offset this.

The trust did better in the previous five-year period from 2013 to 2017, only lagging in emerging markets. This period covers the tail end of Tigue's time in charge and means there isn't a full five-year history for the global strategies brought in by Niven:

Returns from 2013 to 2017

STRATEGY	FCIT	INDEX
UK	59%	58%
North America	160%	141%
Europe excluding UK	93%	88%
Japan	128%	112%
Emerging markets	45%	51%
Global strategies (2015 to 2017 only)	53%	53%
Private equity	91%	n/a

While these figures don't provide any insight into the success or otherwise of the allocation decisions made between the individual strategies, they do suggest that F&C has rarely differed that much from the underlying indices over medium-term periods. They also provide some justification for the weighting towards private equity, although this is an area worth watching more carefully over the next few years, given its likely increased weighting and general valuation concerns.

Portfolio turnover has been fairly consistent in the last few years, typically in the region of 50%. Both 2021 and 2022 saw a reduction in the US growth and global smaller companies categories, with funds reallocated to US value, US core, and global income.

Performance

The next table summarises F&C's performance over the last 20 years:

YEAR ENDED 31 DEC	NAV PER SHARE (P)	DISCOUNT	SHARE COUNT (M)	DIVIDEND (P)	GEARING
2003	217	−13.1%	949	3.7	8%
2004	233	−16.7%	913	4.2	8%
2005	292	−11.4%	827	4.8	4%
2006	321	−11.4%	750	5.3	7%
2007	364	−12.3%	685	5.9	7%
2008	263	−13%	679	6.5	12%
2009	310	−12.2%	632	6.7	6%
2010	351	−11.8%	610	6.8	13%
2011	327	−11.7%	590	7.1	16%
2012	360	−11%	577	8.5	14%
2013	425	−11%	570	9.0	8%
2014	458	−8.1%	562	9.3	9%
2015	483	−7.1%	559	9.6	9%
2016	587	−7.4%	547	9.9	7%
2017	676	−4.3%	542	10.4	7%
2018	643	−1.5%	542	11.0	7%
2019	754	1.5%	543	11.6	10%
2020	832	−5.4%	537	12.1	8%
2021	999	−7.3%	527	12.8	9%
2022	932	−3%	518	13.5	7%

F&C has made steady progress over the last two decades, although the overall return shown in the table is flattered by starting at a low point for markets in 2003 after the dot-com bust.

On a capital-only basis, there have been only four negative years in the last 20: −28% in 2008, −7% in 2011, −5% in 2018, and −7% in 2022, which were all years where global market returns were poor.

Over the 10 years to 2012, F&C's NAV return was 144% – just ahead of the 129% from its composite UK and global benchmark. The FTSE All-World Index produced a 132% return over that same period.

Over the 10 years to 2022, F&C returned 210% while the FTSE All-World Index was a little further back at 191%. Given how hard it can be for diversified global funds to beat an index, especially in recent years with the very largest companies performing so strongly, I would call that a pretty respectable result. Admittedly, the annualised margin of outperformance over the entire 20-year period is quite small at 10.6% a year versus 10%.

F&C shareholders benefitted from a narrowing discount over these two decades although the discount has widened out again to the low double-digits as of summer 2023. F&C's returns have also no doubt been helped by the modest level of gearing in markets that have generally been rising. The trust has also bought back around half its shares since the late 1990s when legislation changes made share repurchases more tax efficient, adding perhaps 0.3% to the annualised return over this period.

The level of buybacks has been a lot slower over the last decade, reflecting the fact that F&C's discount has been a bit narrower than it was in the 2000s. Indeed, in late 2018, with the trust trading at a premium for the first time in its entire history, it was able to issue its first shares since 1959. A few more share issues took place in 2019 before the trust began to trade at a discount once again.

The official stance on discount control is as follows:

> We buy back shares in the market for the benefit of shareholders where we see value and, importantly, in pursuit of a sustainably low deviation between the share price and NAV per share and to dampen discount volatility, in normal market conditions. The policy and the levels within which it has operated are continually reviewed, with the aim of achieving the long-held aspiration of the company's shares trading at or close to NAV per share.

So far, 2023 is shaping up to be a more difficult year for F&C. The NAV is trailing the trust's benchmark by three percentage points and the share price by 10, due to the discount widening once again. That may be partly because of the general decline in the ratings across the whole trust sector and partly because of investor concern about any trust that has any unquoted exposure. The discount has been quite a lot more volatile in the last few years than it has been for some time so this may be something the board seeks to address.

Given its wide level of diversification, it would be surprising to see F&C be the best-performing global trust over any sustained period, but its returns measure up pretty well against the rest of the sector in my opinion.

Over the last 10 years, most of which have been on Niven's watch, F&C's 11% annualised NAV return places it fourth out of 13 trusts. Scottish Mortgage and Lindsell Train are way ahead at 16.8% and 16%, but F&C is only just behind Mid Wynd's 11.6%. F&C sits ahead of Monks, Alliance, Brunner, Bankers, Martin Currie Global, AVI Global, and Witan, which have returned between 10.3% and 8.4%.

F&C's longer-term performance back to 1995 is a little more middling. I only have share price total return data for this period and on this basis, it trails Scottish Mortgage, AVI Global, Monks, Mid Wynd, and Alliance but is ahead of Bankers, Brunner, and Witan.

Dividends

F&C can pay dividends from capital but says it has no intention to do so. Over the last decade, dividends have roughly matched the underlying income from the portfolio, with F&C adding to its revenue reserves in some years and drawing them down in others.

The 2022 dividend of 13.5p was covered by earnings of 13.9p, and there is a further 18p in revenue reserves. That means F&C should have little trouble in continuing to increase its dividend in future, as it has done every year since the early 1970s. It sits in sixth position on the AIC's list of Dividend Heroes with a 52-year record of rising dividends. I believe F&C has also paid a dividend for all 155 years it has been trading, which is arguably even more impressive.

F&C's yield is 1.6%, pretty much in line with its average for the past five years, and similar to the yield you would get from a global index tracker. The average yield for the last 20 years is around 2% with F&C yielding a little bit more when it had a greater weighting towards UK equities.

Gearing

F&C's average level of gearing over the last 20 years has been 9%, so its current level of 4% is a little lower than usual. As at June 2023, F&C held around £300m in cash and short-dated gilts offset by £580m of structural gearing in the form of loan notes.

There are currently 13 separate loan notes repayable at various points from 2026 to 2061, so there is no significant near-term refinancing risk. The average interest payable is just 2.4%. If we turn the clock back a decade, before these loan notes were issued, the average rate payable was in the region of 7%, so F&C has done an excellent job in securing cheap borrowing for the next few decades.

Directors and major shareholders

F&C has eight directors, all of whom are considered independent. Beatrice Hollond joined the board in 2017 and became chairman in January 2020. The longest-serving director joined in 2016.

While there is plenty of experience across the board, there's very little experience of serving on the boards of other trusts mentioned in the annual report, which is a little unusual. The directors owned around 60,000 shares between them at the end of 2022, worth a collective £0.5m. That's a little on the low side for a large generalist trust like this, although quite a few directors are relatively new appointments.

Paul Niven, on the other hand, held 191,697 ordinary shares as of 6 March 2023. He was a shareholder before becoming manager in 2014 and has continued to be invested on behalf of both himself and his family.

Around two-thirds of F&C shares are held through retail platforms, such as Columbia Threadneedle's long-running savings scheme. There is no list of major shareholders over 3% listed in the annual report that I could see and, unusually, no RNS announcements relating to changes in holdings.

Charges

F&C's basic management fee is 0.3% up to a market cap of £4bn and 0.25% above that level, so it's pretty competitive. A decade ago, the management fee was a flat 0.365% so the direction of travel has been downwards in recent years. The use of some external managers means that the ongoing charges are a little higher at around 0.5%. It's good to see the basic fee is measured against market cap rather than net assets, though, so shareholders see some reduction when the trust trades at a discount.

F&C is one of the cheapest global trusts, helped by its large size. On an ongoing cost basis, the likes of Scottish Mortgage, Monks, and Bankers are slightly cheaper, but F&C is a little less expensive than Alliance, Mid Wynd, Martin Currie Global, Brunner, Witan, and AVI Global.

Closing thoughts

F&C has proved to be a remarkably consistent performer over an extremely long period and has managed to outperform global markets, albeit at a fairly gentle pace, over the last two decades with a little help from some modest gearing and regular share buybacks.

The low level of charges, securing a low interest rate across all its structural debt, and the fact that its lead managers usually stick around for at least a decade are other plus points.

It may not be the most exciting trust to own, but many of us no doubt feel that we've had more than our fair share of excitement over the last few years!

Actual investors are focused.

Not frantic.

Search for Actual Investors

Baillie Gifford™
Actual Investors

POLAR CAPITAL TECHNOLOGY

STUART WATSON *profiles Polar Capital Technology (PCT), the largest trust in the AIC's technology sector, which was launched in 1996 and now has assets of over £3bn.*

POLAR CAPITAL TECHNOLOGY made its stock market debut in December 1996. It was originally known as Henderson Technology, and it was the rollover vehicle for a previous technology fund called TR Technology. Brian Ashford-Russell had managed TR Technology from 1988 to 1996 and was also PCT's first lead manager.

PCT started with net assets of around £140m, and its share price closed at 98p on its first day of trading. As at August 2023, the share price had increased to £22, representing an annualised gain of 12.4% over nearly 27 years and making PCT one of the best-performing trusts over this period.

The trust's early performance in the late 1990s was spectacular, and the top holdings of the time included many names that will be familiar to those who were investing during the tech boom and bust, such as America Online, Microsoft, EMC, CMG, Cisco, and Logica. Only one of those names, and no prizes for guessing which one, remains in the portfolio today.

PCT's net asset value (NAV) per share increased by 43% in the year ending April 1998, 34% the following year, and an astonishing 126% in the year ending April 2000. Net assets at this point were a sizeable £669m, and the trust's shares traded at a 10% premium – such was the demand for anything tech-related.

In September 2000, with the share price hitting what turned out to be a long-time peak of 567p, it was announced that Ashford-Russell and Tim Wooley, the trust's co-managers, were leaving Henderson to help set up a new company called Polar Capital. The trust followed them to their new home and changed its name to Polar Capital Technology a few months later.

As we know now, the next few years were brutal for technology investors. The NAV per share declined by 38%, 27%, and then 21% over the next three years. The share price even briefly fell back below its IPO price in October 2002, and it wouldn't be until late 2014 that the share price peak set in 2000 was reached again.

Ben Rogoff joined Polar Capital in 2003, initially taking charge of the trust's US portfolio. After a short sabbatical, Ashford-Russell decided to take a back seat and

Rogoff took on the post of lead manager in May 2006, a position he still occupies today. Rogoff is responsible for switching the investing style from an all-cap fund to what he calls a 'benchmark aware' approach. This means PCT often has sizeable positions in the largest tech stocks – Apple, Alphabet, Microsoft and so on – although its weightings tend to be a little lower than they are in the trust's benchmark, the Dow Jones Global Technology Index.

Rogoff credits Ashford-Russell with teaching him that one of the keys to success in tech investing is trying to avoid the really big losers – crucial in a sector where companies can suffer massive share price declines over short periods. The benchmark-aware strategy builds on this with the theory that you can't afford to miss the big winners either.

PCT's share price recovered to around 250p in early 2007 but then halved to 125p in late 2008 as the financial crisis deepened. However, this set the stage for a prolonged period of extraordinary gains. The share price hit 300p by 2010 and then doubled to 600p by 2015. The shares almost reached £14 before the taper tantrum in 2018. Then there was another extraordinary run from £11 in early 2019 to £27 in early 2022 when the war in Ukraine began, interest rates started to rise and investors turned much more sceptical on growth stocks.

PCT's share price fell from £27 to £17 over the course of 2022. However, by August 2023, it had recovered to £22 thanks to renewed enthusiasm for mega-cap tech stocks, and in particular excitement about the prospects for AI. By contrast, the discount on the shares had increased to 14%, the widest level it has been since 2009.

Key stats

- Launched: 16 December 1996
- Domicile: UK
- Management firm: Polar Capital
- Manager: Ben Rogoff (worked on the trust since 2003 and lead manager since May 2006)
- Ticker: PCT
- AIC Sector: technology & technology innovation
- NAV return over the last 10 years: 19.3% annualised (2nd out of 2 in the sector)
- Benchmark: Dow Jones Global Technology Index
- Market cap: £2.8bn
- Share price: 2,220p
- Share count: 125m
- Discount to NAV: 14%
- Five-year average discount: 7%
- Net cash: 5%
- Charges: 0.81% (OCF) and 1.2% (KID)
- Management fee: 0.8% of NAV up to £2bn, then 0.7% up to £3.5bn, 0.6% thereafter
- Performance fee: 10% of any outperformance of its benchmark subject to a high-water mark
- Discount control policy: no fixed policy but has regularly either issued or bought back shares
- Continuation vote: yes, every five years with the next one due in 2025
- Number of holdings: 90
- Top 10 holdings: 49%
- Year-end: 30 April
- Results released: July (finals) and December (interims)
- Dividends: none paid since the trust was launched

Data as at August 2023.

Investment approach

The portfolio is built around several core themes, although they tend to evolve over time. These weightings are as at August 2023:

- Cloud infrastructure/cybersecurity – 23%

- Data economy/artificial intelligence – 19%

- Digital advertising/ecommerce/payments – 16%

- Connectivity/5G/internet of things – 15%

- Software/digital transformation – 12%

- Mobility and electric vehicles/energy transition – 9%

PCT shifts the weightings between themes based on its evaluation of the balance of risk and reward at any particular time. As of now AI is undoubtedly the key theme, and Rogoff says the entire portfolio has been reviewed to remove companies deemed to be on the wrong side of the AI trade, as he puts it. While not everything in the portfolio has to have a direct AI angle, he says the hurdle rate for inclusion has effectively been raised.

Rogoff reckons that while 19% of the portfolio is directly linked to AI, in practice around 70% of positions have some level of exposure and nearly 90% could be AI beneficiaries in some shape or form. Around a third of the trust's latest presentation deck is devoted to AI and the terms 'AI' and 'artificial intelligence' are mentioned nearly 100 times in the most recent annual report. There have been many false dawns, but this time it looks like the age of AI may have finally arrived.

It's clear that Rogoff, a keen student of history, thinks that AI could be transformative in the same way as the internet and smartphones were in previous decades. Adoption of software like ChatGPT has been much swifter than we've seen with previous major technologies, and Rogoff reckons that one potential outcome of this is that AI disrupts multiple industries much more quickly than many people expect. The fact that the majority of the world's population could soon have access to multiple AI-powered services through their handheld devices could be another factor pointing to fast adoption.

A lot of the trust's positioning towards AI at this stage is via semiconductors, reflecting the need to build out the infrastructure behind this new technology, but this will undoubtedly change as the industry matures and other opportunities present themselves. And it's clear that despite PCT's enthusiasm for the potential of AI, they are still intent on their long-held strategy of not paying too much on a relative basis for individual stocks.

Of course, it's also extremely difficult to predict exactly who will be the biggest winners and losers from AI. Alphabet is a good illustration of why that might be the case – while it was an early investor in this space with its acquisition of Deep Mind, Rogoff suggests we might also see its core search advertising business being bypassed because of advances in AI.

In terms of its actual investing process, PCT has a universe of around 4,000 stocks which it whittles down to around a hundred to make up its portfolio. The thematic overview comes first, focusing on real-world changes in user behaviour.

PCT's managers carry out hundreds of meetings a year, not only with companies in the portfolio but also their rivals, suppliers and sector experts to get a more rounded view of the industry. According to Quoted Data, PCT looks for stocks that can grow 30% to 50% quicker than the average company in its benchmark index but it aims to pay no more than 20% to 30% more in valuation terms to secure those greater growth prospects.

A fair value is calculated for each stock, which is regularly reassessed, and positions tend to be trimmed if the share price approaches these levels. Positions are also sold if the management of a company fails to execute on its plans or there is a fundamental change to its business model.

Portfolio turnover tends to be quite high as a result, as it often is for specialist equity trusts. In the last two financial years, it's been in the region of 80% to 90%. Despite this, PCT has held many of its top positions for a very long time, such as Microsoft from 2007, Apple from 2003 (it was Rogoff's first purchase after joining PCT), Alphabet from 2005, Samsung from 2007, Amazon from 2009, and both TSMC and ASML from 2001.

There are currently around 90 positions in the portfolio with around three-quarters of the portfolio invested in North America. The vast majority of holdings (more than 90% by value) are worth more than $10bn. Rogoff tends to avoid both early stage companies that are yet to become profitable and/or cash-generating and also more mature and slower-growing tech veterans. He prefers to concentrate on businesses that are riding the long uptrend of the emerging/adoption and mainstream stages of the Gartner hype cycle. That means that the likes of Cisco, IBM, Oracle, SAP, and Texas Instruments – all notable components of PCT's benchmark – are unlikely to be found in its portfolio.

While the trust has the authority to invest up to 10% of its portfolio in unquoted companies, there are no such positions at the moment. There are a number of formal investment restrictions that are measured at the time of acquisition or when PCT adds to a position:

- Not more than 10% of gross assets in one company. However, if a company makes up more than 10% of the benchmark, the trust can match the index weighting to a maximum level of 15% (Apple and Microsoft are recent examples of stocks in this category).

- A maximum of 25% in emerging markets – the current level of exposure is not explicitly disclosed but appears to be around 10%.

- There are some regional weighting guidelines which are North America (up to 85%), Europe (up to 40%), Japan and Asia (up to 55%) and the rest of the world (up to 10%) although it's rare for any of these to be needed. Specific limits may be set for countries deemed to have elevated risk, such as Russia.

PCT is authorised to borrow up to 20% of its net assets but only has a small amount of structural gearing at present, consisting of some two-year fixed-rate loans in US dollars and Japanese yen that taken together come to around £50m.

For many years now, the trust has typically held a significant amount of cash and therefore had an overall net cash position in the single digits. As well as providing the firepower to buy new positions, this can also dampen the high level of price volatility that its portfolio typically experiences. NASDAQ put options are also sometimes used to dampen volatility as these can generate a profit should the market fall heavily over a short period.

Despite these two measures, PCT still tends to be quite volatile, with Trustnet showing a beta of 1.3 over the past three years (i.e., the typical share price movement has been 1.3% for every 1% move in the overall market). However, that's less than the beta of similar trusts such as Scottish Mortgage and Allianz Technology.

The underlying yield of the portfolio is in the region of 0.5%, which is less than the trust's management fee and other expenses. As a result, PCT has never paid a dividend since it was launched in 1996 and seems unlikely to do so for the near future.

In terms of measuring its performance, PCT initially used the FTSE World Index as there was no suitable global technology index available in the 1990s. Since around 2001, the trust has measured itself against the sterling version of the Dow Jones Global Technology Index and uses this to calculate its performance fee. This index consists of 900 stocks, but it is very concentrated with around 60% by value in the 10 largest companies. While it is a fairly good match for the trust's portfolio, there are a few major PCT holdings that aren't included within it, most notably Amazon, Visa, and Mastercard.

PCT's website is a useful source of information on the trust with both factsheets and annual reports available for the last twenty years, a far longer history than you typically see. QuotedData produces paid-for research reports and Rogoff is a regular podcast guest both on Money Makers and many other investing shows. You can usually find a fairly recent presentation that he has done on YouTube as well.

Capital structure and discount control

PCT's early capital history was slightly complicated by the fact that it often had a large number of subscription shares outstanding. The last of these was exercised in 2014, making its current share structure a lot simpler.

The trust has no formal discount policy, but there have been several prolonged periods when it has either been buying back its shares, either to reduce its discount or lessen share price volatility, or been issuing new shares when it was trading at a premium to NAV. It holds continuation votes every five years, with the next vote due in September 2025.

The share count was around 150m from 1996 to 2004 but fell to 115m after a large share buyback programme that took place in the year ending 30 April 2005. Around 19m subscription shares were exercised in late 2005, and since then the trust's share count has moved within a fairly narrow range from 125m to 140m.

The most recent period of regular share issuance was from April to July 2020, when the shares were very much in demand during the initial Covid-19 lockdown. However, PCT has been trading at a discount since late 2020 and has been buying back its shares regularly since February 2021. In the two years to April 2023, PCT spent a total of £216m on buybacks, reducing its share count from 136.5m to 126.3m, and it has continued to repurchase shares since then.

PCT's investment adviser

Polar Capital, PCT's management firm, was listed in London in early 2007 and has since grown its assets under management from around £2bn to £20bn. UK investment trusts make up just over £4bn of that total with around £3.2bn in PCT and the remainder in Polar Capital Global Financials and Polar Capital Global Healthcare. There is an open-ended version of PCT, the Polar Capital Global Technology Fund, which has slightly fewer holdings but is a little larger with assets of £4.2bn.

Polar Capital also runs a specialist AI open-ended fund that was launched in 2017 and which has around £300m of assets. This has many direct AI plays that can be found within PCT's portfolio, but it also holds positions like RELX and Baker Hughes that are deemed to be AI beneficiaries but either do not have enough of a technology focus or a sufficiently high growth rate to make it into the PCT portfolio.

A team of 10, which Polar Capital reckons is one of the largest specialised technology teams in Europe and most of whom have been with the firm for at least a decade, look after the three technology funds. Individuals within the team tend to specialise into regions and/or technology sub-sectors. They are primarily based in London, with one individual in North America. Alastair Unwin, who joined Polar Capital in 2019, was appointed as the deputy manager for PCT in early 2023.

Rogoff, the lead manager since 2006, is now aged 51. He started his career at Dean Witter before becoming a technology analyst at Clerical Medical in the mid-1990s. He spent four years at Aberdeen as a senior technology manager from 1998 to 2002 before joining Polar Capital. While his direct holding in PCT is not disclosed, he has said in interviews that he has a reasonable percentage of his net worth in the trust and other funds run by Polar Capital.

Performance

This table shows the last 20 years of PCT's NAV performance against its benchmark:

YEAR TO 30 APRIL	NAV PER SHARE (P)	NAV RETURN	BENCHMARK RETURN	DIFFERENCE
2004	194	37.1%	20.1%	17.0%
2005	190	−2.0%	−9.4%	7.4%
2006	256	34.8%	32.0%	2.8%
2007	240	−6.3%	−2.0%	−4.3%
2008	227	−5.4%	1.5%	−6.9%
2009	217	−4.4%	−5.5%	1.1%
2010	315	45.3%	39.7%	5.6%
2011	369	17.0%	4.7%	12.4%
2012	393	6.5%	8.3%	−1.8%
2013	412	5.0%	6.0%	−1.0%
2014	458	11.2%	13.1%	−1.9%
2015	599	30.7%	29.4%	1.3%
2016	606	1.0%	−0.1%	1.1%
2017	945	56.1%	53.4%	2.7%
2018	1,160	22.7%	17.0%	5.7%
2019	1,446	24.7%	21.4%	3.3%
2020	1,716	18.6%	18.1%	0.5%
2021	2,496	45.5%	46.3%	−0.8%
2022	2,305	−7.6%	−0.9%	−6.7%
2023	2,239	−2.8%	2.9%	−5.7%

Both over and underperformance seem to have come in patches of a few years. PCT has generally done better than its benchmark in bull markets and lagged in bears or sideways markets. That would seem to make sense given its focus on slightly smaller and faster-growing companies, and you tend to see a similar pattern in other specialised equity trusts.

In terms of annualised performance over these 20 years, PCT returned 15.2% on a NAV basis compared to 14% for its benchmark, which is a very respectable level of outperformance. Over the most recent decade, the two are more closely matched with PCT at 20.5% and the benchmark at 20.8%. But it's worth highlighting again that the 12-year bull run in tech stocks from April 2009 to April 2021 saw PCT grow at 23.4% annualised versus 21.4% for its benchmark – this was an incredibly strong and sustained period of returns that is unlikely to be repeated in future, so investors should set their expectations accordingly.

The next table looks at how PCT's share price has fared against Allianz Technology, Scottish Mortgage, Herald, and a NASDAQ 100 ETF (a broad-based passive alternative). The figures start from October 2010, a few months after the ETF was launched.

TRUST (TICKER)	ANNUALISED SHARE PRICE RETURN FROM OCTOBER 2010 TO AUGUST 2023
PCT	16.0%
Allianz Technology (ATT)	18.4%
Scottish Mortgage (SMT)	15.0%
Herald (HRI)	11.4%
Nasdaq 100 ETF (CNX1)	20.0%

Allianz Technology is the most obvious direct comparator, and it takes a slightly more aggressive approach than PCT, typically holding about half the number of positions and with more of a slant towards mid-cap tech stocks. About half the difference between Allianz and PCT over this period is because PCT's discount to NAV has widened whereas Allianz started at a wider discount and is still trading at the same level.

Scottish Mortgage isn't a true tech trust of course, and it was still in the initial stages of adopting its 'disruptive growth' approach back in 2010, so that might have hampered its returns a little over the period in question. It has also had a much more challenging time in the last two years.

Herald sits in the global smaller companies sector, and about half of its portfolio consists of UK companies. I still think it's a useful fund to use as a comparator especially as it was launched in 1994, shortly before Allianz in 1995 and PCT in 1996.

The London-listed Nasdaq 100 ETF comes out top of this group, and it's also beaten just about every single open- and closed-ended fund you could have bought. It's tilted towards both the US and mega-caps, both of which have very much worked in its favour over this period. In the 2000s, it would have been a vastly different story.

Despite the ETF claiming the best record over this period, all these trusts have done exceptionally well. Out of over 250 trusts on the AIC database, Allianz is currently the second-best performer in NAV terms over the last decade, PCT the third, Scottish Mortgage the fifth, and Herald the 32nd.

Portfolio

Rogoff's comments in the trust's annual reports normally cover around a dozen pages and go into a lot of detail about the overall market environment, the prospects for various sub-sectors, and the thinking behind any major shifts in the make-up of the portfolio.

Of the various charts produced in these reports, the two I find most useful show the absolute and relative rating of technology stocks within the S&P 500. Although this is biased towards the US, I suspect a global equivalent would look quite similar. In the 2023 annual report, both charts went back 30 years, giving a perspective on current forward valuations versus the peaks of the late 1990s/early 2000s and in 2020–21.

The relative valuation of around 1.4 times for tech stocks versus the S&P is on the high side compared to the long-term average of 1.2, although it's a lot less than the level of 2.4 hit in 2000.

The chart also shows there are three clear phases, a re-rating higher from 0.8 to 2.4 from 1992 to 2001, a steady but prolonged fall back down to 0.8 by 2013, and another more gentle re-rating higher since 2013. You could argue this means that the current re-rating period is exceedingly long in the tooth and any reversal could provide a headwind for returns from here. However, earnings growth is expected to be strong, so even if there is a gradual de-rating share price returns could still be reasonable. Another factor is that tech stocks dominate the S&P these days, so you would expect the relative weighting to be much closer to 1 than it was in the past.

PCT's largest positions, ranging from 6% to 11%, are Microsoft, Apple, NVIDIA, and Alphabet. But the position sizes become a lot smaller quite quickly. The 10th largest position was 1.8% and once you drop below the top 30 it's less than 1%. The bottom forty positions tend to be 0.5% or less. One thing to watch out for will be when PCT reduces its weightings toward mega-cap tech and adopts a flatter portfolio. That could be the point where its performance starts to diverge from its benchmark a little more. This shouldn't be too hard to spot, but there is little sign of it happening anytime soon.

The average PCT stock tends to have a smaller market cap than the average in its benchmark. It will tend to be more highly valued and faster growing as well, both in terms of sales and profits. Many tech stocks have pretty strong balance sheets right now, with the biggest stocks often sitting on large cash positions and having little in the way of debt. So, although the valuation of tech stocks has come down due to the sharp rise in the risk-free rate, there should be little in the way of refinancing risk at the individual stock level. Indeed, Rogoff was quick to clear out the few stocks in PCT's portfolio that did have significant debts as soon as rates started to rise, reflecting the cautious approach taken.

Rating

PCT has been pretty strongly rated throughout most of its life, and the current double-digit discount is the widest it's ever been for any sustained period.

The discount was usually in single figures during the 1990s, but a premium of around 10% or more was not unusual at the turn of the century thanks to the unrestrained enthusiasm for all things tech at that time. The discount was in the mid-teens from 2003 to 2005 and at a similar level from 2008 to 2010, although it did get a little wider in the very depths of the financial crisis.

PCT mostly traded very close to its NAV for a decade from mid-2010 to mid-2020, with the discount widening gradually over the course of both 2021 and 2022. As I write this, it's been around the same level for the best part of a year, despite the fairly hefty amounts being spent on share buybacks and the recovery in tech stocks seen in the first half of 2023.

Relative to similar trusts, PCT's discount is at around the same level as Herald, a little narrower than Scottish Mortgage, and marginally wider than Allianz. In other words, the wider discount doesn't appear to be a PCT-specific issue, and the two occasions when it has been this wide in the past turned out to be particularly good long-term buying opportunities.

Directors and major shareholders

PCT has a fairly large board with six directors, all of whom are considered to be independent. Catherine Cripps took on the role of chair in September 2022, having been appointed to the board a year earlier. She replaced Sarah Bates, who was on the board for 11 years with the last five of those as chair. The other five directors were appointed in 2015, 2017, 2018, 2018, and 2021, so there are no long-service issues. Most serve on the boards of other investment trusts and three of them have expertise in the technology sector in a professional capacity.

All six directors have a holding in the trust, and they collectively held around 19,000 shares (£0.4m) at the last year-end. Catherine Cripps and Jane Pearce, both appointed in September 2021, bought shares in the summer of 2022, spending £10,000 and £20,000 respectively on their initial positions. At the time of writing, no director had bought shares in PCT in the previous 12 months, despite its wider-than-usual discount.

Five major shareholders, primarily wealth managers, were listed in the latest annual report, all of them holding similarly sized positions to the year before:

- Rathbone Brothers – 10.1%

- Brewin Dolphin – 8%

- Investec Wealth – 5.5%

- Quilter – 5.4%

- Lazard Asset Management – 5.1%

Charges

There has been a gradual reduction in fee rates in recent years, which is always good to see. Polar Capital took on the management of the trust using the same fee structure as Henderson, with a 1% base fee plus a 15% performance fee.

A tiered fee structure was introduced in 2015 and has been tweaked several times since then. The performance fee was reduced from 15% to 10% in 2018.

The latest fee structure is 0.8% up to £2bn of NAV then 0.75% up to £3.5bn and 0.6% over £3.5bn. PCT is a little short of that cheapest tier right now. The open-ended Global Technology Fund run by Polar Capital charges 1% plus a 10% performance fee, so PCT should be a little bit cheaper.

PCT's ongoing charges figure is 0.84%, making it slightly more expensive than Allianz, which is 0.7%. Allianz has a similar tiered structure, but its tiers are a little cheaper and reduce slightly more quickly. Allianz has the same 10% performance fee as PCT so, taking everything together, there is little to choose from between the two tech trusts when it comes to costs.

Closing thoughts

The widespread adoption of AI could play out in many ways for PCT. Over the long term, you would expect it to be a net positive for the sector, and indeed perhaps for the market as a whole thanks to the cost savings it might bring, but it's still incredibly early days and some of the initial exuberance we've seen could turn out to be excessive. Indeed, tech valuations still look relatively high against the wider market, although PCT's discount to NAV could provide some protection on that front.

It's difficult to imagine a future where tech companies become less relevant to our lives and the way we choose to spend our money. But the advent of AI and the widespread disruption it looks likely to bring suggest the road could be just as bumpy as it has been in the past.

You can read Ben Rogoff's expert take on the potential of AI on page 213.

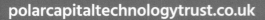

FUTURE OPPORTUNITIES

FORWARD, NOT BACK

EWAN LOVETT-TURNER, *head of investment trust research at Deutsche Numis, reviews a tough year in the markets and looks forward to what happens next.*

How has the investment trust sector performed over the last 12 months?

INVESTORS BUY THE share price of investment companies. Managers manage the net asset value performance. Over the medium term, share prices and asset values tend to move in step, but over shorter periods there can be significant divergence. Over the last year, starting with the UK's 'mini-budget' in late 2022 we have seen several asset classes experience significant share price derating. Some have moved to discounts levels never seen in their history as listed funds.

Concerns around the impact of inflation and rising interest rates have dominated investor attention, weighing on sentiment towards many alternative asset classes. In particular, infrastructure and renewable energy trusts, whose valuations are based on discounting long-term cash flows, have moved from premiums to wider than 20% discounts. In addition, investors have lost faith in several specialist asset classes, such as music royalties, which saw peak-to-trough share price declines of around 40% before M&A activity kicked in.

Interestingly, many private equity investment companies have performed well: 3i Group's share price is up nearly 90% over the last 12 months (to mid-October), whilst the many buy-out funds are up by double-digit percentages (ICG Enterprise +18%, Oakley +12% and HgCapital +16%). Pessimism about potential write-downs was high this time last year, but continued strong earnings growth from portfolio companies has offset declining valuation multiples, leading to resilient NAVs. That said, 'growth capital' strategies, which invest in riskier, early stage ventures, have seen more significant NAV weakness. Their discounts remain very wide.

Rising interest rates have also provided headwinds to 'growth' equity strategies, whilst several 'value' strategies had a strong period in late 2022 and early 2023. However, equity markets in 2023 have been dominated by the AI-driven rally in a small group of US mega-caps. Beneficiaries in the investment trust universe have included Allianz Technology, Polar Capital Technology, Manchester & London and JPMorgan American. However, this has made the US a tough market to beat, given such a narrow list of stocks driving performance.

The UK remains unloved, but cheap valuations have fuelled some M&A activity. Trusts with value-orientated strategies, such as Aurora and Temple Bar, as well as Edinburgh IT, have done relatively well, whilst small caps have struggled as investors have been wary about the economic outlook.

Several trusts that invest in Japan have performed well, although sterling strength and yen weakness have dampened returns for UK investors. Consolidation has also helped discounts narrow. European markets may have surprised many with returns of around 14% in sterling terms over the last 12 months. European Investment companies run by Henderson, JPMorgan and BlackRock have outperformed, whilst growth-orientated strategies such as Baillie Gifford's and smaller companies struggled.

China had a strong late 2022 and early 2023 as investors were positive about the prospects for a post-Covid re-opening of the economy, but it has disappointed since then, and the sector is down around 20% from its peak in January 2023. This has hurt the performance of JPMorgan China Growth & Income and Baillie Gifford China Growth. In contrast, Indian stocks, in particular small and midcaps, have performed well, which has helped India Capital Growth and Ashoka India Equity.

In emerging markets, specialist funds such as Georgia Capital, BlackRock Frontiers and Mobius IT have led the way over the last year, whilst the quality growth bias for JPMorgan Emerging Markets has dampened performance.

What has happened to discounts and where might they go from here?

Average discounts across the trust universe at the time of writing in mid-October are currently around 19%, excluding 3i Group. They have not been this wide for a meaningful period since the aftermath of the global financial crisis. The biggest driver of change over the last year or so is the derating of infrastructure and renewable energy trusts triggered by concerns about rising interest rates. These trusts were trading on average at a premium in mid-September 2022, but now trade on an average discount of 23%. Alternative asset trusts have moved overall from a 4% premium to a 28% discount over the same period.

Equity investment companies have fared better, and are trading on an average discount of 13%, a similar level to mid-September 2022. Discounts tightened to around 8% in Q4 2022 before drifting wider throughout 2023. Growth equity strategies remain out of favour, with many Baillie Gifford strategies remaining on wide discounts, including Scottish Mortgage (market cap £9.4bn) on a 16% discount, whilst Smithson, another previous quality-growth darling, is on a double-digit discount.

There are two ways to close a discount: either the share price recovers or the NAV declines. We are hoping for the former, but there will undoubtably be a few cases of value destruction, as the sorry case of Home REIT appears to be demonstrating. Overall, we expect plentiful investment opportunities, given that the baby tends to be thrown out with the bathwater at times of weak sentiment.

In alternative assets, the key is to understand the quality of the underlying assets and the trust's approach to valuation, which is more subjective than in the case of listed equities, while focusing as well on funds with low levels of debt and strong balance sheets. We believe there are plenty of high-quality assets and cash flows in the infrastructure and private equity sectors, which will ultimately produce attractive returns given current discounts.

We expect that corporate activity will serve as a floor to valuations and we have already seen the pace of takeover activity pick up, as specialist private assets investors seek out bargains in the listed market. Industrials REIT was acquired by Blackstone this year, whilst Round Hill Music Royalty has been acquired by Apollo-backed Concord.

Boards are also seeking to address discounts through reviewing their capital allocation policies, realising assets, in order to prove the validity of valuations and returning excess capital to shareholders via buybacks and tenders. Pantheon International, the listed private equity fund, has been a leader in this regard, returning £200m through a tender and buyback programme that is intended to run until May 2024. The trust is committing to share a proportion of future cash flows from portfolio realisations with investors. HICL Infrastructure has sold several assets, whilst private equity funds, such as HgCapital Trust, continue to make realisations significantly above stated valuations.

There are still no IPOs of any note – how long can the new issue drought last?

There have been two tiny investment company IPOs this year (Onward Opportunities and Ashoka WhiteOak Emerging Markets), after a barren year in 2022, which is believed to be the first since the 1970s. Investors are focused on sorting out the problem children within their existing portfolios, rather than new opportunities. We expect that the lean period may continue for some time, particularly given investors are nursing losses on the late-cycle crop of IPOs, some of which have experienced corporate governance concerns.

It will be a high bar to get an IPO over the line in the near future. Ashoka Whiteoak Emerging Markets has demonstrated that a well-structured trust with a differentiated approach still has the chance of getting away, but the company will need to grow in order to be considered a success. We expect investors will take some convincing to back the next batch of IPOs, managers will have to have strong track records, whilst terms may have to be shareholder friendly and boards able to demonstrate the skills and experience to challenge managers in specialist asset classes.

What will it take for primary/secondary issuance to pick up again?

Few investment companies are able to issue new shares at present, which requires the shares to trade on a premium to NAV. At the time of writing, only around 15 of the 400 shares of London-listed investment companies (ICs) are trading at a premium to NAV, and a further 15 are on a sub-2% discount, meaning few have scope to issue. As a result, we expect secondary issuance to be limited in the near term.

To return to premiums, trusts will have to restore the faith of investors. Equity trusts need to demonstrate they can outperform their benchmarks, even if macro-conditions are not entirely favourable. In addition, alternative trusts will have to deliver strong cash flows and a return profile that remains attractive versus the return available on government bonds. Those that can deliver on pledges of linkage to interest rates and inflation are likely to be rewarded.

A return to significant issuance may require a pick-up in buying from retail investors, who have been a strong source of demand for investment companies in recent years. Covid-19 led to a pick-up in savings and investment by many individuals, but now much of the spare cash has been spent and tight finances resulting from the cost of living crisis means that there has been less free capital to invest.

What is driving consolidation across the sector – and how far has it got to go?

The largest buyers of trusts are increasingly focused on size, trading liquidity and cost. This is particularly impacting private wealth managers, who are increasingly running money in large, aggregated model portfolios that need liquid underlying investments to deal with investor flows.

As a result, boards are becoming more willing to undertake consolidation, seeking to grow the size of an IC where in the past a manager or mandate change may have been viewed as a sufficient shake-up. There have been a number of in-house mergers, namely by abrdn (New Dawn and Asia Dragon), whilst JPMorgan Global Growth & Income has been a successful consolidator in recent years, including the rollover from the Scottish Investment Trust and JP Morgan Elect. In-house solutions do not always work. The proposed merger between GCP Infrastructure and GCP Asset Backed Income fell through as the boards could not sufficiently demonstrate the benefits to all investors.

We expect the consolidation to continue, through a range of measures, including mergers and outright acquisitions, as well as funds adopting wind-down strategies. After a number of years of active IPO markets, a period of consolidation is not unusual. Investment companies which have proved to be based more on story than substance will fall by the wayside. We believe this is a healthy feature of the investment company sector, where underperforming trusts are either reconstructed or wound-down.

Are boards doing enough to put shareholders first and reduce discounts to a minimum?

The picture is mixed. On the one hand, we are seeing a significant number of strategic reviews, wind-ups and mergers, but other boards are often accused of being slow to act. In practice directors face a difficult task when an asset class falls out of favour, and there will never be a silver bullet for solving a discount. However, we believe it is better that boards are on the front foot and seek to demonstrate that they care about the share price and are acting in shareholders' best interests.

It is promising that we have seen a pick-up in share buybacks, especially in new asset classes such as infrastructure and private equity. We have been particularly impressed by measures from Pantheon International, which has listened to, and then acted on, shareholder concerns.

Which methods of discount control are proving to be most effective?

There is no one-size-fits-all discount control. The best approach varies by company, depending on the nature of their portfolios, cash flows, balance sheet and shareholder register. Ultimately, a discount/premium is about ensuring that an investment company is attractive to a wide range of buyers and will depend on factors including performance, mandate, marketing, fees, transparency and corporate governance.

That said, we believe that share buybacks can be a flexible and easy to implement way for boards to signal that they are focused on shareholders' interests and capital allocation, as it can be difficult to justify a new investment versus effectively buying your own portfolio on a wide discount. For example, buying back 10% of share capital on a 30% discount generates a 3.3% uplift to NAV. To generate the same return, new investments would have to deliver nearly a 50% return – a tough target to hit.

Buybacks are unlikely to 'march in' a discount, but we believe they can be valuable in demonstrating capital discipline and that a board is focused on the share price. It can help reduce discount volatility, provide liquidity and narrow spreads. We note that periodic exits have also proved reasonably successful for a number of trusts with exposure to less-liquid asset classes or those with specialist strategies.

What is the outlook for dividends from here – are we facing more cuts? If so who is most vulnerable?

Investment companies have the ability to smooth dividends using reserves, which has contributed to many building multi-decade records of dividend growth. As a result, most equity income trusts were able to maintain or grow their dividends through Covid. Almost all have now returned to full dividend cover, meaning we expect most of them to continue these dividend growth records.

The picture is more mixed for alternative trusts, which reflects the individual circumstances of each company, meaning it is difficult to make broad-brush statements about an asset class. Some funds have seen strong cash flows supporting dividend growth. Renewable energy trusts that continue to benefit from elevated power prices, or infrastructure funds with contracted and/or inflation-linked cash flows are examples. Some specialist debt funds are benefiting from higher interest rates, because of their exposure to floating-rate assets.

Other areas have been more challenged, with dividends particularly under threat where leverage is an important part of the business model, meaning the rising cost of debt has put a squeeze on income streams. Several property companies have cut dividends in recent years, but we now believe that debt levels are manageable and the majority of funds should be able to continue covering their current dividend targets. Some specialist funds have recently announced cuts, including an overdue cut from Digital 9 Infrastructure, whilst Hipgnosis Songs Fund withdrew its dividend to prevent a breach of debt covenants.

Which sectors look well placed to deliver attractive returns over the next three to five years?

We believe that buying equity trusts with strong long-term track records after a period of underperformance is often an attractive strategy. They have the potential to benefit from improved NAV performance, as well as discount narrowing. For investors seeking equity market exposure, we believe it is an attractive time to invest in trusts with the potential tailwind of narrowing discounts over coming years.

In addition, we believe a higher rate environment may be a period when active stock picking can show its worth after a period of dominance by tracker funds. Investors are becoming more engaged, and we expect pressure to mount on boards to address discounts. This may be accelerated by the emergence of a new activist investor, Saba Capital, on the register of several trusts.

Shifts in sentiment tend to be exaggerated, with markets moving from periods of over-optimism to excessive pessimism. As a result, we believe the discounts on infrastructure, renewables and private equity are offering particularly attractive entry points.

How big an issue is cost disclosure for the future of the sector?

The direction of travel with fees remains downwards, with funds that are underperforming typically facing the most pressure. Many equity trusts now have tiered fees that reduce as the level of assets increases. Notwithstanding this welcome trend, we believe that onerous cost reporting has been one of the biggest headwinds to demand in the sector in recent years.

We are in favour of low fees and clear reporting, but we believe current regulations have penalised investment companies and given investors a misleading picture of the costs of a fund. This has led some investors to ration or remove trusts from their portfolios solely on (misleading) cost ratios, with little regard to the return potential they offer. We are hearing positive noises about the potential for change. This would be a significant positive development for the sector, opening up investment companies again to a wider range of investors.

What have been the most positive and most disappointing features of the past 12 months?

Governance failures are always a huge disappointment when they occur. We have seen this in some of the relatively recent vintages of IPOs, such as Home REIT or ThomasLloyd Energy Impact, where apparent management failures appear to have led to a destruction of value for shareholders. In addition, the conflict of interests in the proposed portfolio sale by Hipgnosis Songs Fund and subsequent continuation vote failure highlights how investors need to look very carefully at the terms of management agreements and be willing to pass up on 'the next big thing' if the interests of managers are not suitably aligned to the interests of shareholders.

Independent boards often take a lot of flak in these situations. Sometimes this can be justified when there appears to be a lack of oversight, but in other situations it is good to see board members putting significant effort into remedying difficult situations.

More generally it has been encouraging to see shareholders becoming more engaged. Difficult situations have been the catalyst for more investors to become vocal. In addition, more formal engagement processes, such as that recently undertaken by Quilter Cheviot, provide boards with concrete feedback. The bold action by the board of Pantheon International to put in place a capital allocation policy could act as a call to arms for other boards.

Cost disclosures are inadvertently leading investors to ration their exposure to investment companies, which is a huge disappointment. In particular, some retail investor platforms have been restricting new investment into specific trusts on the basis of flawed cost disclosures, something we believe is harming customer choice.

How do you assess the outlook for ITs from here? How to attract buyers back into the market given the structural issues?

We believe investment companies are excellent investment vehicles that should appeal to a wide range of buyers. Equity trusts have long histories of outperforming their open-ended sister funds, which we believe demonstrates that allowing managers to take a longer-term approach adds value.

In addition, investment companies also give private investors access to asset classes such as private equity, infrastructure, property and specialist debt that are otherwise hard for them to invest in without huge minimum investment sizes, long lock-up periods and specialist expertise. Listed private equity helps to democratise access to private assets, a key aim of regulators.

Often overlooked is that trusts are strategically important to the UK economy. Their assets represent approximately 16% of the UK's installed renewable energy capacity. In addition, specialist life sciences funds offer the potential to invest in transformational, life-saving treatments.

There are always exceptions to the rule, and not all investment companies will deliver on their expectations. However, the process of consolidation, mergers, takeovers and wind-ups is accelerating. This natural selection means that the sector will become focused on the highest quality managers and assets, which positions it well to continue to thrive in the long term. While the IPO market is currently quiet, we expect that the sector will continue to innovate to meet investors' needs, which will ultimately lead to more trusts being launched.

DOWN, NOT OUT

JONATHAN DAVIS *talks to fund manager* ABBY GLENNIE *about the trials of UK smaller companies trusts and her thoughts on taking over as lead manager of the abrdn UK Smaller Companies Growth Trust (AUSC).*

Patience needed

I**T IS A** tough ask to take over management of a trust from one of the most respected managers in your field, as Abby Glennie did at the start of 2023 when she took over from Harry Nimmo at the helm of abrdn's flagship smaller companies investment trust. It is doubly so when UK smaller companies are unloved and out of favour and the quality growth style which the trust has always consistently employed is not performing well.

Market analysts have been saying for years that the UK market appears undervalued and underappreciated, but the promised turnaround in sentiment, style and performance that will happen in due course has yet to materialise as this article went to press. abrdn UK Smaller Companies Growth Trust is therefore no exception in having suffered drawdowns.

Glennie, who had been working on the trust alongside Nimmo for seven years, puts a brave face on the ongoing struggles of her sector. Like other small cap managers, she has good arguments for believing that small cap's fortunes will be restored but acknowledges that patience is needed while waiting for the long-overdue turnaround to arrive.

The evidence that the sector is due a break looks compelling, as she illustrates with reference to a thick deck of helpful slides. The starting point is that UK small cap shares have been outstanding performers over time. According to the London Business School academics Dimson, Marsh and Staunton, in their annual Global Investment Returns Yearbook, UK small cap stocks have outperformed the UK market by 2.8% per annum over the past 68 years, more than compensating for the added volatility that comes with the territory.

Secondly it is undoubtedly the case that the UK equity market is cheap by historical standards and that smaller capitalisation companies are the cheapest of the lot. Whether you look at price to earnings ratios, price to book or dividend yields, the sector is shouting "potential bargains". The PE ratio, for example, for many stocks has fallen almost as low as it did during the global financial crisis.

The third argument is that AUSC has enjoyed one of the best reputations for performance in its sector for many years. Over the last 20 years, it has produced an annualised NAV total return of 12% per annum, 2.8% ahead of its benchmark. [1]While it has experienced many ups and downs along the way, the volatility has historically been compensated for by those sustained double-digit, longer-term returns. And while dividends have never been a priority for this growth-focused trust, the payout has increased by 9.8% per annum over the last five years. The current yield is 2.7%.

Finally, Glennie can also point to the fact that AUSC itself trades on an unusually wide double-digit discount, underlying the scope for a rerating when the market for smaller companies comes back to life. The trust tends to underperform in the first few months of a new bull market, as markets experience a 'dash for trash', but it has typically performed well once a new bull market is established. With inflation in the UK falling, and interest rates seemingly nearing their peak, the chances of that happening again soon are certainly increasing.

Challenges for UK equities

Some challenges remain. One is that when experienced and popular managers like Nimmo retire, it always takes time for the market to place the same faith in their successor, however well trained and involved in the management of the trust he or she may have been. Glennie, who studied economics and finance at university, has been working in UK equities since 2007 and part of the trust's management team since 2016. The investment process of the trust is unchanged, so there is no real reason for that to justify any market scepticism.

Secondly it is hardly news that the UK equity market is dwindling in importance on the global market stage. Twenty years ago the FTSE All-Share Index accounted for 7% of the world's total market capitalisation. Today that figure has shrunk to just 4%, for several reasons. A combination of factors, including globalisation, changes in pension fund investment habits, over-zealous regulation and the ever-greater dominance of the US stock market, have all contributed to this diminishing role.

Not for nothing did Jeremy Hunt, the chancellor, express his concern at the demising importance of the UK equity market and float the idea of making pension

---

[1]   The benchmark is the Numis Smaller Companies plus AIM (excluding investment companies) index. The trust switched to this benchmark with effect from 31 December 2017, having previously used a similar index that excluded the AIM market.

funds commit more of their billions of assets into supporting UK companies in his autumn 2023 Mansion House speech. That neglect is particularly marked in the small and midcap universe of stocks, which barely register on the radar of international investors.

Thus, while the FTSE 100 Index has essentially traded sideways since January 2022, with a gain of 3% before dividends, the FTSE 250 and Small Cap indices have both declined in value, by 22% and 28% respectively on the same basis. The AIM 100 Index has fallen by more than 40% over the same time period.[2]

One explanation for that decline is a shortage of liquidity across large areas of the market. Any broker will tell you that this year there has been something of a buyers' strike in smaller company shares and funds that invest in them have seen significant outflows. When the market turns, some of that liquidity will return.

Another factor is context – the fact that small caps performed unusually well in the 'sugar rush' markets that followed the Covid-19 pandemic. In its marketing materials, the trust notes that on the basis of rolling 12-month rates of return, which looks through shorter-term volatility, it has outperformed in all types of markets, including 70% or more of all positive market periods.

Average rolling 12-month performance over the last 20 years (to 31 July 2023)

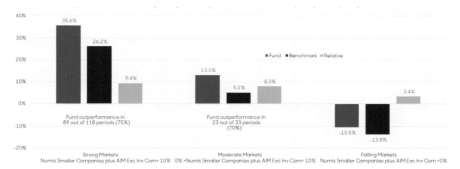

Source: abrdn, Lipper.

Between 2019 and November 2021, AUSC was one of the best performers in the small cap sector, returning 86% in less than three years. Since then, its relative performance has suffered more than most of the 15 investable smaller company specialist trusts and its discount has moved out to 15%, its widest level since the global financial crisis. The board, which looks to defend a discount around the 8% level in normal market conditions, has been buying back shares in recent months.

---

2   As at 1st October 2023.

Bouncing back

The fact that the trust has gone through difficult periods before is one of the reasons why Glennie says she is approaching the future in a positive frame of mind. She makes the point to clients that there has been no change in strategy or in the way that the portfolio is structured. It continues to be built around a proprietary valuation and momentum tool known as the Matrix, first deployed in the 1990s and modified only slightly since.

"I think the thing that has been reassuring for clients is that nothing's changed about our investment process. We're always looking to see if the factors used by the Matrix are still the most relevant for markets and there have been some small changes over its history, but the overall picture and the focus on quality, growth and momentum has remained consistent". It is an effective screening tool, in other words, that continues to identify stocks that merit further fundamental research.

As for the UK market, she says that "the UK has been cheap relative to other geographies ever since Brexit. But even if you want to be negative on UK politics or the UK economy, in the small cap space about 50% of revenues are generated overseas, so that cannot be the whole story. The key thing for us is that the macro story – high inflation, rising interest rates and slower growth – has been dominating the whole market and that will not last forever".

"If you look at the UK, the inflation picture has been a lot worse than other key geographies. Every month for 18 months (from January 2022) it has been worse than people expected. That creates a risk-off environment, and of course we are now living in a world where you have attractive 5% risk-free rate. That is clearly a challenge and a potential alternative to equities generally".

The first thing the trust needs, therefore, is for macro data to improve. Glennie is hopeful that the interest rate cycle may finally be peaking in the UK while the signals suggesting recession remain mixed rather than conclusive. For evidence she points to reported company earnings and the trend in revisions, which has been quietly and slowly improving for more than six months. "We think a lot of the negativity in terms of earnings is actually behind us, but there are still challenges that companies need to navigate".

What has hurt AUSC particularly badly is that in periods of higher inflation and interest rates, everyone automatically discounts stocks with strong future growth prospects. The trust has one of the most pronounced growth tilts of any of its peers, which is one reason its recent performance has suffered more than most. The emphasis on quality stocks, those with above average returns on capital and resilient earnings, will however prove its worth if the UK slows or goes into recession.

"By the same token" says Glennie "we have the evidence of history that if we move to an environment where inflation and interest rates are moving in the right direction, that should be positive for our style". Because of its bias towards growth and quality stocks, the portfolio normally trades at a PE premium to the market, but the premium has rarely been as narrow as it is today, suggesting more upside when style factors revert to normal.

"The key thing for us is that we have stuck to our investment process, which clients know has always delivered value in the long term. We have had tough periods before. This is probably the toughest period we've had because it has lasted so much longer, but we've continued to stick to our process. We have seen more positive earnings revisions when our companies have reported their results, underlining their resilience. We will be helped as and when we move back to a world in which stock specifics matter more than the top-down macro factors and I am sure that is coming".

History shows that UK small cap stocks follow a regular cyclical pattern, with five-year rolling returns ranging from +25% to −5% per annum. The current figure has been hovering around zero, close to past cyclical lows and typically the precursor to a strong recovery. When the cycle reverses, contrarian investors will note, it will be a huge surprise if this trust does not return to its excellent form of the past.

Long-term horizon in small and midcap companies

Source: Morningstar Direct.

abrdn

To invest with confidence, seek out experience.

abrdn Investment Trusts

Now more than ever, investors want to know exactly what they're investing in.

abrdn investment trusts give you a range of 21 carefully crafted investment portfolios – each built on getting to know our investment universe through intensive first-hand research and engagement.

Across public companies, private equity, real estate and more, we deploy over 800 professionals globally to seek out opportunities that we think are truly world-class – from their financial potential to their environmental credentials.

Allowing us to build strategies we believe in. So you can build a portfolio with real potential.

Please remember, the value of shares and the income from them can go down as well as up and you may get back less than the amount invested.

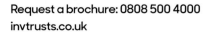

Request a brochure: 0808 500 4000
invtrusts.co.uk

DOUBLY CHEERFUL

JONATHAN DAVIS *talks to* MARCUS PHAYRE-MUDGE, *manager of* TR *Property, about the value opportunities now emerging in listed commercial property companies.*

Down but not out

COMMERCIAL PROPERTY HAS been a 'look away now' sub-sector for most of the past two years, with falling capital values and widening discounts, and only the resulting higher-than-customary dividend yields to compensate. It is encouraging to learn therefore that Marcus Phayre-Mudge, the manager of TR Property (ticker: TRY), is more excited about the upside potential for the sector than he has been for many years.

His investment trust, which he has been involved in since the 1990s and sole manager of since 2011, is a unique vehicle in the investment trust universe, the only one that invests almost exclusively in the shares of commercial property companies, rather than directly into steel, bricks and mortar. Another 8% of the assets of the trust are in direct property.

Its mandate covers listed European property companies, not just UK ones, which gives it broader and more diversified property exposure than most of its peers, and while the period since the start of 2022 has been a painful one, with the shares falling around 50% from peak to trough, and the discount widening at one point to around 11%, the share price and discount have both stabilised more recently.

If 2022 was by his admission "a nightmare year", the good news now is that his universe has rarely in his long career, he says, offered such good potential value.

That is essentially because the derating which has spread right through the commercial property investment trust sector has reached historically extreme levels.

Going into the final quarter of 2023, the average discount at which the companies he owns were trading was 30%. With the near 10% discount at which TR Property itself was trading, shareholders were therefore being offered the chance to buy a well diversified portfolio of property investment companies managed by a respected industry lifer for little more than 60p in the pound.

Nothing says for sure that this double discount could not go wider in the near term, and it could do if the peak in the current cycle of interest rate increases has still to be reached, but any improvement in the macro-environment would be a game-changer, in his view. When that happens, shareholders in the trust will be looking at the happy combination of a double whammy of higher net asset values and a narrowing discount across the trust's 60-stock portfolio.

Historical extremes

The 40% combined discount is wider than it has been at any previous point in Phayre-Mudge's near-25-year career, with the except of the global financial crisis. To illustrate how extreme things have become, he shows me a chart of the discount to net asset values that goes back to 1990 when he started out as a young surveyor. "When we have reached this point in previous cycles, you have always had a sharp correction as the market suddenly realises that net asset values have fallen too far and you start to get bid activity".

There have been at least four examples already this year of M&A activity in the property listed investment trust sector: Blackstone's private equity bid for Industrials REIT, CT Property Trust merging with LondonMetric, Ediston Property selling all its assets to a US property company and Civitas Social Housing being acquired by its largest shareholder, a Hong Kong property company. The premiums involved or implied in these cases strongly suggest that the latest inflexion point has been reached. In three of these cases TR Property was among the largest shareholders and in at least two influential in promoting these outcomes in dialogue with the boards.

As with other sectors, scale is an important challenge facing commercial property investment trusts, with plenty of them having market capitalisations below £200–£225m. Phayre-Mudge says that further consolidation is necessary and coming, even if some boards have to be pushed harder in the right direction than others. He says he would prefer it if that took the form of mergers between trusts rather than their being taken private, as a strong and healthy listed property sector is the more desirable outcome.

The key difference between this cycle and previous bad downturns in commercial property, he thinks, is that this one has been all about the deteriorating macro-environment, one in which rising interest rates have led to sharp declines in capital values and driven up the cost of capital. Unlike a normal business cycle, the economy is not overheating. The blame lies mainly in a raft of external factors, ranging from post-Covid supply shortages to the inflationary impact of the war in Ukraine. They have pushed up inflation and caught central banks on the hop. "We can't get away from the fact that we had a decade of gloriously zero or effectively zero cost of money and that particular punchbowl has been taken away".

There has however so far not been any sign of the rash of speculative development with borrowed money that has helped to predicate the worst property downturns of the past. Operationally, in other words, although there are sub-sectors with specific issues to deal with, such as Canary Wharf, where financial institutions no longer need so much concentrated office space, and the secondary office market generally because of the working from home phenomenon, the fundamentals of property companies in the main remain sound.

Balance sheets too are in better shape than they were in the run up to the global financial crisis, he points out, with average loan-to-value ratios, currently around 30% across the European property sector and even less in the UK, being much lower and well below comparable in other alternative sectors. "Many a private equity firm would kill for those sorts of loan-to-value figures", he says. While interest costs have risen sharply, the smartest finance directors were successfully locking in low-cost, fixed-rate debt during the cheap money decade that has now ended.

In past cycles the mismatch between supply and demand from overdevelopment as the economy goes into recession has driven down capital values, while property companies with poorly managed balance sheets have run into financial distress. "We haven't seen that this time round", he notes. Rental income has remained resilient, and dividends, which normally make up the majority of commercial property's total returns, remain reasonably well covered in most cases, although there have been some reductions this year.

Capital values hit

The hit to capital values was mostly concentrated into a short few months in the second half of 2022, not helped by the fiasco of the short-lived Truss administration, which sent gilt yields shooting up to 4.5%. In 2023, while the shares of commercial property trusts have continued to fall, that has been mainly down to further derating as interest rates have continued to rise. Capital values remain broadly unchanged.

Because net asset values are backward looking, some have argued that current NAVs are out of date and cast doubt on how wide the latest reported discounts might actually be. Phayre-Mudge points out however that there has recently been a relaxation in the professional guidance to valuers in the UK market, which allows them to take note of market sentiment and mark down net asset values more realistically, even when there are no transactions on which to base valuation changes.

"I would argue that the equity market is missing the point that asset values have already corrected quite significantly". In the fourth quarter of 2022 alone, the average capital decline was an eye-catching 14%. The fact that his open-ended fund has been able to sell some assets at net asset value this year he sees as further evidence that valuations are not overstated.

When gilts repriced dramatically in Q4 2022, the high-growth but low-yielding logistics and industrials sectors were among the most dramatically impacted, derating sharply from premiums to big discounts. Once interest rate expectations started to stabilise in the summer, their shares began to find some buyers again. Tritax Big Box, for example, moved back from a discount of more than 40% to nearer 25%, still a long way from the premium its shares have traded at for most of its nine-year life as a listed vehicle, but evidence of improving sentiment.

Risks do remain

There is of course still a risk of a recession in the UK, Europe or both, so property is not out of the woods just yet. A modest recession tends not to be that bad for commercial property, Phayre-Mudge says, because property income is protected by long leases and there is always scope to make short-term cost savings. A deep recession would be more damaging, leading to bankruptcies, vacancies and loss of rental income, but there are still segments of the property universe which are either immune or even can do well in a recession, such as student accommodation and state-funded healthcare.

Subsidised German residential property is another example of a potential European diversification which could do okay in harsher economic times. Holdings like these also speak to a wider point about the outlook for a specialist property investment trust like TR Property, which is that it has the freedom to invest across what has increasingly become a much more varied landscape of opportunities. In Phayre-Mudge's experience, many of the newer specialist investment trusts manage their balance sheets more effectively than the old diversified commercial property trusts.

"Traditionally a lot of your readership's exposure to property would have been a diversified UK-only physical property fund. They no longer exist, and for good reason. The words 'open-ended' and 'daily dealing in real estate' shouldn't be in the same sentence". The strength of TR Property, in contrast, is that "it's pan-European, it's multi-sector and has access to the whole alternatives group".

"When I was a boy, the alternative group was tiny – the odd hotel, etc. Now we're talking student accommodation, self storage, elderly care, primary care and data centres, among others. We break UK retail down into edge of town, out of town, mega shopping centres, city centre and so on. I'm free and able to move around between the sectors looking not only for mega trends, but for shorter cycles as well. And then I'm always playing the tactical valuation game as well".

An optimistic outlook

His optimism, in a nutshell, stems from the happy circumstance of the shares of commercial property companies trading at an unwarranted discount while their fundamentals remain solid. "We are, I think" he sums up "in a moment where the sector is unloved, unfairly so, and for no other reason than the interest rate cycle, and in that game I think we can all accept that we're closer to full time than half time".

Phayre-Mudge is at pains to add that he is no perma-bull. "I'm not some property evangelist who only ever goes long; bear in mind that in Q2 2008, the quarter before the collapse of Lehman Brothers, both my two funds had 20% in cash. I can do miserable and bear market, no problem at all!" Rather than having a large net cash position, the total gearing in the trust when we spoke in early autumn was about 13%, and he has been buying shares in the trust for himself and his family. It remains his largest financial asset outside his home and pension.

While it has been a difficult couple of years, Phayre-Mudge in other words is putting his money where his mouth is, always an encouraging sign for anyone looking for an investment trust bargain, and hoping that the dramatic downturn in fortunes of the last two years is indeed reversing as and when interest rates start to normalise.

MARCUS PHAYRE-MUDGE has been manager of the TR Property investment trust (TRY) since 2011. The trust has net assets of £950m as at 1 October 2023. The full year dividend, 15.5p in the year to 31 March 2023, has grown at a compound rate of 8% per annum over the past 10 years. TR Property is now managed by Columbia Threadneedle Investments following its recent acquisition of BMO's investment trust business.

Imagine your future.
Invest for your lifestyle.

Whatever future you imagine, your investments should help make it possible.

At Columbia Threadneedle Investments, we provide a broad range of actively managed investment trusts and savings plans to suit your lifestyle needs.

With our savings plans, you can invest as little as £25 per month or make a single contribution of £100. And you choose your investment goal: Are you looking for regular income, long-term capital growth or both? Our broad range of funds includes UK small- and mid-sized companies, global diversified portfolios, private equity and property.

Your capital is at risk and you may not get back the original amount invested.

Learn more at ctinvest.co.uk

COLUMBIΛ
THREADNEEDLE
INVESTMENTS

UPSIDE IN JAPAN

NICHOLAS PRICE, *manager of the Fidelity Japan investment trust (FJV), gives his verdict on the outlook for Japanese equities, one of the best performing markets of the past 12 months, at least in local currency terms.*

Why invest in Japan today?

THE SIMPLE ANSWER is that Japan is one of the world's major economic powers with a high level of industrial competitiveness and the second largest country in the MSCI World Index. Yet despite the many opportunities on offer, Japanese equities remain under-appreciated and under-owned, and there is significant change occurring in Japanese companies' corporate governance, which is good for shareholders.

Japan is home to many globally competitive companies in sectors such as capital goods, technology hardware and automobiles. Owing to its geographic proximity, Japan is closely tied to Asia's growth trends, and consumer-related companies with strong brands are well positioned to capture demand from the expanding middle class. It also offers a wealth of smaller market leaders in growing niche industries that often fly under the radar.

Demographically and economically, Japanese companies are tackling challenges that many other countries will soon face. Providers of software and IT services are helping Japanese companies overcome labour shortages and increase productivity. Factory automation solutions utilised at home are being exported globally. Meanwhile, companies that tackle the rising cost of healthcare – from the development of new treatments for age-related conditions to medical devices and equipment for minimally invasive surgeries – also represent potential investment opportunities.

Over the past decade corporate Japan has made significant progress in enacting governance reforms and strengthening dialogue with shareholders. The introduction of the Stewardship Code in 2014 and the Corporate Governance Code in 2015 has been instrumental in driving this change. Key developments include greater board independence and diversity, a reduction in cross shareholdings and record levels of shareholder returns. The Tokyo Stock Exchange's (TSE) reorganisation in April 2022 and its more recent efforts to boost capital efficiency are also contributing to the positive momentum.

Why then is the Japanese market not loved more?

For some time now, global equity portfolios generally have been underweight the Japanese stock market. I suspect that this mostly reflects misplaced perceptions that date back to Japan's 'lost decades', the 20 years of stagnant growth and deflationary fears that followed the years of 'the Japanese miracle'. But that hasn't been Japan for some time. The Japanese economy has been experiencing a recovery since around 2012 that has been as steady as it is low profile, while a structural improvement in operating profitability remains under-appreciated. The weakness of the yen has however limited the returns for overseas investors.

Another factor is that many Japanese stocks are undervalued because of a lack of sell-side coverage and limited information disclosure, especially in the mid/small cap space. This creates a wealth of overlooked and differentiated opportunities for the trust. We provide exposure to companies across the market-cap spectrum. Secular growth trends such as automation and digital transformation underpin many of the portfolio's holdings, alongside fast-growing niche industries that have yet to be fully appreciated by the market.

Where is the catalyst for Japanese equities to rerate?

Japan's equity markets have seen a resurgence in 2023. The broad-based TOPIX has returned around 25% YTD in yen terms as of October 2023, though sterling-based returns are far more muted. As noted above, there has been a steady stream of corporate-governance-related developments, spurred most recently by reform measures from the Tokyo Stock Exchange. Since the first quarter of this year, the TSE has required most listed firms, and especially those whose shares are trading below book value, to 'properly identify' their costs and the efficiency of their capital allocations.

The exchange has recently published a number of follow-up requirements that aim to expand the governance focus beyond companies that trade below book value, increase pressure on companies to unwind cross-shareholdings and encourage the restructuring of non-profitable business units. While this will be a multi-year process, we are optimistic that this initiative to tackle companies' tendency to de-prioritise cost of equity and returns on invested capital will foster a permanent change in corporate mentality and help to lift the profitability and share prices of Japanese companies.

How do today's valuations compare to history?

It is not widely appreciated that Japanese stocks, along with their US counterparts, have been among the strongest performers over the past ten years or so. Despite that, valuations have actually compressed as it has been earnings growth rather than higher multiples which have done the heavy lifting. Although the broad-based TOPIX index has generated strong returns so far this year, valuations remain below the historical average of the past 10–15 years.

Moreover, many small and midcap growth stocks, which have faced significant style headwinds in the face of the Fed's rate hiking cycle, are now trading at similar multiples to the market, despite offering faster earnings growth. What is unusual is that the trust now trades at a forward price-to-earnings discount to the market despite delivering double the rate of mid-term earnings growth. Given that the trust has historically traded at a premium on this measure, this anomaly suggests that there is latent alpha potential in our portfolio.

Why invest in Fidelity Japan to do it?

Fidelity is one of the most experienced global investment specialists in the Asia-Pacific region. From our first office in Tokyo in 1969, we have expanded into Australia, mainland China, Hong Kong, Korea, Singapore and Taiwan. We have a highly experienced Japanese equity team based on the ground, with 12 Tokyo-based research analysts (as at 30 September 2023), including three small cap specialists. Fidelity's analysts are all Japanese speakers. Collectively, we typically undertake around 3,200 company contacts each year.

The trust has the flexibility to invest across the market-cap spectrum and is not restricted in terms of size or sector. Environmental, social and governance (ESG) factors are embedded in the research process, using Fidelity's proprietary sustainability ratings and a locally based sustainable investing team who identify and monitor engagement targets among investee companies.

How have you changed the portfolio over the last three years?

The positioning of the portfolio is a reflection of the ideas generated by our proprietary bottom-up research and my focus on discovering divergent drivers and sources of secular growth. Over time, this will affect how the portfolio looks from a sector perspective, though it maintains a consistent tilt towards small and midcap growth stocks, an often-overlooked area of the market. Moreover, high-conviction names often remain among the top active holdings for an extended period.

Entrepreneurial activity is increasing in Japan, compared with five to 10 years ago, and we remain active in the pre-IPO space. Being on the ground here in Tokyo and seeing many different companies means that we are well placed to help entrepreneurs in the latter stages of their IPO journey.

While there have been opportunities to add oversold technology-related companies that are approaching the trough of their respective cycles, the portfolio is, on balance, bottom-up weighted towards companies that are likely to benefit from a strong yen, such as retailers, domestic growth names and beneficiaries of post-Covid reopening. Key active holdings in the portfolio include a mix of global industry leaders with high market share and pricing power, reopening names that are beneficiaries of economic and societal normalisation, and defensive growth companies with stable earnings and shareholder returns.

What, if anything, are you doing differently from normal?

I remain consistent in my bottom-up investment approach and continue to look for companies where the market is underestimating future growth, including companies at an early stage of their development. I typically find more opportunities among smaller and medium-sized companies, where lower levels of analyst coverage provide greater scope for mispricing of cheap sustainable growth stocks. Shifting macro and market dynamics also create opportunities. For example, rising interest rates in Japan mean that I am actively looking at banks for the first time in many years.

When does the trust tend to perform better/less well?

The trust tends to do well when growth and small/midcaps beat the market. By identifying some of the next growth winners early, the fund is often able to achieve high returns in a market led by growth stocks. Conversely, extreme style reversals can hurt performance. For example, value stocks outperformed their growth counterparts by more than 20% during the first half of 2022 while long-duration growth stocks vulnerable to changes in interest rates corrected sharply amid the prospect of further monetary tightening in the US and Europe.

While we have seen a strong value market over the past two years or so, the valuations of growth stocks, particularly small and midcaps, have come down to value levels and we don't see this dichotomy continuing. If the view that long-term rates have peaked gains traction, this would help to put a floor under growth stocks, and we would expect some of the names which have performed poorly to come back quite strongly.

The discount has widened – how are you dealing with that?

The board has an active discount management policy, the primary purpose of which is to reduce discount volatility. The board's intention is to aim to manage the discount so that it remains in single digits in normal market conditions. However, markets have been particularly volatile and discounts have been wide across the entire investment companies sector. In the six-month period ending 30 June 2023 the trust brought back 0.4% of the issued share capital and a similar amount since.

How significant is the recent shift to inflation in Japan?

Although more economic data over the coming quarters is needed to confirm a long-term trend, the early signals of 'good inflation' bode well for Japan's economy and potentially for investment returns. Goods and services have seen broad-based price hikes this year, and workers are now demanding pay rises, which, if they materialise on a consistent basis, will boost consumption and support further price gains.

Moreover, this new inflationary era is creating investment opportunities among Japanese firms that are able to expand their profit margins. We have seen margin expansion driving stock rallies for some companies that successfully raised prices this year, but more could come if reflation becomes sustainable.

Many Japanese stocks are still priced for deflation or stagnation. Japan Inc. was (in)famous for sitting on large cash piles that reduced capital efficiency, but a change from a deflationary mindset could bring an investment recovery with more companies putting their capital to work. Indeed, we're already seeing signs of this, as dividends and share buybacks both hit record levels in the most recent year.

What is the outlook for the yen now?

From a macro-perspective, we are likely moving towards a peak in US rates at some point in the near future, as well as some policy normalisation from the Bank of Japan. As a result, we are likely to see a trend towards a stronger yen over the next 18 months or so. UK investors who are investing in sterling could potentially benefit if the yen strengthens.

Are you likely to add more gearing – if so when and how?

I have the discretion to be up to 25% geared. Portfolio leverage is currently around 23%, slightly higher than 21% last year. As always, our gearing is dependent on bottom-up conviction in the available investment opportunities, particularly among our top active positions, and their valuations.

What are the major risks that you see to your portfolio?

In my view the biggest economic risks are still around inflation and how interest rates can impact market valuations and levels. Continued signs of weakness in China's recovery and the risk of US recession also represent potential headwinds that could prompt a near-term adjustment in Japanese stocks.

Can you match or improve on the 10-year returns of the last decade?

Past performance is not of course a reliable indicator of future returns but there are always opportunities. As noted previously, it is very unusual for the trust to be trading at an earnings discount to the index, which implies that there is latent alpha in our holdings. Ultimately, bottom-up stock-picking underpinned by a strong research base and on-the-ground expertise provides a strong base for future performance.

NICHOLAS PRICE *has been running Japanese equity portfolios for domestic and overseas clients since 2000. He has been the manager of the Fidelity Japan investment trust (FJV) since 2015.*

WHY INDIA?

GAURAV NARAIN, *manager of the India Capital Growth Fund, makes the case for investing in the fast-growing Indian sub-continent.*

What are the core arguments for investing in Indian equities?

INDIA IS ENTERING a period of high GDP growth. We believe that it will be the fastest growing large economy in the world for the next few years. The factors for growth are already in place. Reforms have made the business environment robust, and infrastructure has improved. Corporate balance sheets are strong, with low leverage, and the banking system is sound.

At the macroeconomic level, forex reserves are strong at US$600bn, currency volatility is low and inflation is under control, with interest rates having peaked and likely to decline by the end of 2023. The government is also focusing on growth through direct investment in infrastructure and favourable policy announcements to incentivise investment in the corporate sector. Geopolitical factors are also having a positive impact. The de-risking of global supply chains and 'China Plus One', the global shift to channel investments in manufacturing away from China, are benefitting India.

Aren't Indian equities more richly valued and therefore more risky than other emerging markets?

India has always looked expensive and continues to do so. There are a few structural reasons why this is the case. The equity market is broadly diversified and not a commodity-heavy market. It has a higher return on equity (ROE) and return on capital employed (ROCE) than most of its emerging market peers, in part down to a high share of technology and consumer companies.

The economy has consistently delivered growth, with nominal GDP having grown at an average of 10%–11% per annum over a 10-, 15- and 20-year period. Confidence in the markets that the growth momentum can be sustained has never been higher. My sense therefore is that the market will remain expensive. It could see some short-term volatility, but the long-term direction is positive as earnings growth will propel the market forward.

How would you describe the investment style of ICG?

We are bottom-up investors. We focus on the quality of the business, cash flows and the management team. We like businesses which are scalable yet have built entry barriers which give them a competitive edge. We invest with a long-term mindset and consequently have a reasonably concentrated portfolio with low turnover. Within the portfolio there is a growth bias. We have a very high active position. Being a concentrated portfolio with a growth bias, it tends to outperform in a rising market.

How do you aim to use the advantages of the investment trust structure?

The biggest advantage of having a trust structure comes when constructing the portfolio. It enables us to take concentrated positions in some less-liquid names. Currently around 45% of the portfolio is invested into smaller companies, as at 31 August 2023. The structure also allows us to invest in stocks at an early stage when valuations are reasonable, so that as the story plays out we benefit from earnings growth and a rerating. We are not forced sellers, or buyers, as a result of fund flows. All these factors result in low portfolio turnover, around 10%–12% per annum, and an extended holding period. We have held over 65% of portfolio stocks for more than five years.

What differentiates your trust from other Indian trusts, or open-ended equivalents?

Our pure small and midcap focus is the clearest differentiator.

What are your ambitions for the trust?

Our ambition is to reduce the discount on behalf of shareholders. Today the average range of the discount is around 6%–9% and we have come a long way from the 14%–15% discount at which the shares traded a few years back. We want to keep reducing this, which means broadening the investor base and delivering performance. We also want to grow the fund sustainably and believe we can achieve that without impacting our ability to cherry pick the right stocks.

How would you compare the claims of India and China as a home for investor capital?

There are clear commonalities between India and China. Both are very large, populous countries. However, unlike China, India has a very young population. China is 10 times the size of India in most sectors, its per capita income is six times that of India and from that perspective India is a decade behind China, underlining the scale of the opportunity. India is now growing faster than China and the China comparison has given us an insight into the potential of the domestic market in India.

Economically and politically China and India couldn't be further apart. As a democracy, things may take longer in India, but there is a level playing field, continuity in policy and companies have legal recourse. India has a well-developed regulatory environment with a strong and independent judiciary and legal system, a strong capital market regulator and respect for intellectual property.

There is a well-developed capital market too. The Bombay stock exchange is over 100 years old and has a faster settlement cycle, at T+1, than many Western markets. There is a strong history of foreign companies operating in India and in most sectors there is a level playing field for foreign companies, in which wholly owned subsidiaries are allowed. Multinational companies have been in India for over 50 years, so there is strong historical track record and, unlike China, global companies like Amazon, Uber etc. dominate alongside strong local competitors.

Recent reforms have made India competitive with China and South East Asian countries. Tax rates are among the lowest in the region and labour costs are as little as a third of those in China. That is why India is emerging as a good alternative to global companies looking to reduce their exposure to China on risk grounds.

Do you have any private companies in the portfolio?

We do not have any private companies in the portfolio. Why? Private markets are competitive and as in many parts of the world, global private equity funds are investing heavily in India, meaning that valuations are not compelling. Investing in the unlisted space requires a different skill set and we don't find the efforts needed commensurate with the potential returns. There are enough opportunities in the listed space, with a large number of new listings each year as well.

The ongoing charge looks high relative to some peers. What is the board's policy here?

We play in a niche segment of the market, small and midcap stocks, and run a concentrated portfolio but the board is conscious of the fee and it was changed from one based on a percentage of assets under management to a percentage of market capitalisation to align with the interest of the shareholders. This means that if the discount is high, the fee automatically comes down.

What are your policies on buybacks and discount control?

The board is conscious of the discount and has the authority to buy back up to 14.99% of issued capital if the discount exceeds a comfortable level. The company also has a redemption facility in place that gives shareholders the right to request redemption of part or all of their shareholding at an agreed exit discount to NAV every two years.

What difference will the acquisition by AssetCo make to the trust?

AssetCo [a business led by industry veteran Martin Gilbert and others that has acquired a number of specialist investment management firms] announced the completion of its acquisition of Ocean Dial Asset Management Limited in October 2023. The acquisition will enable the Ocean Dial team to leverage the broader resources of the group, including sales and marketing, research, risk, compliance and the ESG team.

What impact could the 2024 election have on the Indian equity market?

Current expectations are that the Modi government will return to power. This is likely to be viewed positively by the market as the government is focused on development. If it loses or the result is a coalition government, the impact is likely to be negative. In the short- to medium-term, we would still expect growth to continue as the reforms already put in place cannot be readily reversed. Sustainability of growth beyond the next three to four years will depend on the policies being adopted by the new government.

What are the main investment themes in the portfolio?

Almost every sector in the Indian market is seeing positive growth, which enables us to play our core themes in a diverse way. Our largest exposure is in consumer sectors, a mixture of staples and discretionary, such as quick service restaurants, electronic manufacturing and retail. We also have a reasonable exposure to cement companies, which benefit from higher infrastructure spend and housing demand, and in turn also underpin much of the consumer sector themes. Financials are our second largest exposure. China Plus One is another core theme of our portfolio and the final theme is digitalisation.

GAURAV NARAIN has been co-manager of the India Capital Growth Fund (ticker: ICG) since 2011. The trust is the smallest of the four trusts in the India sub-sector but unlike them specialises in the small and midcap segments of the market. That has helped it achieve the strongest performance record, with an annualised total return of some 18% per annum (as at 30 September 2023). The discount at that date was 9%.

POSITIVE CHANGE

KATE FOX, co-manager of Keystone Positive Change Investment Trust, managed by Baillie Gifford, explains what positive impact investing is and how the trust measures its performance against what is a unique dual mandate in the global investment trust sector.

What differentiates your strategy from other global trusts?

K EYSTONE POSITIVE CHANGE (**KPC**) is the sole global investment trust to have dual objectives: (1) to deliver attractive long-term investment returns and (2) to create positive change by contributing to a more sustainable and inclusive world. We look for exceptional companies delivering measurable positive change through their core products and services.

When we were appointed the managers of Keystone Positive Change in February 2021, we outlined our ambitions, which involve investing in innovative growth companies whose products and services are helping to address global sustainability challenges. It is our firm belief that profit and purpose go hand in hand. Global events have shown the necessity of transitioning towards a prosperous, sustainable, and inclusive world. At the same time, technological progress is enabling innovative solutions to global challenges.

What has been the record of the 'positive change' strategy since you launched it in 2017?

The Positive Change Fund UK OEIC, the first fund to adopt this strategy, has returned 19.4% per annum, net of fees, since its launch in 2019. That is 7.7% per annum ahead of its benchmark, the MSCI All Countries World Index. The portfolio is constructed without reference to the benchmark, however, and as you would expect from a concentrated and high-conviction portfolio, the active share is high – typically 97% or above – while volatility has been around 20% since inception.

The recent performance of the trust been disappointing – why is that?

Last year's financial market swings impacted short-term performance. Inflationary pressures, supply chain dislocation, and geopolitical tensions created a challenging backdrop. As bottom-up stock-pickers, we focus on finding superior growth companies to invest in for multiple years, rather than trying to predict macroeconomic developments. Growth companies generally saw share price declines, impacting our portfolio. Some companies, like Beyond Meat, Peloton and Teladoc, did not meet expectations and were sold.

Have you changed your approach or strategy in the light of the derating?

We have reflected on lessons learned over the period – which we will refer back to – we have a learning mindset. However, we have not altered the overall approach or strategy. In periods of extreme flux, like the one we have experienced in recent years, we do take a step back and consider the implications and relevance of these near-term challenges on the long-term prospects for the companies we own. We need to be sure that we still own growing companies whose products solve global challenges, in line with our dual objectives.

What changes have you made to the portfolio and why?

While near-term market volatility does not alter our long-term investment philosophy, we do not ignore its effects. We have analysed the portfolio's exposures to inflation, interest rates, and geopolitical risks and continue to perform in-depth, fundamental research on individual companies.

Throughout the year, we reviewed some holdings whose share price had fallen significantly. We distinguished between companies facing operational challenges and those performing well operationally, but whose share price declines, in our view, were mostly attributable to changes in market sentiment rather than fundamentals.

While turnover remains low, we used this as a prompt to move on from companies where we had lost conviction, such as plant-based protein producer Beyond Meat. We redeployed capital towards companies where the divergence between share price and operating performance created an attractive opportunity, such as MercadoLibre, the Latin American e-commerce platform and fintech provider.

Please give an example of how your impact assessment process works.

We evaluate portfolio companies based on three main measures: their product impact, their intent and their business practices. Remitly, for example, provides mobile-based remittance services for migrants. It is driving change in the $650bn payments industry. In terms of product impact, Remitly's lower fees, improved user experience, and accessibility help alleviate poverty and improve household resilience. For intent, Founder CEO Matt Oppenheimer is committed to putting customers at the heart of the company's long-term strategy: his vision is to transform the lives of immigrants and their families.

Finally, on business practices, Remitly ranks well in key areas such as stakeholder treatment, board independence, data security and environmental footprint.

Alongside its impressive impact, the company continues to grow its subscriber base and revenues. It is exactly this synergy between the long-term impact and the investment case that we want to see in portfolio companies.

Can you quantify the positive social and environmental impact of the strategy?

As impact investors, we monitor and report on the impact of our portfolio companies through our annual Impact Report, which is available from our website. The most recent report was published in September 2023. We collect company-level data for each stock, mapping activities to the 17 United Nations Sustainable Development Goals (SDGs) and using the 169 specific targets which underpin the SDGs. Our rigorous approach ensures that companies genuinely contribute to the changes needed to achieve the sustainability goals. In 2022 our portfolio contributed to 15 of the 17 SDGs.

By aggregating the data, we can demonstrate the portfolio's impact on environmental and social challenges. We produce 12 aggregate statistics for the portfolio. For example, our companies provided access to education for nearly 180 million learners and access to financial services for 400 million people. Portfolio companies enabled the avoidance of 110 million tonnes of CO_2e emissions in 2022.

We believe that transparent communication will encourage more assets to be directed towards companies driving positive change. We use a third party to provide independent assurance that the methodology we use in the Impact Report is robust and our data accurate.

What is the currency exposure in the portfolio and how do you manage that?

We do not take active currency positions. Our approach to currency risk is to consider this when carrying out our fundamental analysis of each stock in the portfolio.

How do the fundamentals of your portfolio compare to the comparator MSCI ACWI ETF?

The portfolio displays the characteristics you would expect of a concentrated growth portfolio that is well positioned for attractive long-term returns. The active share is high at 97%, so the trust looks and is very different to the benchmark. The trust's forward PE is higher at 25.5 times, compared to the benchmark's 16.5 times. The one-year forward price-to-sales ratio is 4.4 times, against 1.9 times for the benchmark. One-year forward earnings growth is 11.9% against 4.6% for the benchmark. The portfolio companies are in robust health, with relatively little debt in comparison with the benchmark and are reinvesting three times more in their businesses than the benchmark.

Strong fundamentals for future growth

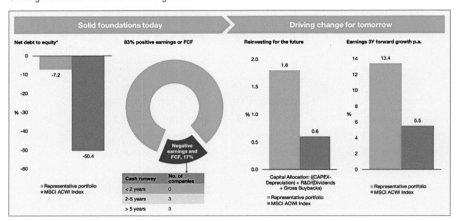

Source: Baillie Gifford & Co, FactSet, Revolution, MSCI. As at 30 June 2023.

Has enthusiasm for ESG waned in the last 18 months, as many seem to believe?

ESG investing is a broad term which covers many different approaches. Within that broad realm, impact investing is one of the most clearly defined and measurable. It continues to attract global demand. Our positive change strategy has seen net positive cash flows over the past 18 months.

What is the outlook for the trust from 2024 onwards. Can you still meet your performance objective?

Over our investment horizon we believe we can meet our performance objective, which is to deliver returns that are 2% per annum ahead of the MSCI ACWI index, net of fees. We have limited insight into what the short-term market environment will be in 2024, but we are committed to finding and investing in the best structural opportunities for the next decade.

We believe that well-run and well-capitalised companies with long-term growth plans which address global challenges will be better positioned to navigate the evolving environment.

Our portfolio consists of exceptional growth companies trading at a price/earnings premium of approximately 1.5 times the market. These companies have demonstrated impressive five-year earnings growth, more than double that of the index. Consensus forecasts, which are potentially underestimated, suggest their earnings growth over the next three years will be nearly four times that of the index.

Despite short-term market volatility, we maintain strong conviction in their ability to deliver robust long-term returns.

Given the discount, why does the board think that reinvestment is a better option than share buybacks? Are you concerned that the trust remains sub-scale?

The company has the power to buy back its own shares and will do so if the board considers that such activity will benefit shareholders. The board has a range of options at its disposal to address the discount at which the company's shares trade. We are not concerned by the size of the trust, but we would like to grow it over time, recognising the benefits that size confers on shareholders in terms of liquidity and costs.

Would you expect the investment trust to outperform the open-ended equivalent over time?

The closed-ended structure enables the managers to seek out and invest in companies at an earlier stage than the open-ended fund can do. The trust can also invest in private companies and include smaller listed companies (with a minimum $500m market capitalisation, instead of $1bn). We expect the trust and the open-ended fund will continue to diverge in portfolio composition as a result. The trust's ability to use gearing also serves to differentiate the investment returns from the OEIC fund and we expect that to benefit KPC shareholders over the long term.

Do you expect the private listed component of the trust to grow – and if so by how much?

The maximum amount which can be invested in private company securities is 30% of the gross asset value of the company, measured at the time of investment.

As at the end of August 2023, the figure was less than 5%, but we expect it will grow steadily over time to reach double figures.

Which of your holdings have the greatest growth potential at present?

We run a high-conviction portfolio, and competition for capital is fierce. Our largest weighted positions are the ones we believe have the highest potential for future growth and impact. I would highlight companies such as MercadoLibre, which is strengthening its position in Latin American e-commerce and financial services; Tesla for its progress in scaling up vehicle production and battery manufacturing; Bank Rakyat, Indonesia's largest bank, which has a competitive advantage in micro-finance thanks to its extensive rural branch network; Dexcom, a continuous glucose monitor manufacturer, with strong revenue growth that is expanding into international markets; and Deere, the agricultural equipment manufacturer, a leader in the growing field of precision agriculture, contributing to sustainable food production.

Some younger companies in the portfolio also have great potential to meet our dual objectives. Duolingo, an online learning platform, continues to grow its user base, enabling further education and employment, and Remitly continues to meet key operational milestones and is helping to maximise the vital role remittances play in socio-economic development.

Keystone Positive Change is listed in the global equity sector of the AIC's classification. It adopted its new positive impact strategy when Baillie Gifford was appointed as the new manager of the trust in 2021. The annual Impact Report can be found at www.bailliegifford.com and is well worth a read.

DISCOUNT HEAVEN?

JOE BAUERNFREUND, *manager of AVI Global Trust (AGT), explains how it seeks to make money from investing in deeply discounted global securities. The trust currently focuses on three main areas: large holding companies (often family-controlled), UK-listed investment trusts and Japanese equities.*

Why should someone invest in AVI Global? Is it appropriate for private investors?

AVI GLOBAL OFFERS investors of any kind a differentiated approach to global investment. We focus on areas of the market that are neglected and overlooked by other investors. We believe we can find good-quality companies trading at discounts to their intrinsic value, a policy that has served Warren Buffett and others very well over the years.

Why do you have a world excluding US benchmark rather than a world index benchmark?

Historically, the fund had no exposure to the US, and thus an ex-US benchmark was chosen. The board monitors the performance of the trust relative to a range of different benchmarks, and the question of what is the appropriate benchmark is kept under regular review. Bear in mind however that our approach is entirely benchmark agnostic. The choice of benchmark will not have any impact on portfolio construction.

What changes have you made in the portfolio in 2023?

We have added to opportunities within the UK investment trust sector, particularly within private equity. Princess Private Equity (PEY) and Pantheon International (PIN) have both become substantial holdings for us. We made additional investments into portfolio names where we believed there was likely to be an idiosyncratic driver of returns.

Two examples would be FEMSA, a Mexican retailer, and Schibsted, a Norwegian holding company with interests in advertising companies. Both companies have announced strategic reviews. In a generally challenging market environment, where we have seen extreme moves to the downside, we have taken advantage of that by adding to some beaten up names, such as private equity firm Apollo and media investor IAC Inc., which have since recovered very strongly. We have reduced some other positions, including Pershing Square Holdings and Exor, and sold Third Point Investors, Fujitec and Eurazeo among others.

Your trust's portfolio currently sits on a 'double discount' of around 40%, with portfolio companies trading at an average 30% discount and the trust itself trading at a 10% discount. What is the catalyst for bringing that back in and what is a reasonable target for this metric?

That will depend on the particular holding. In some cases, such as Japan or closed-end funds, it could be activism on our part. In the case of Schibsted, News Corp and IAC it is likely to be management action. Another holding, Exor, recently announced a tender offer which saw its discount narrow by around 5% in a day.

There are two drivers of returns for us. One is NAV growth and the second is discount contraction. While we always buy on wide discounts and sometimes exert pressure on the company to narrow the discount, we will never buy something if we don't believe that the NAV will go up as well.

While discounts tell you how cheap a company is, our investment thesis is typically predicated on there being growth in the value of the business, regardless of what the discount does. The discount is icing on the cake, not the only reason for investing.

NAV gains will typically be the larger driver of returns, particularly over longer holding periods. This is why we emphasise that the strategy is about buying good-quality business at discounts, rather than simply buying cheap companies.

AGT double discount

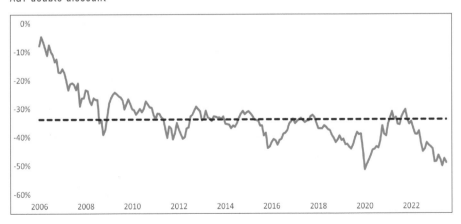

Are the wide discounts in the UK investment trust sector justified?

On the whole our view is that they are not justified. You have a market where a large cohort of buyers, namely wealth managers, have been de-risking their portfolios in favour of gilts. The selling pressure is putting downward pressure on discounts. In the case of alternatives, the discounts reflect uncertainty about valuations and a misguided perception that we will see a repeat of what happened in 2008–2009. In both cases, it means that we have been able to find plenty of interesting opportunities.

How long could it take for those discounts to narrow or even disappear?

I've been active in this sector for long enough to know that predicting when discounts are going to narrow or disappear is a fool's game. But tackling the discount is clearly the right thing for the board and manager to do if they want to demonstrate to the market that there is value in their portfolio. Buying back shares on a wide discount is accretive to the NAV and often the best investment that a trust can make. So we think it's a good thing to do, but how long it will take for those discounts to normalise is difficult to judge.

There's been a lot of discussion about whether cost disclosure requirements are keeping wealth managers and others from buying trusts they might previously have owned. How important has that been in producing these wider discounts?

It is certainly one factor in understanding what's going on in the sector. You have a swathe of the investor base restricted or prevented from buying trusts due to the artificial cost reporting requirements that are being imposed upon them. When you think about it, discounts reflect a mismatch in supply and demand and if a chunk of the demand is removed from the market, that creates pressure on the discount. So yes, it has been a problem for the sector to grapple with. Absolutely.

Do you expect to invest more in the UK investment trust universe?

Quite possibly. Our exposure has been increasing throughout the year. And whilst they are not the only area of extreme value in our universe, there are certainly lots of trusts for us to look at, given the widespread derating that we have seen over the last two years. Bear in mind that our aim with the trust is to run a fairly concentrated portfolio. We are not looking for a large number of smaller tail positions. Opportunities are cropping up across the world, but there's only a limited amount of capital available. Right now we are monitoring, comparing opportunities within the investment trust sector against other options.

Share buybacks don't seem to be having much impact in reducing the discount on your own trust. Does that concern you?

Buybacks are a way of buying more of our existing portfolio, and given where discounts are now, we think that stacks up as a very attractive investment for us. It does depend how you measure the impact, however. Without the buybacks, our own discount could be approaching the very high teens or early twenties that some of our peers are trading at.

I agree that we would have hoped that our discount would be narrower given our performance relative to peers and our active buyback programme. The trust has bought back nearly 40% of its shares over the last 10 years and we have been buying back more shares this year than we've done in the previous few years. Given the broader environment however it is perhaps not surprising that we haven't yet made major inroads into the discount level.

Within the portfolio which are your highest conviction investments?

The largest holdings are the highest conviction ones. They are Schibsted, Oakley Capital, Femsa, KKR, Apollo and the two listed private equity trusts I have already mentioned.

What is your approach to taking interests in family-run holding companies, where your ability to influence behaviour is more limited?

As a general rule, what we're looking for is families that have done good things for minority shareholders as well as themselves, rather than having abused the structure of a listing to their own advantage and to the detriment of minority shareholders. Where you find examples of bad behaviour it's safe to assume that may be repeated at some point in the future, in which case the discount will be justified, rather than an opportunity for us.

But when you find families that have done good things for all their shareholders, and their minority shareholders have become richer as the family have become richer, you can assume that they do have broader shareholder interests at heart and they're likely to repeat that behaviour, subject to the timing being convenient for them. It is those kinds of companies that we would choose to invest in.

The key driver of return in these situations is the NAV growth, and very often that NAV growth has been spectacularly strong, certainly stronger than you will find in most markets. Exploiting the discount and benefiting from some normalisation can generate a few basis points of additional return over the long term, and that is very helpful. But it is finding those really good-quality, undervalued businesses that is the real driver of returns. It has been very successful for us.

The other point to highlight, in the context of our discussion about investment trust costs, is that many of these holding companies are run very efficiently and on tight budgets, 0.1% to 0.2% on average. There's a great alignment of interest between minority shareholders and the families. It's not that families are using the listing to pay themselves huge salaries. They are pretty modest in terms of the cost and that's an added benefit to minority shareholders.

Turning to Japan, what is your approach there?

Japan is part of the special situations leg of our portfolio. It's a collection of asset-backed companies that are trading at discounts to their value. Right now the key focus is on cash-rich Japanese small-cap companies trading at very low valuations, where there's not only an opportunity to benefit from rerating in that valuation but also an opportunity, given the corporate governance reforms in Japan, to engage with the management of those companies constructively to push them to introduce measures to improve their share prices. There are different approaches, some more hostile, some more aggressive, some more private and more constructive. The key point is that engaging with companies has clearly and demonstrably helped to unlock huge amounts of value.

How important is the recent change in monetary policy there for those investments?

At the company level it is not that important. Our approach is more about valuation, corporate governance improvement and our engagement with companies. However, on a macro-level it is hugely important. The weak yen has been a drag on performance for sterling investors and we expect that situation to reverse as monetary policy reverses course, as we think it will in due course. There are indications that the end of yield curve control is in sight. Having said that, it's well known that the government has a lot of debt. The Bank of Japan will be reluctant to allow interest rates to increase rapidly since that would put more pressure on the market. So a steady easing of the very extreme monetary policies that we've seen over the last few years or the last few decades is the most likely way forward, I would say.

Can you evidence the improvements in corporate governance in Japan?

Absolutely. A large and growing proportion of Japanese companies are doing share buybacks and boosting their dividend payout ratios. We are also seeing many more independent directors on boards. Companies are engaging extensively with shareholders on how they can boost shareholder returns. Recent efforts by the Tokyo Stock Exchange to get companies to boost share prices, particularly those trading below book value, is helping to accelerate these trends.

Are you still involved in public activist campaigns outside Japan, like the one in 2022 involving Third Point Investors, the UK-listed trust managed by US hedge fund manager Dan Loeb?

Watch this space! [The trust has since our conversation issued an open letter advocating changes at Hipgnosis Songs Fund, the troubled music royalties company]. We did go public with Third Point Investors. Our preference is always private engagement initially. If we need to go public we will, but we don't do it for the sake of getting our names in lights.

Which of your three main strategies holds out the prospect of the best returns? How correlated are they to each other and global markets?

They are all very attractive at the moment, in the sense that we find attractive valuations and wide discounts across the board. They are all long-only equity positions and to the extent that there is a degree of correlation across equity markets, there will be a high degree of correlation for us too.

Having said that, the concentration on sources of idiosyncratic returns has been deliberately designed to boost exposure to opportunities that have less sensitivity to changes in market levels. In the same way shareholder activism, where we employ that, can deliver positive returns regardless of what the markets are doing.

JOE BAUERNFREUND has been the manager of AVI Global (known until 2019 as British Empire Securities) since 2015. Asset Value Investors, the manager of the trust, is also responsible for the management of AVI Japan Opportunities Trust and this year was also awarded the mandate to run MIGO Global Opportunities Trust (MIGO), another trust that specialises in identifying trusts on attractively wide discounts. AVI Global has delivered a share price total return of 9% per annum over the last ten years (as at 30 September 2023).

WHAT ABOUT AI?

BEN ROGOFF *assesses the potentially revolutionary impact that artificial intelligence may have on the modern world and its implication for investors.*

A pivotal moment

WE HAVE BEEN excited about the potential of AI for many years, highlighting the remarkable progress the technology has made in narrow fields. This was led by Google's DeepMind acquisition which achieved 'superhuman' ability in games such as Go (2016) and Chess (2017) before solving one of the grand challenges in biology during 2021 when AlphaFold was able to predict 3D models of protein structures described at the time as "the most important achievement in AI ever".

That lasted until ChatGPT used a transformer model trained on 175TB of text to generate human-like responses to seemingly any question. Able to take on different personas, write poems or programming code, even offer opinions, ChatGPT is already the first AI to 'viably compete with humans'. This is likely to prove a pivotal moment for AI with Microsoft's $10bn investment in ChatGPT maker OpenAI best understood as one of the 'opening shots' in an AI war that has just commenced.

We have long argued that the semiconductor industry looks well positioned, with McKinsey arguing this sector might capture as much as 40%–50% of the value associated with AI. This view was seemingly supported following recent record-breaking July quarter guidance from chipmaker Nvidia that was more than 50% ahead of consensus driven by AI-related strength. On the earnings call, CEO Jensen Huang spoke to a $1trn opportunity over 10 years to replace CPU-based infrastructure with more efficient, accelerated computing based around GPU architectures as generative AI becomes the "primary workload of most of the world's data centres". Nvidia stock rose 24% on the day, despite having already gained 109% on a year-to-date basis prior to the report.

Of course, there are myriad risks associated with AI. However, the fact that ChatGPT makes mistakes (so-called 'hallucinations') is not one of them; most disruptive technologies begin as 'good enough' and trading accuracy for speed worked wonders for the telegraph, Encyclopaedia Britannica, and the biro. Moral and legal questions posed by AI are more difficult to dismiss, especially those regarding bias and the potential for it to 'industrialise plagiarism'.

While eventual regulation of AI seems inevitable, the industry would likely welcome the introduction of legislative guardrails. However, this will not be straightforward; rather than a restrictive set of regulations applied suddenly, we believe regulation may follow a 'governance by accident' approach that has underpinned the development of the airline industry; if aviation is any guide, it is possible that by reducing risk, regulation actually accelerates the adoption of AI, rather than stymies its progress.

As such, the focus on regulation – so soon after the advent of generative AI – might say more about investor fatigue around 'technology disruption' than it does about the risk regulation poses to the development of this nascent industry. This is understandable, following a period that has witnessed more than its fair share of investment hyperbole, much of which was catalysed by the pandemic. In contrast with blockchain and the metaverse, which are early stage technologies in search of a problem, artificial intelligence might be "the most profound technology humanity is working on". From a historical perspective, generative AI could prove another key moment in human history when codification and dissemination of knowledge is accelerated.

What AI could do

In the ancient world, these key moments included the development of writing systems (such as cuneiform and hieroglyphics) around 3500 to 3000 BCE, as well as advanced mathematics and philosophy in Ancient Greece from the eighth century BCE onwards. Libraries, historical record-keeping, and translation of ancient texts were other key developments in the codification and preservation of knowledge, aided by breakthroughs that enabled information to be stored (e.g., papyrus, paper), retrieved (e.g., cataloguing systems, encyclopaedia) and distributed (e.g., libraries, printing press). Advances in science, technology and communication during the Modern Era have "led to the codification of knowledge on an unprecedented scale", epitomised by the internet, which has facilitated knowledge sharing and democratised access to information in a manner that has changed the world.

Generative AI offers similar – if not greater – promise. Built using 'foundation' models which contain "expansive neural networks inspired by the billions of neurons connected in the human brain", generative AI applications are able to process extremely large and varied sets of unstructured data and perform more than one task. This allows them to "augment human creativity, automate labour-intensive tasks and generate novel solutions to complex problems". They can also understand natural language, which means that generative AI could "change the anatomy of work" by automating activities that today account for as much as 60%–70% of employees' time.

However, in contrast with historic patterns of technology automation, disruption is expected to be disproportionately felt by knowledge workers. While Goldman Sachs estimate that more than 300m jobs could be at risk, we remain optimistic that humans will graduate to higher value work just as 60% of workers today are employed in occupations that did not exist in 1940. Furthermore, McKinsey forecast that generative AI could deliver $2.6–4.4trn annually to global GDP driven by productivity gains that could be as high as 3.3% per annum when generative AI is combined with other technologies. This would be remarkable given current labour market tightness, ageing Western populations and below-average productivity growth achieved during the past 20 years.

Artificial intelligence also has the potential to become a transformative 'general purpose technology' (GPT) which – like electricity, steel, and the internet – may "reshape economies, drive innovation and create new opportunities". If so, history suggests that bold, early predictions about AI may prove extremely conservative. This is not just because humans struggle with non-linear change (an observation that has long informed our investment approach), but also because as yet unknown technology improvements subsequently transform the opportunity set. If early applications for steel were predictable (e.g., bridges, ships, rails), later and significantly larger market opportunities represented by skyscrapers, cars and home appliances could not be known in 1855 when Bessemer perfected his steelmaking process.

The same was true for aviation when the jet engine (and other avionic developments) transformed the cost and safety profile of flight, resulting in passenger traffic growth compounding by more than 10% per year between 1950 and 1970 and helping travel and tourism become one of the world's largest sectors. More recently, the confluence of internet, cloud and smartphone has presaged widespread disruption and exponential change well beyond late 1990s predictions that were only able to peer into a near and incomplete future that was yet to feature Google, AWS, and iPhones. Today, the app economy is worth around $63trn, more than 60 times greater than the value of the handset market in 2007, the year that Apple introduced the iPhone.

The impact of generative AI is likely to be felt more rapidly than either the internet or the smartphone. In part, this reflects the role that both earlier pervasive technologies will play as AI-enablers with access to ChatGPT (and other natural language 'chat' interfaces) only requiring an internet connection and a smartphone. These low barriers to adoption have already supported an unprecedented rate with ChatGPT taking just 2.5 months to reach 100m users, as compared to Instagram which took 2.5 years (in itself extraordinary).

Speed and scale

Another major difference between AI and prior technology shifts is the astonishing speed of AI improvement. This is most evident when comparing the capability of two OpenAI large language models (LLMs) – GPT-4 (the latest version) and the earlier GPT-3.5 (ChatGPT) released approximately a year apart. While GPT-3.5 was trained on 175bn parameters (akin to internal variables the model learns during its training phase), the newer GPT-4 may have been trained on as many as 170trn.

In addition, GPT-4 also has a much larger context window – 25,000 words versus around 3,000 for its predecessor – which means it is able to retain far more information from earlier conversations. Aside from its 'mastery of natural language', GPT-4 "can solve novel and difficult tasks that span mathematics, coding, vision, medicine, law, psychology and more, without needing any special prompting". In all of these tasks, model performance is "strikingly close to human-level performance", evidenced by consistently high exam scores across a diverse range of disciplines.

The improvements in GPT-4 have been so remarkable that Microsoft recently posited in a white paper ('Sparks of artificial general intelligence') that the LLM "could reasonably be viewed as an early version of AGI system". The concept of AGI was popularised in the early 2000s to differentiate between 'narrow AI' being developed at the time and 'broader notions of intelligence'. Until recently, AGI remained a popular science fiction topic and long-term aspirational goal within AI. That is until the range and depth of GPT-4's capabilities "challenged our understanding of learning and cognition" with the model said to "exhibit many traits of intelligence". Naysayers argue that large language models do not 'understand' concepts and are merely adept at 'improvising on the fly'. However, like Microsoft, we believe the question is moot. After all, one might ask "how much more there is to true understanding than 'on-the-fly' improvisation?".

BEN ROGOFF *is the lead manager of the Polar Capital Technology Trust.*

WIND IN THE SAILS?

Greencoat UK Wind, the investment sector's first and largest renewable energy trust and a bellwether for the specialist sector, celebrated its tenth anniversary as a listed company in 2023. STEPHEN LILLEY, *co-founder and co-manager of the trust, answers questions about its track record and the outlook from here.*

The trust's objective is to provide investors with an annual dividend that increases in line with RPI inflation and real NAV preservation. Why did you choose the dividend as a primary objective?

YOU HAVE TO remember that the development of Greencoat UK Wind as a publicly listed asset class was a child, if you like, of the back end of the credit crunch and the global financial crisis. There wasn't a lot of income to be had elsewhere at the time, as interest rates were so low and coming down.

Governments were not keen to see interest rates go up after a credit crunch which required a lot of debt to be issued. Inflating it away – allowing inflation to erode some of its value in real terms – was not a bad thing to do.

Against that background we set out to create a company that had a dividend which we knew we could always increase in line with inflation, whilst preserving shareholders' capital in real terms. The combination of real capital preservation and an inflation-proofed income turned out to be a great product at the time, good for wealth managers, good for multi-asset managers and good for renewable energy developers and operators.

But it was not an accident that we framed the trust as we did, with an initial 6p dividend and the promise of an RPI-linked yield and real NAV preservation. You may not know that we had a dry run at creating a vehicle like this in 2011, but just failed to get it away. We were aiming to raise £200m, but only got to around £180m. We decided that if we listed with a new type of trust that nobody had done before and only just about managed to get it over the line, it would not trade well, so for this and other reasons we called it off.

The benefit of failure is that, if you are wise and learn from it, you can make the product better next time round. Our first effort in retrospect may have not been explained as well as it could have been, so we formulated something better the

217

second time round. We worked out who the likely investors were and what they needed. The coalition government, advised by the Green Investment Bank, gave us £50m, which also helped, and sold out at a profit a couple of years later.

Ten and a bit years on from IPO, how would you measure your success in meeting the twin objectives?

I think the track record speaks for itself. The trust has grown from a market cap of £260m at launch to £3.2bn today. We have raised £2.5bn through secondary equity issues and increased the dividend each year in line with the RPI, as we said we would. This year's full-year target dividend is 67% higher than the initial 6p (10p is the target for calendar year 2023). The NAV per share has meanwhile risen from 98p to 165.8p (as at 30 September 2023), which is also comfortably ahead of inflation.

Even though the shares have derated to a discount since September 2022, along with the great majority of investment trusts, for most of the period since IPO they have traded at a premium. Of the original half-dozen renewable trusts that launched in 2013–14 we remain the largest and have the best performance record. The annualised NAV total return since IPO is 11.4% (including assumed dividend reinvestment).

Can that unique RPI-linked dividend be sustained, as it has been so far?

For sure. The dividend is very well covered by earnings for the foreseeable future. In our latest results we showed that it would be covered by earnings until at least 2028 even if the price we receive for the power our wind farms generate were to fall to £10/MWh, which – although future power prices are expected to fall after the Ukraine War – is a long, long way below the current price and practically impossible. The average price we received in the first half of 2023, which was a relatively poor period for wind generation, was £104.06/MWh.

What are your competitive advantages compared to your most comparable peers?

As well as the superior long-term performance, I think that our initial pricing of the shares and rate of dividend was well thought out. The explicit RPI linkage is not matched in the listed peer group. As the largest listed renewable energy trust, we also have the advantages of scale and our pure focus on operational UK wind assets also helps to differentiate us. We've acquired or invested into wind farms from almost everyone in the sector. We're well known and understood.

We do not invest in riskier wind development projects, nor do we intend to diversify away from the UK's onshore and offshore wind sectors, as some of our peers have done. As a manager, we launched a second investment trust, Greencoat Renewables, in 2017 which has a broader mandate, investing in European wind projects and other types of renewables, such as solar. Greencoat UK Wind continues to do what it says on the tin.

That was a deliberate choice. We did not want to add currency risk to Greencoat UK Wind by investing in other regions, nor did we want to blur the proposition by moving away from a pure UK wind focus. The trust remains the largest single fund in the total £10bn of renewable energy investments that Schroders Greencoat now manages for pension funds, other institutions and private investors.

You are generating substantial amounts of cash, but is reinvestment still the best use of your cash, compared to the alternatives: higher dividends, debt repayment or share buybacks?

Since listing on the London Stock Exchange in March 2013, we have generated £1,764m of cash flow, paid £887m of dividends and reinvested £877m of excess cash generation. Reinvestment is clearly an important part of the story and will continue to be. There remains a £100bn pool of assets that we can buy from, so we're not short of opportunities. Reflecting our confidence in our outlook, in October this year we decided to increase our annual dividend target to 10p, an increase of 14.2%, and also commenced a share buyback programme up to £100m, which we feel achieves an optimal use of cash to deliver value for our shareholders. Excess cash generation might be used to reduce debt, but it is mostly fixed rate and has an average cost of 4.1%, which is not onerous and well below our projected rates of return.

While NAV progression has been in line with your total return target (7–9% p.a.), the shares have recently gone to a discount for almost the first time since launch, reducing shareholder returns. Why is that and what can you do about it?

It is only since September 2022 that the shares have moved to a discount, which I think is largely the result of the surge in inflation and rising interest rates that has caused derating across almost every investment trust sector. It's a frustration that we're not trading at a premium because there are a lot more transactions we could do if we were.

I am confident that we can get back to trading around par in due course. What some investors have overlooked, I think, is not just that the inflation-linked dividend is very secure – it has been covered on average 2.0x by earnings since IPO – but that that 2.0x coverage also means that a lot of reinvestment has been going on. There are still good returns to be made from reinvesting our excess cash flow.

It is true that higher yields on gilts and corporate bonds now offer income-seeking investors an alternative source of yield, but our potential returns are still significantly higher. The return on our business at NAV has risen – at 11% it is now 1% higher than at the time of our IPO – but our cash flows, unlike those of a gilt, are also highly correlated to inflation. For every 1% increase in inflation, our cash flows increase by roughly the same amount.

Since we launched the trust, the amount we have reinvested in new assets has been more or less the same as the amount we have paid out in dividends. With significant surplus cash flow, we can continue to self-finance future growth projects without needing to issue more debt or equity. That is the message that we have been taking to investors over the last few months.

How do you plan to change your approach, if at all, from here?

We don't intend to change our approach. We will continue to focus solely on investing in operational UK wind projects. Rising costs have put pressure on developers of new offshore wind projects, some of whom have been paused as a result. Although that might threaten the government's renewable energy targets, it has also given us the opportunity to acquire further assets at attractive prices from developers who need to sell assets.

This year we have added interests in two new farms and will be completing two more planned investments by the end of the year. In terms of acquisitions, I would say there has almost never been a better time. There are a massive number of projects out there, which is not surprising since the build-out needed to meet the government's renewable energy targets by 2030 is massive.

Have the potential returns from UK wind assets deteriorated compared to 2013, given that the early Government subsidies are being phased out and the Government last year imposed a windfall levy on your profits?

The potential returns from investing in UK wind remain attractive, in our view. Although coming down, power prices are significantly higher than when we launched the trust and our assets will also still be generating subsidised revenues for many years to come, given the average life is only seven years. Some newer wind farms have shown they can make money without subsidy. Given the government's target for increasing offshore wind generating capacity to 50GWA by 2030, the demand for new investment remains. There's a lot of need for capital, and therefore opportunities for us.

Looking ahead at the overall portfolio, we calculate the projected total return after taking account of leverage is around 11%, which reduces to 10% per annum after taking account of fees, if the share price was trading at NAV. The return is obviously higher than that currently. That represents a significant premium over the potential return from gilts, which have been trading on yields of 4–5% and have no inflation protection.

Was the Government decision to charge an electricity levy in 2022 justified in your view and how will it affect the trust?

Once investors understood that the Government's real reason for imposing the levy was the impact that the Russian invasion of Ukraine had on power prices, and not a tax on profits per se, it became easier to justify. As to the impact, we will likely pay a lot less than was forecast at the outset, largely because power prices have come down since then. We expect to pay less than £20m this year and almost nothing next year. It is likely that power prices will be below the threshold after that, in which case we won't be paying anything further. So it has some effect, but it's not been massive.

While the Government decision to end the restriction on new onshore wind farms is a positive, should not investors be worried by the cancellation of big offshore wind projects by Orsted and other developers and the failure of the UK's September auction? What does it say about the economics of new developments?

I think it was obvious that no offshore projects were going to be included in the auction for two reasons. Firstly, as much more capacity is built, it would seem likely that turbine prices will increase. Secondly, and perhaps more significantly, the cost of capital has increased for all and thus the return requirement for the builders of new offshore capacity and those, like us, that might buy in the secondary market has also increased. Thus, the cap also looked too tight for new offshore capacity.

From our perspective, there are currently approximately 29GW of operating UK wind farms (15GW onshore plus 14GW offshore), which equates to approximately £100bn. We currently have about 6% of that market, so regardless of rates of future onshore and offshore wind build-out, there is no shortage of investment opportunities available to us.

Editor's note: about Greencoat UK Wind

The renewable energy infrastructure sector today numbers more than 20 companies with combined net assets of £17bn, a mature and significant important part of the investment trust universe. Greencoat UK Wind became the first renewable trust to complete an IPO on the London market, raising £260m in an oversubscribed IPO in March 2013. As at 30 June 2023, it had equity interests in 46 wind farms with a total generation capacity of 1.65GW, valued at around £5bn, equivalent to 1.6% of the UK's total electricity consumption. The portfolio is partly funded by £1.1bn of debt at the trust level. The combined gross loan-to-value ratio is 31%. Since its IPO, the trust has acquired from 21 separate sellers, buying both from utilities and private developers. In 2021, Schroders bought a 75% stake in Greencoat Capital for £358m and it has options allowing it to acquire the remaining 25% over time.

THE UPSIDE IN BONDS

RHYS DAVIES, *the manager of Invesco Bond Income Plus Limited, the largest trust in the investment trust debt sector, explains how the dramatic rise in interest rates is creating opportunities in the high yield bond market.*

Bond markets have been anything but boring over the last couple of years – what happened?

THEY'VE BEEN EXCITING – and painful – for investors. We all know what happened in 2022. Inflation, which is the nemesis of bonds, was a lot higher than most people expected. Interest rates were hiked in reaction. Many people criticise the central banks for being late to the game, but when they did start, they were certainly very aggressive.

In the UK the base interest rate has gone from 0.1% to 5.25%. The bond market had to adapt to that. In Europe, for example, yields had become very low. The high yield bond market was only offering a yield to maturity of 3.4% at the end of 2021.[1] So there were many bonds with coupons that were uncompetitive versus interest rates.[2]

There were a lot of sub-investment grade bonds, those with a rating of BBB– or below, with coupons of 3% or 4%. These bonds should offer a higher yield than government bonds, to reflect the extra risk of investing in a corporate bond compared to a government bond. But with government bond yields rising to 5% and beyond, it means that prices of high yield bonds have had to fall sharply in order to ensure that the yield on high yield bonds remained higher.

By the end of 2022, the yield to maturity in the European high yield market had risen to around 8% and the average price of bonds in the index had declined from 101 to less than 86.[3] That meant a lot of pain for bondholders last year – it was the biggest calendar year price move since 2008 – as we moved from a world of low

---

1 The yield to maturity is the total expected return on a bond investment, taking into account the purchase price, the coupon payments and the re-payment of principal at par, or amount of money the issuer will return to bondholders at maturity.

2 A coupon is the annual interest payment a bondholder will receive from the bond issuer from the date of issuance until the date of maturity of the bond. It is expressed as a percentage of the face value of the bond.

3 Sterling denominated bonds are typically issued at a price of £100.

yields to high yields. That shouldn't be played down, but in terms of finding income in the bond market, I believe it has left us in a very good position now.

Do you think the interest rate hiking cycle is near an end?

The short answer is yes, I think we're near the end. A couple of months ago, market pricing suggested that investors were expecting several more hikes, particularly in the UK. But expectations have since reduced. In part, that's due to falling inflation. The market is now being priced on the expectation that the central banks are finished, or nearly finished, with their interest rate increases.

We've all just experienced a very aggressive hiking cycle. In some ways, the economy has held up better than predicted. For example, the labour market, as measured by unemployment levels and wage growth, is still looking positive. That's the case in the US as well as the UK. My main issue is that a lot of this positive data is backward-looking. If you look at some of the leading indicators, there is more reason to be pessimistic about growth. Levels of activity are deteriorating and even some labour market data is now getting weaker.

We also have to bear in mind that there is a lag between the imposition of interest rate hikes and their full effects on the economy being felt. Given the size and pace of the interest rate increases we have seen, there is potential for economic conditions to weaken further from here, which would tend to create the conditions not just for the hiking cycle to end, but for interest rates to be cut.

Where would a weaker economy leave the high yield bond market and your portfolio?

It's an important question. The prospect of reaching a peak in interest rates is very good news for bonds. When interest rate expectations fall, the coupons available from bonds that have already been issued at fixed rates become more valuable. So just as bond prices fell when interest rate expectations rose last year, so they could rise if interest rate expectations fall this year and next.

We call the sensitivity of bond prices to interest rates 'duration'. I've been adding to the duration of the portfolio over the last year, for example buying longer-maturity bonds. But we have to think about growth as well as interest rates. The high yield bond market, which is where the BIPS portfolio invests, is more sensitive to the growth environment than other parts of the bond market. This is because high yield bond issuers are typically more indebted companies.

It also means that they are more exposed to a rise in the interest payments on their debt, which is now happening across the board. For the moment, heading into the fourth quarter of 2023, corporate earnings are okay. The high yield sector is not particularly highly indebted, and many companies issued bonds when interest rates were low and they were able to borrow on good terms. But these conditions could change.

Lower economic growth tends to depress earnings and so reduce companies' ability to service debt. At the same time, when it comes to refinancing their debt, they are likely to have to pay significantly higher interest rates. We have seen some examples of that already. These two risks – lower earnings and higher refinancing costs – are definitely clouds on the horizon.

But, as I said earlier, yields are a lot higher now than they were, and we want to take advantage of that. The key for us is to manage the portfolio actively. It is about aligning risk and reward. For that reason, I've been raising the credit quality of the portfolio in recent months. About a quarter is now in investment-grade corporate bonds, where credit risk is lower. We have also reduced our exposure in CCC-rated bonds, the highest risk area.

While some companies may struggle in the coming quarters, we want to be picking up the good levels of yields that the bonds of better-quality companies are now offering. Our investment decisions are driven by research into both individual securities and their issuers. We use our excellent credit research resources to identify companies that are more or less equipped to handle the risks we see in the market.

What is the yield on your portfolio today?

There are a few ways of thinking about the yield. The simplest and most visible is the dividend yield. That's what the shareholders receive. The dividend is decided by the board of the trust. The BIPS board's annual dividend target right now is 11.5p per share. At the current share price (164p at the time of writing), that is equivalent to a 7% yield.

Remember that the level of the dividend is not guaranteed. However, that dividend is more than covered by the income which the BIPS portfolio is generating. The excess income is kept within the trust and can be used to smooth dividends in a lower-yielding environment. In addition to that, the average price of the bonds is 87, so well below the redemption price of 100 that the portfolio will receive if the bonds are held until they mature.

The yield to maturity is a measure which combines both the coupon payments and the potential capital gain. On the assumption that the bonds will be repaid at par (100), it is higher than the portfolio yield and is currently about 9.5%. We also have some gearing, meaning borrowing that enables us to make additional investments, in the portfolio. Gearing is 20% of NAV and the effect of that is to increase the yield further.

That all adds up to a considerable yield. I've been involved in these markets for 20 years. After a long time, during which interest rates were low and central banks were buying bonds as part of quantitative easing, I'm now seeing the sort of yields that I used to see when I started my career. These are more like the yields that I was trained to believe high yield bonds should be paying investors.

Does the ability to gear the portfolio make the trust structure a good one for managing bonds?

I think that the investment trust structure is great. The first big advantage is that being closed-ended, BIPS has a fixed number of shares, so I'm never under pressure to sell holdings just to fund redemptions. I can really focus on taking a long-term view and act boldly during times of market stress.

That's what we did when Covid-19 hit. In March and April 2020, the bond markets experienced a lot of indiscriminate and forced selling. It was what I would describe as a dysfunctional time. Being able to manage a portfolio through that, without having to worry about redemptions, was great. We were in a position to be buying and picking up some really attractive-looking opportunities.

The use of gearing is also an attraction of the closed-ended structure. It would be pretty scary to be managing an open-ended fund if it had gearing and clients could take their money out overnight. I don't think my nerves could cope with having to deal with both the gearing and redemptions at the same time. Gearing has to be managed prudently, of course, and we've got a lot of experience of doing that on the desk.

The other thing I like about the investment trust structure is the ability to set a dividend target. For BIPS, it is presented very simply as a pence per share target. That means that I can put together the portfolio with 11.5p in mind. Every quarter, when I meet the board, we can have a discussion about how comfortable we are with the target.

If I feel like hitting the target would mean taking more risk than I'm happy with, I can say that. Today, there's plenty of income out there to cover the dividend and there are good opportunities to lock in attractive coupons, with the prospect of capital gains on top. Right now, we're in a good place.

RHYS DAVIES *has been a manager of the Invesco Bond Income Plus Limited (ticker: BIPS) since 2014. BIPS was created from the 2021 merger of City Merchants High Yield and Invesco Enhanced Income but can trace its roots back to 1991. That makes BIPS by far the oldest debt trust and one of only a handful that predates the global financial crisis.*

It invests in high-yielding fixed-interest securities and other debt instruments, primarily in the UK and Europe. It aims to hold the majority of the positions it buys until they mature, and the average maturity of its portfolio is roughly five years. BIPS has total assets of around £340m spread over around 170 different issuers and it currently uses gearing in the high teens after several years of adopting a more conservative net-cash position. You can find a full-length profile of the trust on the Money Makers website. Data as at 26 September 2023 unless otherwise stated.

Invesco

Capital at r

Investment trusts:
A closer look

Why invest with us?

- We're completely focused on finding investment opportunities for you that others might have missed. We do this through meticulous research backed by decades of experience

- We believe our long-term approach to seeking out the strongest returns could help you make the most of the growth and income potential from financial markets.

- Almost all our investment trusts pay an income decided on by the board, which can be paid from income earned or from capital, so may provide a consistent level of income.

Investment risks
The value of investments and any income will fluctuate (this may partly be the result of exchange rate fluctuations) and investors may not get back the full amount invested.

Our range of investment trusts

We offer four investment trusts across a larg and diverse range of seven strategies.

These are:
- Invesco Asia Trust plc **(Ticker: IAT)**
- Invesco Bond Income Plus Limited **(Ticker: BIPS)**
- Invesco Perpetual UK Smaller Companies Investment Trust plc **(Ticker: IPU)**
- Invesco Select Trust plc:
  - Invesco Select Trust plc UK Equity Sha Portfolio **(Ticker: IVPU),**
  - Invesco Select Trust plc Global Equity Income Share Portfolio **(Ticker: IVPG),**
  - Invesco Select Trust plc Balanced Risk Allocation Share Portfolio **(Ticker: IVP**
  - Invesco Select Trust plc Managed Liquidity Share Portfolio **(Ticker: IVPM**

Scan the QR code or speak to your financial adviser to find out more.

ANALYSING INVESTMENT TRUSTS

by JONATHAN DAVIS

TRUST BASICS

For first-time investors in trusts, here is an overview of investment trusts – what they are and how they invest – from editor JONATHAN DAVIS.

What is an investment trust?

I NVESTMENT TRUSTS, ALSO known as investment companies, are a type of collective investment fund. All types of fund pool the money of a large number of different investors and delegate the investment of their pooled assets, typically to a professional fund manager. The idea is that this enables shareholders in the trust to spread their risks and benefit from the professional skills and economies of scale available to an investment management firm. Funds are able to buy and sell investments without paying tax on realised gains.

Collective funds have been a simple and popular way for individual investors to invest their savings for many years, and investment trusts have shared in that success. Today more than £250bn of savers' assets are invested in investment trusts. The first investment trust was launched as long ago as 1868, so they have a long history. Sales of open-ended funds (unit trusts, OEICs and UCITs funds) have grown faster, but investment trust performance has been superior over most periods.

How do they differ from unit trusts and open-ended funds?

There are several differences. The most important ones are that shares in investment companies are traded on a stock exchange and are overseen by an independent board of directors, like any other listed company. Shareholders have the right to vote at annual general meetings (AGMs) on a range of things, including the election of directors, changes in investment policy and share issuance. Trusts can also, unlike most open-ended funds, borrow money in order to enhance returns. Whereas the number of units in a unit trust rises and falls from day to day in response to supply and demand, an investment trust is able to deploy capital on a permanent basis.

What are discounts?

Because shares in investment trusts are traded on a stock exchange, the share price will fluctuate from day to day in response to supply and demand. Sometimes the shares will change hands for less than the net asset value (NAV) per share of the company. At other times they will change hands for more than the NAV per share. The difference between the share price and the NAV per share is calculated as a percentage of the NAV and is called a discount if the share price is below the equivalent NAV and a premium if it is above the NAV.

What is gearing?

In investment, gearing refers to the ability of an investor to borrow money in an attempt to enhance the returns that flow from his or her investment decisions. If investments rise more rapidly than the cost of the borrowing, this has the effect of producing higher returns. The reverse is also true, meaning that gains and losses are magnified. Investment trusts typically borrow around 5–10% of their assets, although this figure varies widely from one trust to another, and many trusts do not use the opportunity to gear at all.

What are the advantages of investing in an investment trust?

Because the capital is largely fixed, the managers of an investment trust can buy and sell the trust's investments whenever they need, rather than having to buy and sell simply because money is flowing in or out of the fund, as unit trust managers are required to do. The ability to gear, or use borrowed money, can also potentially produce better returns. The fact that the board of an investment trust is directly accountable to the shareholders is important. So too is the ability of boards to smooth the payment of dividend income by putting aside surplus revenue as reserves.

Another advantage of having permanent capital is that investment companies are free to invest in a much wider range of investments than other types of fund. In fact, they can invest in almost anything. Although many of the largest trusts invest in listed stocks and bonds, the biggest growth in recent years has been in a range of more specialist areas, such as renewable energy, infrastructure, music royalties, shipping and doctors' surgeries. These are not the kind of assets that other types of fund can readily invest in. Investment trusts offer fund investors a broader choice and greater scope for diversification, in other words.

And what are the disadvantages?

The two main disadvantages are share price volatility and potential loss of liquidity. Because investment trusts can trade at a discount to the value of their assets, an investor who sells at the wrong moment may not receive the full asset value for their shares at that point. The day-to-day value of the investment will also fluctuate more than an equivalent open-ended fund, as we have seen happen dramatically over the last two years. In the case of more specialist trusts, it may not always be possible to buy or sell shares in a trust at a good price because of a lack of liquidity in the market. Investors need to make sure they understand these features before investing.

How many trusts are there?

According to the industry trade body, the Association of Investment Companies, there were just over 370 investment trusts with more than £260bn in assets (as at the end of September 2023). They are split between a number of different sectors, reflecting the regions or type of investments in which they invest. Scottish Mortgage, the largest trust, has approximately £14bn in assets. If you include venture capital trusts, as the AIC does, some of the smallest trusts have just a few million pounds in assets.

What are alternative assets?

While investment trusts have traditionally invested primarily in publicly listed stocks and shares, whose values are known every day, the last decade has seen significant growth in so-called alternative assets. These are trusts which invest in longer term assets which are mostly not traded daily and therefore can be valued only at less frequent intervals. As noted above, examples include commercial property, renewable energy, infrastructure and private equity. Many of these alternative trusts have become popular because of their ability to pay higher levels of income, at a time when the income on savings paid by banks or government bonds has been very low (but has risen sharply in the last two years).

How are investment trusts regulated?

All investment companies are regulated by the Financial Conduct Authority. So too are the managers the board appoints to manage the trust's investments. Investment trusts are also subject to the Listing Rules of the stock exchange on which they are listed. The board of directors is accountable to shareholders and regulators for the performance of the trust and the appointment of the manager and are legally bound by the requirements of successive Companies Acts.

How do I invest in an investment trust?

There are a number of different ways. You can buy them directly through a stockbroker or via an online platform. A few larger investment trusts also have monthly savings schemes where you can transfer a fixed sum every month to the company, which then invests it into its shares on your behalf. If you have a financial adviser, or a portfolio manager, they can arrange the investment for you.

What do investment trusts cost?

As with any share, investors in investment trusts will need to pay brokerage commission when buying or selling shares in an investment trust, as well as stamp duty on purchases (something that the industry has long campaigned to have abolished). The managers appointed by the trust's directors to make its investments charge an annual management fee which is paid automatically, together with dealing and administration costs, out of the trust's assets. These management fees typically range from as little as 0.3% to 2.0% or more of the trust's assets.

What are tax wrappers?

Tax wrappers are schemes which allow individual investors, if they comply with the rules set by the government, to avoid tax on part or all of their investments. The two most important tax wrappers are the Individual Savings Account (ISA) and the Self-Invested Personal Pension (SIPP). The majority of investment trusts can be held in an ISA or SIPP. There are annual limits on the amounts that can be invested each year (currently £20,000 for an ISA). Venture capital trusts (VCTs) are a specialist type of investment trust which also have a number of tax advantages, reflecting their higher risk. VCTs invest in start up and early stage businesses.

Who owns investment trusts?

Twenty-five years ago life insurance companies were the biggest investors in investment trusts, which they used to manage their client funds and pensions. These days such institutional investors mostly manage their own investments directly. Other than some specialist types of trust, the largest investors in trusts today are wealth management firms (many of them former stockbroking firms), other types of professional investors and, increasingly, private investors. The growing number of individual investors reflects the growing influence of online platforms, which give individual investors the ability to choose their own investments for ISAs, SIPPs and taxable share/fund accounts.

Are they as difficult to understand as some people say?

Investment trusts are a little more complex than a simple open-ended fund, but no more difficult to understand than most types of listed company. It is important to understand the concept of discounts and premiums before you start to invest, but buying, selling and following the fortunes of your investment could not be easier. If you like the idea of making the connoisseur's choice when investing, you are sure to find the effort of understanding investment trusts worthwhile.

Key terms explained

Investment trusts (aka investment companies) pool the money of individual and professional investors and invest it for them in order to generate capital gains, dividend income, or both. Here are some of the most common jargon terms.

SHARE PRICE

The price (typically in pence) you will be asked to pay to buy or sell shares in any investment company. Your interest is to see it go up, not down.

SPREAD

The difference between the price per share to pay if you want to buy and that you will be offered if you wish to sell – can be anything from 0% (good) to 5% or more (bad). The bigger the trust, the tighter the spread should be, and the lower the cost of making changes to your portfolio.

MARKET CAPITALISATION

The aggregate current value of all the shares a trust has issued – in essence, therefore, what the market in its wisdom thinks the investment company is worth today. (The market is not always wise and would be a duller and less interesting place if it were.)

NET ASSET VALUE (NAV)

The value of the company's investments, less its running costs and the value of any debt it has taken on, at the most recent valuation point – typically (and ideally) that will be yesterday's quoted market price, but for some types of investment trust, whose assets are not traded on a daily basis, it might be one or more months ago.

NET ASSET VALUE PER SHARE

This is calculated, not surprisingly, by dividing the NAV (see above) by the number of shares in issue. You can compare it directly with the share price to find the discount or premium.

DISCOUNT/PREMIUM

When the share price is below the investment company's net asset value per share it is said to be trading 'at a discount'; if it trades above the NAV per share, then the trust is selling 'at a premium'.

RATING/RERATING

Rating is a common piece of jargon that refers to the discount or premium on an investment trust. When the discount widens, we talk about the trust "derating" and when it narrows we say it is "rerating". The idea is that, as share prices of any trust is set by supply and demand, the discount/premium it commands is a measure of how positively or negatively the market currently values it.

LIQUIDITY

This is another much-used term that essentially seeks to capture how easily and how efficiently a trust's shares can be traded. It captures both the quantity of shares that can be bought and sold at any time and the spread between the buying and selling price. In general, the smaller the trust, the more difficult it will be to buy or sell shares in large lots and the wider the spread will be.

SHARE BUYBACKS

Although it was not possible until a helpful change in the regulations in 1999, investment trusts are free to buy back their own shares, subject to maximum limits agreed by the shareholders. Boards of directors will typically do this in an attempt to reduce the discount at which its shares are trading. Any shares bought back can either be cancelled, meaning they are eliminated, or 'held in Treasury', meaning they can be issued again later if a trust's shares return to trading at a premium.

DISCOUNT CONTROL POLICY

Share buybacks are the most common way in which the board of a trust can implement a discount control policy. Alternatives include redemption schemes and tender offers. Discount control policies typically involve setting a level of discount at which the board pledges to start buying back shares. For some trusts this is zero, for others a higher figure. Many trusts do not have a formal policy at all, however.

DIVIDEND YIELD

How much a trust pays out as income each year to its shareholders, expressed as a percentage of its share price. The usual figure quoted is based on the dividends a company has paid in the previous 12 months. Over time you hope to see the dividend increasing at least in line with inflation. Many alternative asset trusts publish a target dividend at the start of their financial year.

DIVIDEND HERO

A catchy term invented by the industry trade body to describe trusts which have increased their dividend every year for more than 20 consecutive years (see the data section for a full list). This has proved to be a popular marketing approach, even though the percentage increases from one year to the next can be minimal in some cases.

FUND MANAGER

The person (or team) responsible for choosing and managing the investment trust's capital. Will typically be professionally qualified and highly paid. How much value he or she really adds is a lively source of debate. Boards can and sometimes do change the management firm they appoint to look after the trust's investments.

THE BOARD

Investment companies are listed companies, so they must comply with stock exchange rules and appoint a board of independent directors who are legally responsible for overseeing the company and protecting the interests of its shareholders, which ultimately means replacing the manager or closing down the trust if results are not good.

GEARING

A fancy word for borrowing money in order to try and boost the performance of a company's shares – a case of more risk for potentially more reward. A number of different types of borrowing (e.g., with fixed or variable interest rates) can be used. Some trusts use complex derivative securities to achieve the same effect.

FEES AND CHARGES

What it costs to own shares in an investment trust – a figure that (confusingly) can be calculated in several different ways. More important than it sounds on first hearing, as the cost of an investment can have a material impact on the results it is able to achieve over time.

OCR

Short for Ongoing Charge Ratio, one of the most commonly used formulas used to measure the annual cost of owning a trust. Expressed as a percentage of the NAV. Total Expense Ratio is another cost measure you may come across.

SECTORS

Investment trusts come in many shapes and sizes, so for convenience are categorised into one of a number of different sectors, based on the kind of things that they invest in.

PERFORMANCE

A popular and over-used term which tells you how much money an investment trust has made for its shareholders over any given period of time – by definition, a backward-looking measurement. It does not guarantee future performance will be as good.

BENCHMARK

The outcome against which a trust and its shareholders have agreed to measure its performance. For conventional equity trusts this is typically a stock market index relevant to the area or style in which the portfolio is being invested (e.g., the FTSE All-Share index for trusts investing in UK equity markets). You will come across other types of benchmarks as well. Be careful when a trust decides to change its benchmark: sometimes this can make its past performance record look better.

TOTAL RETURN

A way of combining the income a trust pays with the capital gains it also generates (you hope) over time, so as to allow fair comparisons with other trusts and funds.

Shown either as a simple percentage gain over the period or as an annualised gain, the compound rate of return per annum.

RISK AND RETURN

Riskier investments tend to produce higher returns over time, typically at the cost of doing less well when market conditions are unfavourable and better when they are more helpful. Risk comes in many (dis)guises, however – some more visible than others.

CONTINUATION VOTE

When new investment trusts are launched, it is common for shareholders to be offered a continuation vote at periodic future intervals. This means that shareholders will have an opportunity every so often to vote on whether the trust should continue to operate. In some cases this just happens automatically. In others the vote will only be triggered if a trust fails to meet some given performance criteria.

WINDING UP

One of several terms that describes how a trust may come to the end of its life, typically after serval years of disappointing performance. The board asks shareholders for approval to shut the company down, with any remaining assets returned to shareholders as cash. In practice shareholders are often offered an alternative of 'rolling over' their holding into another investment fund, as doing so does not trigger a capital gains liability, which might otherwise apply.

BETA

This is a term used in financial economics to measure the extent to which the shares of a company rise or fall relative to the stock market as a whole. The stock market has a beta of 1.0, so if the market rises 10%, then a trust with a beta of 1.2 is expected to rise by 12% (=10 × 1.2). If it falls by 10%, the shares should also fall by 12%.

ALPHA

A statistical measure of the additional returns that a trust has made after adjusting for the relative risk of its portfolio. It is often used (not entirely accurately) as shorthand for fund manager skill. The idea is that you can distinguish between the gains a trust makes purely as a result of the stock market going up and down (measured by the beta) and and the additional return which a trust's fund manager has generated by his or her efforts (the alpha).

ACTIVE MANAGEMENT

What is going on when the investment manager of a trust makes a conscious decision not to include in its portfolio all the stocks or shares that make up its benchmark index. The latter can be easily and much more cheaply replicated by a computer – what is known as passive management. All investment trusts are actively managed.

INVESTMENT STYLE

An attempt to characterise the way in which the manager of a trust chooses to invest. One common distinction is between value and growth. The former style aims to find companies whose shares are cheap relative to their competitors or historic price. The latter concentrates on finding companies with above average sales and profit growth prospects. Other style factors include size, quality and momentum.

IS THERE ANY DIFFERENCE BETWEEN AN INVESTMENT COMPANY AND INVESTMENT TRUST?

Basically no. Strictly speaking, investment trusts are investment companies but not all investment companies are investment trusts. Feel free to use either term interchangeably, without fear of embarrassment.

CLOSED-END FUNDS

Investment trusts are an example of what is called a 'closed-end fund', meaning that its capital base is intended to be fixed and permanent (unlike unit trusts, OEICs and horribly named UCITs 3 funds, which take in and return money to investors on a daily basis and are therefore called open-ended). The distinction is no longer quite as important as it was, as it has become somewhat easier for successful investment companies to raise new money through regular share issues.

USEFUL SOURCES OF INFORMATION

INDUSTRY INFORMATION
The Association of Investment Companies | www.theaic.co.uk

DATA, NEWS AND RESEARCH
Money Makers | www.money-makers.co

Morningstar | www.morningstar.co.uk

Trustnet | www.trustnet.com

Citywire | www.citywire.co.uk

PLATFORMS
Interactive Investor | www.iii.co.uk

Hargreaves Lansdown | www.hl.co.uk

A.J.Bell | www.ajbell.co.uk

Fidelity International | www.fidelity.co.uk

SPONSORED NEWS AND RESEARCH
Edison | www.edisoninvestmentresearch.com

QuotedData | www.quoteddata.com

Trust Intelligence (Kepler Partners) | www.trustintelligence.co.uk

SPECIALIST PUBLICATIONS
Investment Trusts Newsletter (McHattie Group) | www.tipsheets.co.uk

Investment Trust Insider (Citywire) | www.citywire.co.uk

PUBLICATIONS THAT REGULARLY FEATURE INVESTMENT TRUSTS
Financial Times | www.ft.com

Investors Chronicle | www.investorschronicle.co.uk

Money Makers newsletter | www.money-makers.co

MoneyWeek | www.moneyweek.com

The Telegraph | www.telegraph.co.uk

UNDERSTANDING ALTERNATIVES

EMMA BIRD, *head of investment trust research at Winterflood Securities, answers reader questions about the way that alternative asset trusts are valued and trade.*

How are the NAVs for alternative asset trusts calculated and how does that differ from those of equity investment trusts?

THE FIRST KEY difference between the NAVs of alternative and conventional equity investment trusts is that the latter are based on publicly available stock prices, whereas the valuations of the former are based on a variety of inputs and use a range of methodologies, the mix of which depends on the asset class.

The underlying valuations of alternative assets are not immediately verifiable, as is the case for equity funds, because there are no up-to-date market prices available. The fact that they are often based on assumptions, or models, can lead to scepticism over the accuracy of the NAVs.

Another significant difference is that equity investment trusts generally publish daily NAVs, with less than a 24-hour time lag. In contrast alternative asset funds tend to publish their NAVs quarterly, or in some cases semi-annually, with a lag of up to three months from the period end.

This is because the valuation process is more complex and time-consuming and there is no daily trade in the underlying assets. When it comes to publishing interim and full-year results, the requirement that valuations of investment trusts, like those of all listed companies, are independently audited by a third party also adds to the time lag.

What is the role of the board in valuations?

The role of the board is important, as it is ultimately their responsibility to approve and publish a trust's NAV. All valuations need to be scrutinised by the board on an ongoing basis and are also reviewed by external auditors once a year. Some funds engage an external third-party valuation agent, either to submit valuations or to challenge the valuation process.

Boards need to include at least some directors with relevant knowledge and experience to review and, if necessary, challenge the valuations put in front of them. However, the fact remains that valuations of most alternative assets ultimately rest in part on assumptions rather than observable facts and inevitably involve an element of judgement.

What do we mean by mark-to-model and mark-to-market?

Mark-to-model is a pricing method for an asset (or portfolio of assets) that is based partly or wholly on a financial model. The method is generally used for investments when there is no liquid tradeable market to provide accurate pricing. This contrasts with mark-to-market valuations, in which market prices are used to calculate values, as happens with long-only equity investment trusts. Most mark-to-model valuations involve discounting estimated future cash flows by an appropriate discount rate.

How are alternatives' NAVs calculated?

As with conventional equity investment trusts, the NAV of an alternative asset trust is based on subtracting its total liabilities from its total assets. Liabilities include outstanding debt, tax owed and so on. Total assets include the value of the portfolio of investments, plus cash and any other assets. The NAV can then be divided by the number of shares in issue to give the NAV per share.

However, as will soon be discussed in more detail, the inputs into the valuation of the investment portfolio for alternative assets are not only different from those used to value equity funds, but also vary from sector to sector and from trust to trust.

How is gearing factored into NAVs?

Alternative asset investment trusts also often use gearing/leverage. A fund may combine its equity with additional debt in order to acquire a larger, more diversified portfolio of assets, which is important for asset classes where individual investment sizes are often large due to the lack of fractional ownership opportunity (you cannot generally purchase half of a building, or a quarter of a wind farm). This debt is a liability and is therefore deducted from total assets to arrive at the net asset value figure.

Gearing enhances movements in NAVs, both positive and negative, as well as having an impact on a trust's revenue. It is important to remember that the trust will incur interest costs on the debt it has taken out, which may rise as general interest rates increase, unless the interest rate payable on the debt has been fixed or hedged.

What are the key inputs that go into valuations?

PRIVATE EQUITY TRUSTS

In the private equity sector, the predominant valuation method is comparative analysis, not discounted cash flows. The value of portfolio companies in the private portfolio is compared to the valuations of similar companies listed on public markets, as well as the valuations involved in any recent transactions. The methodology applies comparable multiples to portfolio company earnings and revenues to arrive at a 'fair value'.

For private equity investment trusts that invest in unquoted companies directly, it is not unusual for some portfolio companies to remain in the portfolio even after they have completed an IPO and become publicly listed. For this listed share of the portfolio, valuations are marked-to-market.

Initial valuations are submitted by the investment manager, often generated by a valuation team that works separately from the fund managers. Valuations are scrutinised by the board on an ongoing basis, generally through its audit/valuation committee, and then again by external auditors. Many funds also engage an external third-party valuation agent on an annual basis.

For private equity investment trusts that adopt a fund-of-funds approach, valuations are received from the funds they invest in, based on formal audited financial statements and interim updates. These are then generally adjusted for factors such as rights/protections built into the particular investment agreement, as well as any significant changes in cash flows, exchange rates, or other circumstances that have occurred since the last available valuation date.

Across the private equity investment trust sector, it is customary for funds to disclose the mix of valuation sources they have used and the dates that the reported NAV relates to. So a trust might say that 80% of its portfolio is valued at the most recent reporting date (say 30 March) and 20% as at an earlier date (say 31 December).

INFRASTRUCTURE TRUSTS

Infrastructure funds' portfolios are primarily valued using a discounted cash flow (DCF) analysis of the forecast cash flows from each project/investment. The resulting valuation is often checked against other valuation benchmarks, including, for example, earnings multiples, recent transactions and quoted market comparisons.

External factors that feed into the forecast cash flows include inflation rates, interest rates, GDP growth rates and applicable tax rates, while investment-specific drivers are also taken into account. Valuers need to make forecast assumptions for each of these metrics. The fair value for each asset is then calculated by applying an appropriate discount rate and year-end currency exchange rate (if applicable).

The discount rate comprises a risk-free rate and a risk premium, with the latter taking into account a number of factors, such as the predictability of revenues and the phase of its life that an investment has reached – for example, whether in construction or already in operation. As at 18 September, the discount rates used by infrastructure trusts range from 7.2% to 14.2%, with a median of 8.7%.

RENEWABLE ENERGY INFRASTRUCTURE TRUSTS

Renewable energy infrastructure funds also generally use a DCF methodology to value their portfolios. However, in this sector, the key drivers of the forecast cash flows are the remaining life of the asset, a forecast of future power prices, the energy yield (the amount of energy produced by an asset) and assumptions about inflation. Currently, the discount rates used by renewable energy trusts range from 6.2% to 13.7%, with a median of 8%.

COMMERCIAL PROPERTY TRUSTS

The portfolios of property investment trusts tend to be valued by an independent external valuer, in accordance with standards set by the industry's professional body, the Royal Institute of Chartered Surveyors. This methodology values individual properties on a number of factors, including lease length, location, strength of tenant covenants, net initial yields and expected rental growth. Valuations achieved in recent transactions involving similar properties are also taken into account.

DEBT TRUSTS

In the debt sector, a substantial share of corporate bonds and asset-backed securities held by investment trusts are traded publicly and therefore can be marked-to-market. Where funds deviate from the marked-to-market approach, for instance because their mandate requires holding instruments to maturity, this is disclosed and an accompanying IFRS NAV is also regularly published.

Direct loans are debt instruments that are not publicly traded. Where there is no observable market, such assets are generally valued by the investment manager on a DCF basis, as the coupons (income payments) and other cash flows from these instruments are generally contractual and predictable.

Depending on the risk profile of the underlying investment, recently used discount rates range between 8% and 14%. There are also instances in which more advanced valuation methods are utilised, including the Black-Scholes options pricing model, while broker quotes may also be used to ascertain the value of illiquid instruments.

Structured credit products such as asset-backed securities (ABS) and collateralised loan obligations (CLOs) commonly adopt expert valuations, alongside observable price information and broker quotes. Expert input may be provided by the investment manager, as several investment trusts are managed by leading global ABS/CLO issuers.

MUSIC ROYALTIES

In the music royalties sector, NAVs are derived from DCF-based valuations of projected revenue generated by music catalogues from streaming, live performances and other revenue sources. DCF discount rates are derived by an external valuation agent, based on assumptions around the cost of capital, the correlation of the asset class with the wider market and a sector risk premium.

The last of these has been deemed to be decreasing in recent years, as growth in the use and reach of streaming has provided a higher degree of certainty about future revenues. It is fair to say however that investors have been sceptical of valuations in the music royalty sector, which is one reason why the board of Hipgnosis Songs Fund (SONG) appointed Kroll Advisory to review its valuation assumptions in 2022.

Scepticism has been borne out by recent announcements. In September the board of Round Hill Music (RHM) recommended a cash offer for the company at an 11% discount to its prevailing NAV. Hipgnosis Songs Fund announced shortly afterwards that it has agreed to sell approximately 20% of its portfolio at a 17.5% discount to its prevailing NAV. The chairman acknowledged the market's scepticism regarding previously reported net asset values and suggested that the transaction provided a benchmark for a more 'credible' valuation.

What is a bridge?

Alternative asset funds often use bridge visualisations to illustrate the factors influencing the movement in NAV over a certain period. Below is an example from the latest interim results published by Regional REIT, a property investment trust that specialises in regional offices in the UK. This bridge shows the changes that have contributed to (the yellow bar) and detracted from (the grey bar) the movement in EPRA net tangible assets (NTA) per share over the six months to 30 June 2023. An EPRA NTA is an industry standard for valuations, EPRA being a European property industry association.

Movement in regional REIT's EPRA NTA per share over the six months to 30 June 2023

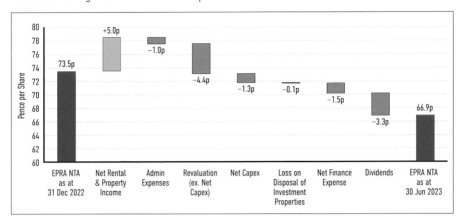

Source: Regional REIT, Winterflood Securities.

What is the relationship between discount rates and bond yields?

The discount rate in discounted cash flow calculations combines a risk-free rate with a premium for other factors specific to the asset class. Government bond yields are used as a proxy for the risk-free rate. As government bond yields rise, as they have done since 2022, it follows that discount rates should also be increased, assuming there is no offsetting reduction in the risk premium.

All else being equal, these higher discount rates will lead to lower portfolio valuations and lower NAVs for investment trusts that use a DCF valuation methodology. Even if trusts are slow to adjust their discount rates, the market may do it for them, by marking down share prices to a level that implies a higher discount rate is required. This broadly is a large part of what has happened to alternative asset share prices over the last two years.

Discounts for alternative asset trusts have widened significantly over the last 18 months. Why?

We think that the widening of discounts in alternative sectors over the last 18 months can be largely attributed to their interest rate sensitivity, with the rising rate environment resulting in negative sentiment towards these asset classes. A key issue for these trusts is that rising interest rates are seen to negatively impact underlying valuations.

For example, within infrastructure and some other sectors, higher interest rates hit asset valuations because the discount rate used to discount cash flow valuations has had to be raised. Property valuations are also impacted by higher borrowing costs, reducing demand for debt-funded acquisitions.

Private equity and growth capital trusts face pressure on their NAVs from a deterioration in sentiment towards venture companies and other stocks with longer-term, and potentially more uncertain, payback periods.

In addition to share prices falling ahead of anticipated declines in NAVs, demand for many alternative asset investment trusts, particularly infrastructure and property, declines as rising gilt yields render the yields offered by these funds comparatively less attractive, exacerbating the discount widening effect.

Finally, we believe that the considerable macroeconomic and geopolitical uncertainty over the last 18 months has weighed on investor sentiment towards risk assets in general, further reducing demand.

How difficult is it to assess whether discounts are justified?

After the derating that has been evident since last year, on the face of it discounts across the alternative asset universe look attractive relative to their history. It is a matter of judgment however whether these discounts are justified or not, for several reasons. One is that markets are forward looking, and therefore current discounts may reflect the expectation of future declines in NAVs, for example as a result of higher interest rates or a recessionary environment.

Secondly, as highlighted previously, discounts may also reflect an element of investor scepticism around the reliability of portfolio valuations and NAVs. If investors believe the true NAV to be lower than stated, this will be factored into the share price. Probably the best way for trusts to counter such scepticism is to use transactional evidence, such as selling an asset, to demonstrate the accuracy of its valuations. This should increase investor confidence and may indicate that a particularly wide discount is unjustified.

Another factor to consider is the yield offered by the investment trusts. Many property, infrastructure and renewable energy trusts have sold off significantly in the wake of rising interest rates. In part this is because the yields they offer, which looked very attractive when interest rates on cash and government bonds were negligible, have become less attractive compared to bonds and other yield options.

As long as the dividend paid by a fund remains the same, any fall in the share price automatically increases the yield. The adjustment is necessary to keep the premium over government bonds at a similar level. Investors generally require such a pick-up to justify the additional risk of an investment trust when compared to 'risk-free' government credit.

On the other hand, markets often over-react and it may be that the historically wide discounts observed this year have been overdone and represent an attractive opportunity for long-term investors. We would expect an improvement in sentiment towards interest-rate-sensitive asset classes as the outlook for inflation and interest rates becomes clearer, creating the potential for a 'double whammy' of improving NAVs and narrowing discounts for investment trusts in these areas.

What is the difference between debt at fair value and debt at par? Which one should I be looking at?

Investment trusts that have long-term debt in place will often publish multiple NAV figures, valuing this debt both at 'fair' and 'par' value. NAVs with debt at par value/book value simply deduct the amount that the fund borrowed, which is equal to the amount the fund will owe at expiry of the debt instrument, from total assets. NAVs with debt at fair value/market value will deduct the value of the fund's debt instruments based on an estimate of the theoretical cost of repaying the debt today (or conversely, the price an investor would be willing to pay to own the debt). NAV with debt at fair value is the standard measure across the investment trust industry.

The distinction between these two ways of measuring NAVs is particularly important in the current environment, where the significant increase in benchmark rates over the last 18 months has impacted the fair value of investment trusts' debt. For example, as at 30 June 2023, the NAV per share for City of London Investment Trust with debt at par value was 385.22p, whereas it was 391.24p with debt at fair value. Similarly, the decline in NAV per share over the year to 30 June 2023 was −1.4% measuring debt at par value, but was only −0.6% with debt at fair value. This is because the value of the fund's debt at fair value fell over the period, contributing positively to NAV. The fund's long-term fixed-rate debt declined in value over the period as market interest rates and bond yields rose, meaning that an investor would not be willing to pay as much to acquire the debt and receive the interest payable on it as they could get paid higher interest rates in the market.

DATA AND PERFORMANCE TABLES

The largest equity sectors

AIC SECTOR	# COMPANIES	NET ASSETS (£M)	% INDUSTRY NET ASSETS	MARKET CAP (£M)	% INDUSTRY MARKET CAP	MARKET CAP (£M) 2018	5 YR MARKET CAP % GROWTH	AVERAGE GEARING %
Global	13	27,000	11.4%	24,153	12.3%	28,464	-15.1%	5.7%
Flexible investment	20	14,570	6.1%	10,843	5.5%	7,351	47.5%	8.9%
North America*	7	12,689	5.2%	8,969	4.6%	3,051	193.9%	6.1%
UK equity income	19	11,057	4.7%	10,784	5.5%	10,412	3.6%	10.3%
Global smaller companies**	5	5,747	2.4%	4,870	2.5%	257	1792.0%	3.6%
Global emerging markets	11	5,486	2.3%	4,847	2.5%	5,720	-15.3%	4.5%
UK smaller companies	26	5,380	2.3%	4,720	2.4%	4,982	-5.3%	3.7%
Global equity income	6	4,942	2.1%	4,834	2.5%	2,970	62.7%	4.2%
Europe	7	4,313	1.8%	3,962	2.0%	3,500	13.2%	7.0%
UK all companies	8	3,804	1.6%	3,376	1.7%	5,630	-40.0%	6.9%
Asia Pacific	6	3,098	1.3%	2,769	1.4%	n/a	n/a	4.4%
Country specialist	4	2,562	1.1%	2,103	1.1%	n/a	n/a	0.0%
Japan	6	2,349	1.0%	2,142	1.1%	2,314	-7.4%	16.1%
Asia Pacific equity income	5	1,994	0.8%	1,840	0.9%	n/a	n/a	4.4%
China/Greater China	4	1,739	0.7%	1,521	0.8%	n/a	n/a	11.8%
European smaller companies	4	1,979	0.8%	1,704	0.9%	1,720	-0.9%	4.3%
India/Indian subcontinent	4	1,600	0.7%	1,366	0.7%	n/a	n/a	3.0%
Asia Pacific smaller companies	3	1,282	0.5%	1,086	0.6%	n/a	n/a	6.3%
Japanese smaller companies	5	1,074	0.5%	975	0.5%	898	8.5%	6.8%
Financials and financial innovation	2	758	0.3%	599	0.3%	706	-15.2%	2.6%
North American smaller companies	2	429	0.2%	367	0.2%	789	-53.6%	3.3%
UK equity and bond income	1	210	0.1%	208	0.1%	783	-73.5%	23.4%
Latin America	1	135	0.1%	117	0.1%	197	-40.8%	5.1%
Total	**169**	**114,198**	**48.11%**	**98,154**	**50.00%**	**79,746**	**23.08%**	**-**
Average								**6.66%**

Source: AIC/Morningstar, all figures to 30/09/23 unless otherwise stated.

* Please note Pershing Square Holdings which has a current market cap of £7bn, moved from hedge fund to North American sector in January 2022.

** Smithson and Herald are two large companies moving into this sector after 2018 (IPO and sector change respectively).

There are no set rules for what an investment trust can invest in. The trust's strategy does, however, have to be outlined in a prospectus and approved by shareholders if, as does happen, the board wishes to change that objective at a later date. For convenience, and to help comparative analysis, trusts are grouped into a number of different sectors, based primarily on their investment focus. These are listed here and on the following three spreads.

The majority of the sector categories are self-explanatory. It is worth noting, however, that individual trusts within each broad sector category will often have somewhat different investment objectives and benchmarks. The 'flexible investment' sector is a relatively new one that includes a number of trusts which invest across a broad range of asset classes, not just equities. Most of these were previously included in the global sector.

These sectoral classifications are reviewed at regular intervals by a committee of the Association of Investment Companies. In 2019, for example, the AIC introduced a number of changes to its categorisation of Asian trusts and specialist trusts in particular. In 2020 utilities was changed to infrastructure securities. By tradition the sectoral breakdown distinguishes between trusts that invest primarily in large cap stocks and those that focus on mid and smaller companies.

The table on this page summarises the sectors which, together with healthcare, financials and technology, are normally described as conventional equity trusts, to distinguish them from so-called 'alternative assets', such as infrastructure, debt and private equity. If you count commercial property as an alternative asset, the split between equity trusts and alternatives is close to 50-50 today. The balance favoured equity before the global financial crisis, after which many alternatives trusts were launched.

A notable feature of the table is that just under 20% by market capitalisation of these conventional equity trusts have the UK as their primary investment focus. Investment trusts have always had a bias towards investment outside the UK. The aim of the very first trust in 1868, Foreign & Colonial (now F&C), was to enable its shareholders to diversify their portfolios by investing in bonds issued by companies outside the UK, which in practice initially meant mostly railroad company bonds.

The significant overseas focus is one reason why equity investment trusts on average perform quite differently from the FTSE All-Share index. They track world markets more closely than the UK stock market, and for most of the past two decades that has been an advantage, as other markets, the US in particular, have comfortably outperformed the UK. Movements in the pound-dollar and other exchange rates can have a significant impact on returns for UK-based investors.

Comparing the totals for market capitalisation and net assets gives you an indication of the average discount across these trusts. It comes in at 14% for the equity sectors on this page.

Specialist sectors

AIC SECTOR	# COMPANIES	NET ASSETS (£M)	% INDUSTRY NET ASSETS	MARKET CAP (£M)	% INDUSTRY MARKET CAP	MARKET CAP (£M) 2018	5YR MARKET CAP % GROWTH	AVERAGE GEARING %
Private equity	17	33,536	14.1%	30,775	15.7%	16,748	83.7%	0.9%
Renewable energy infrastructure	22	16,581	7.0%	13,140	6.7%	5,088	158.3%	3.1%
Infrastructure	9	15,192	6.4%	11,884	6.1%	9,692	22.6%	2.7%
Growth capital	6	6,019	2.5%	2,846	1.4%	n/a	n/a	0.0%
Biotechnology and healthcare	7	5,290	2.2%	4,470	2.3%	6,073	-26.4%	5.2%
Technology and technology innovation	4	4,344	1.8%	3,794	1.9%	3,517	7.9%	0.0%
Debt – direct lending	6	2,517	1.1%	1,898	1.0%	n/a	n/a	9.1%
Hedge funds*	6	2,459	1.0%	2,121	1.1%	3,768	-43.7%	0.0%
Commodities and natural resources	8	2,239	0.9%	1,826	0.9%	2,015	-9.4%	8.2%
Royalties	2	2,227	0.9%	1,351	0.7%	n/a	n/a	12.4%
Debt – structured finance	7	1,876	0.8%	1,558	0.8%	n/a	n/a	3.5%
Debt – loans and bonds	8	1,331	0.6%	1,281	0.7%	n/a	n/a	4.1%
Leasing	7	1,471	0.6%	919	0.5%	1,965	-53.2%	74.1%
Environmental	3	1,328	0.6%	1,192	0.6%	611	95.3%	3.2%
Infrastructure securities	2	235	0.1%	210	0.1%	135	55.4%	25.1%
Farmland forestry	1	187	0.1%	140	0.1%	150	-6.3%	0.0%
Other	2	100	0.0%	74	0.0%	526	-86.0%	1.4%
Total	117	96,931	40.8%	79,478	40.5%	50,287	58.0%	-
Average								8.2%

Source: AIC/Morningstar, all figures to 30/09/23 unless otherwise stated.

*Please note Pershing Square Holdings which has a current market cap of £7bn, moved from hedge fund to North American sector in January 2022.

The specialist sectors are also clearly identified by their name. Unlike conventional equity trusts, which are mainly defined by their regional focus, the specialist sectors are mostly grouped by industry. The specialist sector gives a flavour of the wide range of investment strategies which are available once you look beyond the traditional equity names.

That range has expanded significantly since the global financial crisis with the launch of many new trusts offering access to new asset classes. Note how for example there are no five-year comparisons for growth capital trusts, royalties and most types of debt fund, as most did not exist until recently. The renewable energy sector has grown since the crisis to more than 20 companies.

The market value of private equity, infrastructure and renewable energy trusts in combination grew rapidly up until the end of 2021, thanks to a combination of strong performance, the arrival of new entrants and considerable secondary share issuance. Together with commercial property, they make up the majority of the so-called alternative asset sector.

The biotechnology and healthcare sector has also seen a significant expansion. It and technology qualify as specialist trusts by virtue of being narrowly focused on one particular sector of the listed equity market. Unlike alternatives, their appeal lies mainly in the potential for capital growth rather than their ability to generate solid and reliable dividend income streams.

Since the end of 2021 however the value of the specialist sectors has fallen sharply as discounts have widened and capital values have also declined in several cases. In aggregate the trusts in the sectors on this page have seen their market value fall from more than £100bn to under £80bn.

The way the universe of listed trusts looks inevitably changes significantly from decade to decade, and we are seeing that process in action today. Recent newcomers include trusts that invest in the space industry, shipping, farmland, digital infrastructure, battery storage and energy efficiency. Even before the market declines of the last two years, hedge funds (with notable exceptions) and many debt trusts were already disappearing. They will be followed by others as the current cycle unfolds.

By comparison to the last spread, the average discount for specialist sectors is 18%, while it is 35% for the property trusts on the next spread, underling just how severe the impact of higher interest rates has been on these sectors.

Property sectors

AIC SECTOR	NET ASSETS (£M)	% INDUSTRY NET ASSETS	MARKET CAP (£M)	
Property – UK commercial	7,605	3.2%	5,246	
Property – UK logistics	5,047	2.1%	3,571	
Property – UK residential	3,090	1.3%	1,018	
Property – Europe	1,552	0.7%	910	
Property – UK healthcare	1,158	0.5%	814	
Property – Debt	945	0.4%	778	
Property securities	967	0.4%	892	
Property – rest of world	187	0.1%	79	
Total	**20,552**	**8.7%**	**13,308**	
Average				

Top 15

COMPANY NAME	TICKER	AIC SECTOR	MANAGEMENT GROUP	
Tritax Big Box REIT	BBOX	Property – UK logistics	Tritax Management	
LXI REIT	LXI	Property – UK commercial	LJ Capital	
Supermarket Income REIT	SUPR	Property – UK commercial	Atrato Capital	
UK Commercial Property REIT	UKCM	Property – UK commercial	abrdn	
Home REIT	HOME	Property – UK residential	AEW UK Investment Management	
Tritax Eurobox	BOXE	Property – Europe	Tritax Management	
TR Property Investment Trust	TRY	Property securities	Columbia Threadneedle	
Balanced Commercial Property	BCPT	Property – UK commercial	Columbia Threadneedle	
Civitas Social Housing	CIVSHP-OR	Property – UK residential	Civitas Investment Management	
PRS REIT	PRSR	Property – UK residential	Sigma Capital	
Urban Logistics REIT	SHED	Property – UK logistics	Logistics Asset Management	
Target Healthcare REIT	THRL	Property – UK healthcare	Target Fund Managers	
Warehouse REIT	WHR	Property – UK logistics	Tilstone Partners	
Regional REIT	RGL	Property – UK commercial	Toscafund Asset Management	
Triple Point Social Housing REIT	SOHO	Property – UK residential	Triple Point Investment Management	

Source: AIC/Morningstar, all figures to 30/09/23 unless otherwise stated.

MARKET CAP (£M) 2018	# COMPANIES	5YR MARKET CAP % GROWTH	AVERAGE GEARING %	AVERAGE YIELD %	AVERAGE DISCOUNT %
6,180	14	-15.1%	31.4%	8.3%	-29.0%
2,440	4	46.3%	75.4%	6.8%	-16.5%
2,141	6	-52.5%	43.4%	9.6%	-50.6%
1,103	4	-17.5%	41.6%	7.3%	-41.6%
1,788	2	-54.5%	23.2%	7.8%	-29.2%
n/a	5	n/a	4.9%	8.8%	-21.1%
1,295	1	-31.1%	13.4%	5.5%	-7.3%
182	2	-56.2%	0.0%	-	-57.4%
15,129	**38**	**-12.0%**			
			33.0%	**7.7%**	**-32.4%**

% YIELD	% 5YR DIVIDEND GROWTH P.A.	GEARING (%)	ONGOING CHARGE %	% 5YR SHARE PRICE TOTAL RETURN	% 5 YEAR NAV TOTAL RETURN	TOTAL ASSETS (£M)	NET ASSETS (£M)	DISCOUNT %
5.0%	1.8%	33.55%	0.76%	17.03%	61.46%	5,063	3,718	-28.42%
7.3%	9.5%	5.39%	0.90%	-0.37%	34.19%	2,295	2,055	-24.25%
8.0%	1.8%	36.23%	1.27%	-2.54%	38.32%	1,700	1,222	-22.38%
6.3%	-1.9%	17.39%	0.70%	-22.58%	3.71%	1,319	1,053	-34.46%
14.5%	-	8.79%	1.41%	-	-	1,219	973	-69.09%
8.5%	-	48.27%	3.15%	-38.40%	8.02%	1,206	714	-42.55%
5.5%	4.9%	13.39%	0.73%	-16.59%	-12.85%	1,156	967	-7.31%
7.1%	-4.4%	29.19%	0.86%	-38.32%	-1.40%	1,130	822	-42.04%
-	13.7%	44.66%	1.75%	4.30%	34.55%	1,034	682	-29.08%
5.9%	-4.4%	51.24%	2.45%	-16.18%	50.65%	999	643	-41.76%
6.9%	12.5%	17.30%	1.47%	17.53%	60.83%	967	767	-32.45%
7.4%	-0.9%	27.96%	1.51%	-9.73%	41.89%	908	689	-31.79%
7.8%	20.7%	42.62%	1.30%	9.92%	51.24%	789	529	-34.00%
18.4%	-3.4%	77.22%	5.30%	-54.58%	-1.49%	776	392	-62.55%
10.9%	40.4%	44.03%	1.60%	-36.49%	63.63%	776	515	-61.63%

The great majority of commercial property trusts invest directly in physical property, meaning they buy, sell or lease out the bricks and mortar themselves. By their nature they are typically illiquid, since buildings such as offices, shops and factories can take many months to purchase and cannot be sold in a hurry, unlike the shares in a property company which can be bought and sold within minutes.

TR Property (TRY) is differentiated from all these trusts by virtue of being the last remaining example of a trust that invests almost exclusively in the shares of other property companies (in its case drawn from across the whole of Europe). The trust's shares trade like other types of share, rising and falling more markedly from day to day than those of trusts which invest directly in property.

Not so long ago most of the biggest trusts in the property sector were generalist trusts, the likes of BMO Commercial Property and Schroder Real Estate, managed by well-established fund management companies. These trusts typically have diversified portfolios of assets across all three of the main property categories, shops, offices and industrial buildings. They have been supplanted in popularity more recently by trusts that specialise in smaller, niche sectors of the market, such as social housing, residential developments, doctors' surgeries and warehouses.

That trend can be seen in the table of the 15 largest property trusts. Tritax Big Box, which invests in the huge distribution warehouses used by Amazon and other retailers to move products around the country, only came to the market in 2013 but, despite a dramatic derating, has since grown to become the single largest trust in the sector. Its sister company Tritax Eurobox was only launched five years ago but already has £1.3bn in assets.

Initially many of these newer property companies traded on premiums, reflecting the appeal in a low-interest-rate environment of their above-average dividend yields and long-term, often partially inflation-linked, income streams. That has all changed in 2022 and 2023 as interest rates have shot up in response to moves by the Federal Reserve and other central banks to head off rising inflation.

The independent valuers who are responsible for valuing property portfolios started reducing capital values sharply in the fourth quarter of 2022, with companies owning offices particularly badly hit, and while that process has not been as severe this year to date, it continues to cast a shadow over the sector, which is down on average by around 18%. The average discount across all the main property sectors was above 30% at the start of Q4 2023, and in the case of residential property, one of the newer sectors, which has experienced some particularly bad news, it was more than 40%.

The average figures conceal significant differences between individual trusts, however. Among the diversified trusts, for example, AEW UK, the one trust to maintain its dividend through the pandemic, is the most highly rated, entering Q3 2023 on a 7% discount, having been as wide as 25%, while Regional REIT, which specialises in regional offices, was on a huge 60% discount.

The effect of the derating in both generalist and specialist property trusts has been to produce significantly more attractive dividend yields. The average yield in the generalist sector stood at 5.8% at the start of October 2022, 5.0% in specialist healthcare and more than 6.5% in the logistics and warehouse sector. A year later, in October 2023, the comparable figures were 7.9%, 8.0% and 5.9% respectively. Some of these dividends are uncovered, however, and three trusts have made dividend cuts in 2023.

What is not in doubt is that discounts on commercial property are very wide by historical standards, and that leaves the way open for opportunistic bids by third parties who decide a portfolio is fundamentally undervalued. Industrials REIT (MLI) and Civitas Social Housing (CSH) both succumbed to agreed third-party bids at premiums to their share prices this year, although in both cases the exit prices were below the most recent NAVs, while Ediston Property (EPIC) also sold its entire portfolio to Blackstone, the US private equity house.

The shares of Home REIT meanwhile were suspended in January 2023 after an activist shareholder raised questions about the trust's reported valuations and claimed (accurately as the board subsequently admitted) that it was failing to collect rent from many of its tenants. The trust has now appointed a new management company for a transitionary period to try and sort out the possibly fraudulent mess, which has so far prevented the annual report and accounts for 2022 from being finalised or the shares to be relisted.

VCT sectors

AIC SECTOR	# COMPANIES	NET ASSETS (£M)
VCT generalist	33	5,202
VCT AIM quoted	6	726
VCT generalist pre-qualifying	3	76
VCT specialist: environmental	2	47
VCT specialist: healthcare and biotechnology	1	15
VCT specialist: environmental pre-qualifying	1	25
VCT specialist: technology	2	34
VCT AIM quoted pre-qualifying	1	3
Total	**49**	**6,126**
Average		

Top VCTs

COMPANY NAME	MANAGEMENT GROUP	AIC SECTOR
Albion Enterprise VCT	Albion Capital Group	VCT generalist
Octopus Titan VCT	Octopus Investments	VCT generalist
Octopus Apollo VCT	Octopus Investments	VCT generalist
Unicorn AIM VCT	Unicorn Asset Management	VCT AIM quoted
Pembroke VCT B shares	Pembroke Investment Managers	VCT generalist
Baronsmead Second Venture Trust	Gresham House	VCT generalist
Foresight VCT	Foresight Group	VCT generalist
British Smaller Companies VCT	YFM Private Equity	VCT generalist
Baronsmead Venture Trust	Gresham House	VCT generalist
ProVen VCT	Beringea	VCT generalist
ProVen Growth and Income VCT	Beringea	VCT generalist
Amati AIM VCT	Amati Global Investors	VCT AIM quoted
Hargreave Hale AIM VCT	Canaccord Genuity	VCT AIM quoted
Foresight Enterprise VCT	Foresight Group	VCT generalist
Albion Technology & General VCT	Albion Capital Group	VCT generalist
British Smaller Companies VCT 2	YFM Private Equity	VCT generalist
The Income & Growth VCT	Gresham House	VCT generalist
Puma VCT 13	Puma Investments	VCT generalist
Molten Ventures VCT	Molten Ventures	VCT generalist
Albion Development VCT	Albion Capital Group	VCT generalist
Octopus AIM VCT	Octopus Investments	VCT AIM quoted
Northern 3 VCT	Mercia Asset Management	VCT generalist
Northern 2 VCT	Mercia Asset Management	VCT generalist

% VCT INDUSTRY NET ASSETS	MARKET CAP (£M)	MARKET CAP (£M) 2018	5 YR MARKET CAP % GROWTH	AVERAGE YIELD %
84.9%	4,885	2,924	67.0%	6.9%
11.9%	657	735	-10.6%	7.4%
1.2%	78	120	-34.8%	-
0.8%	36	157	-77.2%	2.9%
0.2%	14	3	306.3%	13.3%
0.4%	25	n/a	n/a	-
0.5%	30	11	166.5%	10.5%
0.0%	3	n/a	n/a	-
2.6%	**5,728**	**3,952**	**44.9%**	
			69.4%	**7.0%**

TOTAL ASSETS (£M)	MARKET CAP (£M)	NET ASSETS (£M)	NET ASSETS 2018 (£M)	LAUNCH DATE	YIELD %
1,528	1,316	1,528	62	05/04/2007	5.5%
1,075	1,006	1,075	6	28/12/2007	7.7%
389	357	389	125	17/10/2006	5.3%
217	179	217	193	11/04/2007	9.2%
216	204	216	36	01/04/2015	4.7%
207	199	207	n/a	30/01/2001	10.9%
203	188	203	6	02/11/1999	5.8%
202	188	202	84	04/04/1996	7.7%
194	185	194	175	03/04/1998	11.0%
162	154	162	113	10/04/2000	6.3%
157	149	157	n/a	31/05/2001	7.2%
153	142	153	156	22/02/2001	7.4%
152	141	152	7	29/10/2004	7.0%
149	142	149	9	16/03/1998	5.5%
136	129	136	6	16/01/2001	5.5%
133	127	133	55	12/04/2001	2.7%
124	114	124	82	15/11/2000	15.0%
124	113	124	17	02/07/2018	7.8%
124	117	124	n/a	18/05/1998	3.1%
122	115	122	57	27/01/1999	5.3%
119	113	119	148	17/03/2004	7.9%
115	110	115	27	17/12/2001	5.3%
112	107	112	27	21/04/1999	6.0%

COMPANY NAME	MANAGEMENT GROUP	AIC SECTOR
Kings Arms Yard VCT	Albion Capital Group	VCT generalist
Northern Venture Trust	Mercia Asset Management	VCT generalist
Crown Place VCT	Albion Capital Group	VCT generalist
Mobeus Income & Growth VCT	Gresham House	VCT generalist
Thames Ventures VCT 1	Foresight Group	VCT generalist
Mobeus Income & Growth 4 VCT	Gresham House	VCT generalist
Maven Income and Growth VCT 4	Maven Capital Partners	VCT generalist
Octopus AIM VCT 2	Octopus Investments	VCT AIM quoted
Albion VCT	Albion Capital Group	VCT generalist
Mobeus Income & Growth 2 VCT	Gresham House	VCT generalist
Maven Income and Growth VCT 5	Maven Capital Partners	VCT generalist
Maven Income and Growth VCT	Maven Capital Partners	VCT generalist
Maven Income and Growth VCT 3	Maven Capital Partners	VCT generalist
Triple Point Venture VCT Venture shares	Triple Point Investment Management	VCT generalist

Source: AIC/Morningstar, all figures to 30/09/23 unless otherwise stated.

Venture capital trusts are specialist investment companies that exist to support companies at an early stage of their development, in return for which shareholders in the VCTs are offered potentially attractive tax breaks. Most of these trusts will be investing in unlisted securities, although an exception are the AIM VCTs, which own mostly shares listed on the Alternative Investment Market.

By their nature, most VCTs are designed to be relatively small in size and are inherently riskier than conventional equity trusts. Some of the first VCTs to be launched have grown however to become substantial and mature businesses. Of these, Octopus Titan is comfortably the largest and best known, having been early investors in at least four bid successes.

The trust was launched in 2007 and now itself has a market value of just under £1bn. Octopus has subsequently followed up with a number of other VCTs and a renewable energy infrastructure trust. The AIC now breaks down VCTs into 10 different sub-sectors, reflecting the kind of business that they were set up to invest in. Many of these have yet to generate a five-year history.

Although the purpose behind giving tax breaks to investors in VCTs is to encourage the financing of early-stage businesses, many higher-rate taxpayers in the first VCTs found the tax-free dividends a particularly strong attraction. The criteria VCTs must meet in order for their shareholders to qualify for the tax benefits have subsequently been tightened to make sure that the majority of a VCT's investments are genuine higher-risk, early-stage ventures.

TOTAL ASSETS (£M)	MARKET CAP (£M)	NET ASSETS (£M)	NET ASSETS 2018 (£M)	LAUNCH DATE	YIELD %
112	106	112	69	04/04/1996	5.2%
105	98	105	91	01/11/1995	7.1%
97	89	97	6	08/04/1998	6.3%
92	88	92	71	08/10/2004	17.9%
90	86	90	6	30/04/1996	5.2%
87	80	87	57	08/03/1999	13.8%
86	82	86	42	17/02/2005	6.3%
83	79	83	37	25/01/2006	7.4%
71	65	71	6	01/04/1996	5.7%
65	62	65	48	16/12/2005	20.5%
65	62	65	29	04/12/2000	11.1%
61	58	61	27	06/04/2000	5.8%
61	57	61	67	12/12/2001	6.3%
54	51	54	n/a	12/04/2019	5.3%

In September 2022 the Treasury announced that the tax regime for VCTs would continue after 2025, reflecting their significant contribution to funding technology and other businesses, and this has since been reconfirmed. Research by the AIC in 2022 found that in the past five years VCTs have invested £1.7bn into 530 companies.

As the record demand for VCTs shows, the appeal of tax-free dividends remains. Several older trusts have also generated notable capital gains as well. Inevitably, many of the larger equity VCTs have not been immune from the general decline in smaller company and AIM stocks. Five-year share price returns from AIM VCTs are minus 11% on average, for example, at the time of writing. Octopus Titan VCT has given up nearly all of its share price gains of the past five years.

Given that there is very little liquidity in VCT shares – most investors who own them tend to keep them indefinitely to avoid losing the tax breaks – the underlying value of these trusts may be lower than the reported numbers suggest. The dividend yields on offer from the most mature VCTs have, however, increased as share prices have declined.

In the generalist sector the average dividend yield is now around 7.0%, but note that dividend growth on average has been negative over five years. The issue of future dividend capacity will come into question if we enter a recession. A number of the more mature VCTs do however put money aside every year to help sustain their dividend capacity, since that is the key selling point for investors.

Largest management groups

MANAGEMENT GROUP	# COMPANIES	TOTAL ASSETS (£M)	NET ASSETS (£M)	MARKET CAP (£M)	AVG MARKET CAP (£M)	% TOTAL ASSETS 2023
Baillie Gifford	13	21,582	19,139	16,247	1,250	8.2%
3i Group	1	18,547	17,772	20,177	20,177	7.1%
J.P. Morgan Asset Management	19	12,783	11,611	10,733	565	4.9%
Pershing Square Capital Management	1	10,936	8,812	5,585	5,585	4.2%
abrdn	20	10,870	9,745	7,845	392	4.1%
Columbia Threadneedle Investments	9	10,008	8,785	7,815	868	3.8%
Janus Henderson Investors	12	7,511	6,845	6,333	528	2.9%
InfraRed Capital Partners	2	6,636	6,636	5,167	2,584	2.5%
Schroders Greencoat	2	6,522	4,949	4,198	2,099	2.5%
Tritax Management	2	6,269	4,432	3,072	1,536	2.4%
Fidelity	6	5,624	4,825	4,374	729	2.1%
Frostrow Capital	5	4,943	4,706	4,356	871	1.9%
BlackRock Investment Management (UK)	9	4,246	3,768	3,531	392	1.6%
Polar Capital Holdings	3	4,230	4,071	3,578	1,193	1.6%
RIT Capital Partners	1	3,938	3,564	2,867	2,867	1.5%
Goldman Sachs Asset Management, L.P.	1	3,826	3,826	1,712	1,712	1.5%
3i Investments	1	3,331	3,100	2,809	2,809	1.3%
Willis Towers Watson	1	3,328	3,104	2,946	2,946	1.3%
Schroder Investment Management	9	3,262	3,069	2,720	302	1.2%
HarbourVest Advisers L.P.	1	3,067	3,067	1,790	1,790	1.2%
Amber Infrastructure Group	1	2,958	2,929	2,366	2,366	1.1%
Pantheon Ventures	2	2,903	2,903	1,908	954	1.1%
Caledonia Investments	1	2,875	2,875	1,837	1,837	1.1%
Allianz Global Investors	3	2,591	2,456	2,278	759	1.0%
Fundsmith	1	2,391	2,391	2,126	2,126	0.9%
Hipgnosis Songs	1	2,389	1,795	970	970	0.9%
Gresham House	12	2,360	2,173	1,783	149	0.9%
LJ Capital	1	2,295	2,055	1,557	1,557	0.9%
Foresight Group	8	2,206	2,206	1,821	228	0.8%
HgCapital	1	2,165	2,165	1,781	1,781	0.8%
Troy Asset Management	3	2,134	2,114	2,091	697	0.8%
Tetragon Financial Management	1	2,041	2,041	669	669	0.8%

Source: AIC/Morningstar, all figures to 30/09/23 unless otherwise stated.

TOTAL ASSETS 2018 (£M)	% TOTAL ASSETS 2018
13,655	7.2%
7,431	3.9%
11,455	6.1%
3,286	1.7%
7,177	3.8%
9,980	5.3%
6,812	3.6%
3,762	2.0%
2,190	1.2%
2,640	1.4%
4,306	2.3%
5,448	2.9%
3,625	1.9%
2,473	1.3%
3,412	1.8%
-	-
1,688	0.9%
3,018	1.6%
2,754	1.5%
1,438	0.8%
2,010	1.1%
1,389	0.7%
1,945	1.0%
1,604	0.8%
309	0.2%
-	-
109	0.1%
264	0.1%
974	0.5%
768	0.4%
224	0.1%
1,585	0.8%

The management groups with the most trust mandates are listed here. The trust sector is a competitive one, in which no management group has a dominant position. There has, however, been some notable consolidation in the last few years. The 20 largest groups manage just under 60% of total industry assets, up from 47% five years ago, but only six firms manage more than 10 trusts out of more than 300 in total.

In 2018 Baillie Gifford, a private partnership based in Edinburgh, became the largest player in the investment trust sector for the first time, overtaking 3i and J.P. Morgan. After an exceptional year of performance in 2020–21, its growth style of mixed public and private investing has since fallen dramatically out of favour and its share of total assets has fallen from to 12.7% to 8.3%, a dramatic change in fortunes. With notable exceptions, such as 3i, Columba Threadneedle, InfraRed Capital Partners and Schroders, many other management groups have seen the value of their investment trust assets decline as well over the last 12 months.

A period of consolidation is clearly under way. BMO Global Asset Management dropped out of the list in 2022 after selling its investment trust business to Columbia Threadneedle. Aberdeen Standard Investments, now rebranded as abrdn, has started to consolidate its investment trust holdings this year, merging two sets of UK trusts and two Asian ones and disposing of others, including Aberdeen Private Equity Opportunities. Janus Henderson is also proposing to merge two European trusts.

Schroders has meanwhile acquired a majority stake in Greencoat Capital, managers of two renewable energy trusts, and Gresham House, the listed management company behind 12 trusts, including a number of VCTs, has also been bought by a private equity firm for £479m.

Vintage investment trusts

COMPANY NAME	AIC SECTOR	LAUNCH DATE	MARKET CAP (£M)
F&C Investment Trust	Global	19/03/1868	4,533
Alliance Trust	Global	21/04/1888	2,946
Investment Company	Flexible investment	01/01/1868	16
Dunedin Income Growth	UK equity income	01/02/1873	397
Scottish American	Global equity income	31/03/1873	885
JPMorgan American	North America	18/06/1881	1,470
Mercantile Investment Trust	UK all companies	08/12/1884	1,543
JPMorgan Global Growth & Income	Global equity income	21/04/1887	1,877
Henderson Smaller Companies	UK smaller companies	16/12/1887	534
Bankers Investment Trust	Global	13/04/1888	1,206
The Global Smaller Companies Trust	Global smaller companies	15/02/1889	727
Merchants Trust	UK equity income	16/02/1889	793
Edinburgh Investment Trust	UK equity income	01/03/1889	1,072
AVI Global Trust	Global	01/07/1889	934
Law Debenture Corporation	UK equity income	12/12/1889	1,061
City of London Investment Trust	UK equity income	01/01/1891	1,996
abrdn Diversified Income and Growth	Flexible investment	05/01/1898	252
TR Property Investment Trust	Property securities	05/05/1905	892
BlackRock Smaller Companies	UK smaller companies	02/05/1906	609
Baillie Gifford China Growth	China/Greater China	24/01/1907	133
Murray International Trust	Global equity income	18/12/1907	1,482
Witan Investment Trust	Global	17/02/1909	1,425
Scottish Mortgage Investment Trust	Global	17/03/1909	9,414
Hansa Investment Company (A share)	Flexible investment	01/01/1912	148
Hansa Investment Company	Flexible investment	01/01/1912	75
Murray Income Trust	UK equity income	07/06/1923	915
Finsbury Growth & Income Trust	UK equity income	15/01/1926	1,743
Temple Bar Investment Trust	UK equity income	24/06/1926	697

NET ASSETS (£M)	TICKER	YIELD %	1YR AVG DISCOUNT / PREMIUM %	ONGOING CHARGE %	10YR NAV TOTAL RETURN %	10YR SHARE PRICE TOTAL RETURN %
4,777	FCIT	1.5%	-5.2%	0.54%	182.2%	191.8%
3,104	ATST	2.3%	-5.7%	0.61%	168.8%	201.9%
6	INV	0.6%	-11.6%	2.17%	36.7%	41.6%
440	DIG	4.9%	-4.8%	0.64%	73.2%	60.6%
893	SAIN	2.8%	-1.4%	0.59%	198.0%	175.2%
1,458	JAM	0.9%	-3.0%	0.36%	315.3%	315.4%
1,744	MRC	3.7%	-13.8%	0.46%	91.0%	90.8%
1,838	JGGI	4.0%	0.4%	0.22%	223.4%	252.6%
609	HSL	3.6%	-12.0%	0.44%	76.7%	81.2%
1,386	BNKR	2.4%	-9.9%	0.50%	147.0%	115.8%
837	GSCT	1.6%	-12.8%	0.79%	130.8%	99.8%
776	MRCH	5.1%	0.7%	0.56%	83.9%	88.7%
1,122	EDIN	3.9%	-8.0%	0.53%	86.6%	68.5%
1,031	AGT	1.6%	-10.0%	2.22%	146.2%	156.8%
999	LWDB	3.8%	1.3%	0.49%	126.9%	131.9%
1,956	CTY	5.1%	1.9%	0.37%	75.0%	70.9%
337	ADIG	6.8%	-24.6%	1.41%	28.2%	7.1%
967	TRY	5.5%	-7.6%	0.73%	82.5%	85.3%
679	BRSC	3.2%	-13.4%	0.70%	113.6%	102.0%
154	BGCG	0.8%	-10.8%	0.94%	9.2%	10.3%
1,584	MYI	4.7%	-2.0%	0.52%	98.9%	71.0%
1,510	WTAN	2.6%	-8.6%	1.00%	124.1%	127.8%
11,075	SMT	0.6%	-15.9%	0.34%	355.0%	288.0%
254	HANA	1.7%	-42.7%	1.20%	65.0%	42.1%
127	HAN	1.7%	-41.8%	1.20%	65.5%	42.6%
978	MUT	4.5%	-7.6%	0.48%	79.3%	69.1%
1,823	FGT	2.2%	-4.5%	0.60%	128.7%	118.9%
724	TMPL	4.0%	-5.9%	0.54%	54.4%	46.1%

COMPANY NAME	AIC SECTOR	LAUNCH DATE	MARKET CAP (£M)
Brunner Investment Trust	Global	01/01/1927	453
JPMorgan Japanese	Japan	02/08/1927	695
Monks Investment Trust	Global	06/02/1929	2,132
JPMorgan European Growth & Income	Europe	15/03/1929	392
Shires Income	UK equity income	31/03/1929	72
Canadian General Investments	North America	15/01/1930	450
Henderson Far East Income	Asia Pacific equity income	30/05/1930	359
3i Group	Private equity	01/04/1945	20,177
Henderson European Focus Trust	Europe	01/01/1947	334
Keystone Positive Change	Global	19/11/1954	126
Caledonia Investments	Flexible investment	18/07/1960	1,837

Source: AIC/Morningstar, all figures to 30/09/23 unless otherwise stated.

The first investment trust, F&C (FCIT), was formed in 1868 and continues in existence today. It celebrated its 150th anniversary in 2018. A number of other investment companies have also been around for many years. Seventeen can trace their histories back to the 19th century. This is a list of some of the oldest vintage trusts which are still in existence, although their names are rarely the same today as they were when launched. It includes every trust created before 1960 and still in existence today.

A number of these trusts were started by wealthy families looking to invest their fortunes in a tax-efficient manner, but have since expanded to include outside investors as well. The first Scottish investment trust, Dunedin Income Growth (DIG), for example, was founded to provide a home for the savings of wealthy textile merchants in Dundee. Caledonia (CLDN) was founded by the Cayzer shipping dynasty and Brunner by one of the families whose chemical businesses combined to form ICI in 1926.

There is no obvious correlation between age and size or quality of trust, although the mere fact of having survived for so long indicates that a trust has at

NET ASSETS (£M)	TICKER	YIELD %	1YR AVG DISCOUNT / PREMIUM %	ONGOING CHARGE %	10YR NAV TOTAL RETURN %	10YR SHARE PRICE TOTAL RETURN %
511	BUT	2.1%	-12.1%	0.63%	162.0%	176.4%
755	JFJ	1.3%	-7.4%	0.68%	102.2%	115.3%
2,408	MNKS	0.3%	-11.0%	0.43%	155.8%	156.1%
440	JEGI	4.6%	-11.3%	0.66%	129.3%	132.9%
77	SHRS	6.1%	-3.1%	1.17%	77.9%	71.3%
687	CGI	2.7%	-35.6%	1.37%	199.1%	201.0%
367	HFEL	10.9%	2.2%	1.01%	38.2%	33.8%
17,772	III	2.6%	-1.9%	0.89%	792.2%	732.5%
379	HEFT	2.8%	-11.8%	0.77%	159.6%	143.6%
146	KPC	5.5%	-15.0%	0.90%	-5.7%	-15.6%
2,875	CLDN	2.0%	-30.5%	0.77%	184.6%	151.0%

least successfully established a niche in the market. The wide range of average discounts illustrates the disparity in their liquidity, performance and popularity. Trusts with a founding family often take on third-party investors over time, reducing their shareholdings but retaining a measure of control in return for a broader asset base. A long history is no guarantee that the trust will survive without new management.

A number of trusts have changed investment manager in recent years. In 2020 four of these trusts: Witan Pacific (now BGCG), Edinburgh Investment Trust (EDIN), Temple Bar (TMPL) and Perpetual Income and Growth (PLI) moved from one management firm to another. Keystone (now KPC) did the same in 2021. The Scottish Investment Trust (SCIT) was absorbed into JPMorgan Global Growth & Income in 2022 and has disappeared from this list, along with JPMorgan Elect (also merged into JPMorgan Global Growth & Income) and Genesis Emerging Markets which has become Fidelity Emerging Markets after Fidelity was awarded the mandate in 2021.

Long-serving managers

COMPANY NAME	TICKER	AIC SECTOR	
Capital Gearing Trust	CGT	Flexible investment	
Lowland Investment Company	LWI	UK equity income	
City of London Investment Trust	CTY	UK equity income	
Herald Investment Trust	HRI	Global smaller companies	
JPMorgan Emerging Markets	JMG	Global emerging markets	
abrdn Asia Focus	AAS	Asia Pacific smaller companies	
Atlantis Japan Growth Fund	AJG	Japanese smaller companies	
CT UK Capital & Income	CTUK	UK equity income	
JPMorgan UK Smaller Companies	JMI	UK smaller companies	
JPMorgan European Discovery	JEDT	European smaller companies	
CT Private Equity Trust	CTPE	Private equity	
BlackRock World Mining	BRWM	Commodities and natural resources	
European Opportunities Trust	EOT	Europe	
Finsbury Growth & Income Trust	FGT	UK equity income	
HgCapital Trust	HGT	Private equity	
Lindsell Train Investment Trust	LTI	Global	
Aberforth Smaller Companies	ASL	UK smaller companies	
Impax Environmental Markets	IEM	Environmental	
Impax Environmental Markets	IEM	Environmental	
Henderson Smaller Companies	HSL	UK smaller companies	
Schroder UK Mid Cap Fund	SCP	UK all companies	
Artemis Alpha Trust	ATS	UK all companies	
Law Debenture Corporation	LWDB	UK equity income	
Bankers Investment Trust	BNKR	Global	
Global Opportunities Trust	GOT	Flexible investment	
MIGO Opportunities Trust	MIGO	Flexible investment	
Murray International Trust	MYI	Global equity income	
Schroder Real Estate	SREI	Property – UK commercial	
TR Property Investment Trust	TRY	Property securities	
abrdn New India Investment Trust	ANII	India	
Balanced Commercial Property	BCPT	Property – UK commercial	
Biotech Growth Trust	BIOG	Biotechnology and healthcare	
The Global Smaller Companies Trust	GSCT	Global smaller companies	
JPMorgan European Growth & Income	JEGI	Europe	
TR Property Investment Trust	TRY	Property securities	
JPMorgan China Growth & Income	JCGI	China/Greater China	
Polar Capital Technology	PCT	Technology and media	
Merchants Trust	MRCH	UK equity income	
Middlefield Canadian Income Trust	MCT	North America	
abrdn Property Income Trust	API	Property – UK commercial	
Murray Income Trust	MUT	UK equity income	
International Biotechnology	IBT	Biotechnology and healthcare	
abrdn Japan Investment Trust	AJIT	Japan	
Volta Finance	VTA	Debt – structured finance	

MANAGER NAME	EFFECTIVE	YEARS IN SERVICE	10YR NAV TOTAL RETURN %
Peter Spiller	05/04/1982	41 years 6 months	64.14
James H. Henderson	01/01/1990	33 years 9 months	46.12
Job Curtis	01/07/1991	32 years 3 months	75.01
Katie Potts	16/02/1994	29 years 8 months	170.21
Austin Forey	01/06/1994	29 years 4 months	101.95
Hugh Young	19/10/1995	27 years 11 months	95.55
Taeko Setaishi	10/05/1996	27 years 5 months	73.99
Julian Cane	01/03/1997	26 years 7 months	72.55
Georgina Brittain	02/01/1998	25 years 9 months	104.78
Francesco Conte	01/11/1998	24 years 11 months	116.53
Hamish Mair	01/02/2000	23 years 8 months	283.91
Evy Hambro	01/09/2000	23 years 1 month	93.83
Alexander Darwall	22/11/2000	22 years 10 months	127.23
Nick Train	11/12/2000	22 years 10 months	128.69
Nic Humphries	01/01/2001	22 years 9 months	440.07
Nick Train	22/01/2001	22 years 8 months	350.14
Euan R MacDonald	14/05/2001	22 years 5 months	71.21
Bruce Jenkyn-Jones	22/02/2002	21 years 7 months	177.33
Jon Forster	22/02/2002	21 years 7 months	177.33
Neil Hermon	01/11/2002	20 years 11 months	76.70
Andy Brough	30/04/2003	20 years 5 months	72.78
John Dodd	01/06/2003	20 years 4 months	22.65
James H. Henderson	01/06/2003	20 years 4 months	126.88
Alex Crooke	01/07/2003	20 years 3 months	147.04
Sandy Nairn	15/12/2003	19 years 10 months	95.85
Nick Greenwood	06/04/2004	19 years 6 months	105.34
Bruce Stout	16/06/2004	19 years 4 months	98.86
Nick Montgomery	15/07/2004	19 years 3 months	124.82
Marcus Phayre-Mudge	01/10/2004	19 years 0 months	82.48
Kristy Fong	09/12/2004	18 years 10 months	210.60
Richard Kirby	17/03/2005	18 years 7 months	80.63
Geoffrey C. Hsu	19/05/2005	18 years 4 months	87.29
Peter Ewins	31/07/2005	18 years 2 months	130.75
Alexander Fitzalan Howard	02/08/2005	18 years 2 months	129.34
George R. Gay	01/09/2005	18 years 1 month	82.48
Shumin Huang	02/01/2006	17 years 9 months	94.41
Ben Rogoff	01/05/2006	17 years 5 months	469.25
Simon Gergel	01/06/2006	17 years 4 months	83.86
Dean Orrico	06/07/2006	17 years 3 months	79.72
Jason Baggaley	13/09/2006	17 years 1 month	142.04
Charles Luke	03/10/2006	17 years 0 months	79.34
Ailsa Craig	01/11/2006	16 years 11 months	166.64
Chern-Yeh Kwok	10/11/2006	16 years 11 months	97.53
Alexandre Martin-Min	15/12/2006	16 years 10 months	104.53

COMPANY NAME	TICKER	AIC SECTOR
Henderson Opportunities Trust	HOT	UK all companies
Henderson Far East Income	HFEL	Asia Pacific equity income
UIL	UTL	Flexible investment
UIL	UTL	Flexible investment
Real Estate Credit Investments	RECI	Property – debt
Henderson Diversified Income	HDIV	Debt – loans and bonds
Henderson Diversified Income	HDIV	Debt – loans and bonds
Third Point Investors	TPOU	Hedge funds
Third Point Investors	TPOU	Hedge funds
Third Point Investors	TPOU	Hedge funds
Third Point Investors	TPOU	Hedge funds
Third Point Investors	TPOU	Hedge funds
Third Point Investors	TPOU	Hedge funds
Third Point Investors	TPOU	Hedge funds
Third Point Investors	TPOU	Hedge funds
Third Point Investors	TPOU	Hedge funds
abrdn New India Investment Trust	ANII	India
Asia Dragon Trust	DGN	Asia Pacific
Asia Dragon Trust	DGN	Asia Pacific
Fidelity Japan Trust	FJV	Japan

Source: AIC/Morningstar, all figures to 30/09/23 unless otherwise stated, excludes companies with <£50m market capitalisation.

Some individual trusts are notable for having long-serving managers who have been running the trust's investments for many years. In many cases the managers also have significant personal shareholdings in the trust. This is typically regarded as a good omen for other shareholders, since it should establish a close alignment of interest between the manager and the shareholders.

Because fund management is an extremely well-paid profession, the fact that a manager continues to manage a trust after many years in harness can be interpreted also as demonstrating exceptional commitment to the business. While some successful fund managers retire early to do other things, those who remain in post for decades are typically the enthusiasts who cannot think of anything more interesting or rewarding to do (look at Warren Buffett, still running Berkshire Hathaway in his 90s).

Against that, sometimes situations arise where managers have such a large personal shareholding in a trust that they effectively control the running of the company, and as a result may not always make the interests of other shareholders as high a priority as the other shareholders might wish. They are effectively being paid to look after their own money, often with a longer-term perspective that makes them worry less about short-term performance or the persistence of a wide discount.

MANAGER NAME	EFFECTIVE	YEARS IN SERVICE	10YR NAV TOTAL RETURN %
James H. Henderson	24/01/2007	16 years 8 months	61.59
Michael Kerley	02/02/2007	16 years 8 months	38.21
Charles Jillings	20/06/2007	16 years 3 months	68.19
Duncan Saville	20/06/2007	16 years 3 months	68.19
Richard Lang	25/06/2007	16 years 3 months	103.88
John Pattullo	18/07/2007	16 years 2 months	39.55
Jenna Barnard	18/07/2007	16 years 2 months	39.55
Daniel S. Loeb	20/07/2007	16 years 2 months	78.57
Munib Islam	20/07/2007	16 years 2 months	78.57
Brad Radoff	20/07/2007	16 years 2 months	78.57
Neel Devani	20/07/2007	16 years 2 months	78.57
Timothy S. Lash	20/07/2007	16 years 2 months	78.57
Brigitte M. Roberts	20/07/2007	16 years 2 months	78.57
Jim Carruthers	20/07/2007	16 years 2 months	78.57
Jeff Perry	20/07/2007	16 years 2 months	78.57
Rob Schwartz	20/07/2007	16 years 2 months	78.57
Pruksa Iamthongthong	01/08/2007	16 years 2 months	210.60
Adrian Lim	31/08/2007	16 years 1 month	59.62
Flavia Cheong	31/08/2007	16 years 1 month	59.62
Cenk Simsek	01/09/2007	16 years 1 month	121.70

Experience is a vital quality when it comes to choosing someone to manage your money, and many of these long-serving managers have strong performance records. There have been some notable departures in the past two years. Managers who have got into retirement include James Anderson at Scottish Mortgage (SMT), Simon Knott at Rights and Issues (RII: taken over by Jupiter), Max Ward at the Independent Investment Trust (IIT: now absorbed into Monks), Harry Nimmo at abrdn UK Smaller Companies Growth (AUSC: replaced in-house by Abby Glennie) and Simon Edelsten at Mid Wynd International (MWY).

Those who have announced but not yet taken their retirement include Bruce Stout at Murray International (MYI), Hugh Young (abrdn Asia Focus) and John Bennett (Henderson European Focus (HEFT). The managers of Atlantis Japan Growth (AJG) also drop out of the list as the trust is being absorbed into Nippon Active Value (NAVF). Dame Kate Bingham has also stepped back from her role at International Biotechnology Trust to concentrate on her firm's venture capital activities, while the trust's management contract has been moved to Schroders.

The longest serving manager still managing a trust now remains Peter Spiller at Capital Gearing Trust (CGT), who in 2022 celebrated 40 years of running the portfolio.

Dividend heroes

COMPANY	AIC SECTOR	NUMBER OF CONSECUTIVE YEARS DIVIDEND INCREASED
City of London Investment Trust	UK equity income	57
Bankers Investment Trust	Global	56
Alliance Trust	Global	56
Caledonia Investments	Flexible investment	56
The Global Smaller Companies Trust	Global smaller companies	53
F&C Investment Trust	Global	52
Brunner Investment Trust	Global	51
JPMorgan Claverhouse	UK equity income	50
Murray Income Trust	UK equity income	50
Scottish American	Global equity income	49
Witan Investment Trust	Global	48
Merchants Trust	UK equity income	41
Scottish Mortgage Investment Trust	Global	41
Value and Indexed Property Income	Property – UK commercial	36
CT UK Capital & Income	UK equity income	29
Schroder Income Growth Fund	UK equity income	27
abrdn Equity Income Trust	UK equity income	22
Athelney Trust	UK smaller companies	20
BlackRock Smaller Companies	UK smaller companies	20
Henderson Smaller Companies	UK smaller companies	20

Source: AIC/Morningstar. Correct as at 30/09/2023.

To qualify as one of the AIC's 'dividend heroes' an investment trust has to have increased its annual dividend payout each and every year for at least 20 years. Given that markets wax and wane, this is only possible because the investment trust structure allows boards to hold back up to 15% of the portfolio income each year as revenue reserves (effectively 'rainy day' money).

This means the trust can usually call on its reserves during recessions (or indeed pandemics) to continue to pay a dividend. Only during really difficult periods will they be forced to cut it below the previous year's figure. Qualifying as a dividend hero has proved particularly popular with shareholders since the global financial crisis and the subsequent decade of very low interest rates and minimal yields from cash and bonds.

Dividend hero status is not a guarantee that the income from a trust will persist indefinitely. Three trusts that featured on the list before the pandemic had to take an axe to their dividends and subsequently lost their place in the rankings. In 2022 the Scottish Investment Trust fell out of the list following its absorption into the JPMorgan Global Growth & Income Trust. Since the last edition of the *Handbook* three new trusts have joined the list, namely Henderson Smaller Companies (HSL), managed by Neil Hermon, BlackRock Smaller Companies (BRSC), managed by Roland Arnold, and the tiny Athelney Trust (ATY).

It is fair to say that some years trusts are only able to preserve their place on the list by making almost insignificant annual increases in the dividend. You occasionally hear mutterings from fund managers that the need to preserve dividend hero status can have an inhibiting effect on their ability to maximise returns. Prioritising income obligations is not always optimal from a total return or taxation perspective.

Nevertheless, for many shareholders that does not seem to be much of a concern. Trusts such as the City of London, which heads the list, remain very popular despite not having the best long-term track record on other counts. As the table shows, 20 trusts can claim 20 or more years of consecutive dividend increases and 13 of them have been in that camp for 40 years or more.

Coming up behind them are another 28 trusts (see next page) with between 10 and 19 years of consecutive dividend increases. One (Lowland) was in the original list but later demoted. You can be sure that not all of these will move up into the top tier, given the inevitability of another recession/bear market.

As at 30 September 2023, the average trailing 12-month yield of the 20 trusts was 3.6%, having grown by an average of 5% per annum over the past five years. Yields ranged from 7.6% (abrdn Equity Income Trust) to 0.6% (Scottish Mortgage). What hero status does do very effectively is differentiate investment trusts from open-ended funds, which lack the flexibility to ensure a consistently growing dividend policy.

Next generation dividend heroes

COMPANY	AIC SECTOR	NUMBER OF CONSECUTIVE YEARS DIVIDEND INCREASED
Artemis Alpha Trust	UK all companies	19
Murray International Trust	Global equity income	18
Henderson Far East Income	Asia Pacific equity income	16
BlackRock Greater Europe	Europe	16
Schroder Oriental Income	Asia Pacific equity income	16
CQS New City High Yield Fund	Debt – loans and bonds	16
International Public Partnerships	Infrastructure	15
abrdn Asian Income Fund	Asia Pacific equity income	14
Fidelity Special Values	UK all companies	13
Lowland Investment Company	UK equity income	13
Law Debenture Corporation	UK equity income	13
Invesco Select Trust - Global Equity Income Shares	Global equity income	13
TR Property Investment Trust	Property securities	13
Chelverton UK Dividend Trust	UK equity income	13
Aberforth Smaller Companies	UK smaller companies	12
Henderson Opportunities Trust	UK all companies	12
Fidelity European Trust	Europe	12
North American Income Trust	North America	12
Dunedin Income Growth	UK equity income	12
CT Global Managed Portfolio Income	Flexible investment	12
Fidelity China Special Situations	China/Greater China	12
Lindsell Train Investment Trust	Global	12
CT Private Equity Trust	Private equity	11
Mid Wynd International	Global	10
Henderson High Income Trust	UK equity and bond income	10
CT UK High Income Trust	UK equity income	10
Mercantile Investment Trust	UK all companies	10
ICG Enterprise Trust	Private equity	10

Source: AIC/Morningstar. Correct as at 30/09/2023.

Investment trust champions for generations

SHARES AWARDS 2022 WINNER Best Investment Trust Group

Allianz Global Investors and its predecessors have been managing investment trusts since 1889. Our trusts span investor aims – from income, to growth, to the specialist sector of technology – and offer a path to investment opportunities around the world. We're delighted to have been named Best Investment Trust Group in the 2022 Shares Awards. So whatever your investment goals, please take a closer look and discover what our investment trusts could bring to your portfolio.

Please note: investment trusts are listed companies, traded on the London Stock Exchange. Their share prices are determined by factors including demand, so shares may trade at a discount or premium to the net asset value. Past performance does not predict future returns. Some trusts seek to enhance returns through gearing (borrowing money to invest). This can boost a trust's returns when investments perform well, though losses can be magnified when investments lose value. A ranking, a rating or an award provides no indicator of future performance and is not constant over time. You should contact your financial adviser before making any investment decision.

0800 389 4696   uk.allianzgi.com/investment-trusts

Largest/most liquid trusts

COMPANY NAME	AIC SECTOR	MANAGEMENT GROUP	
3i Group	Private equity	3i Group	
Scottish Mortgage Investment Trust	Global	Baillie Gifford	
Pershing Square Holdings	North America	Pershing Square Capital Management	
F&C Investment Trust	Global	Columbia Threadneedle	
Greencoat UK Wind	Renewable energy infrastructure	Schroders Greencoat	
Alliance Trust	Global	Willis Towers Watson	
RIT Capital Partners	Flexible investment	RIT Capital Partners	
3i Infrastructure	Infrastructure	3i Investments	
Polar Capital Technology	Technology and technology innovation	Polar Capital Holdings	
Tritax Big Box REIT	Property – UK logistics	Tritax Management	
Renewables Infrastructure Group	Renewable energy infrastructure	InfraRed Capital Partners	
HICL Infrastructure	Infrastructure	InfraRed Capital Partners	

Source: AIC/Morningstar, data to 30/09/23.

While a small minority of investment trusts are managed directly by the board of directors, the great majority delegate the management of their portfolios to specialist fund managers, employed on annual or multi-year management contracts with a mandate to meet the trust's investment objectives. Those objectives are set by the board of directors and need to be approved by shareholders before any significant changes can be made.

The investment trust with the greatest total assets a year ago, Scottish Mortgage (SMT), has since been overtaken by 3i, the private equity group. The fortunes of these two largest names in the trust universe have moved dramatically in opposite directions. Scottish Mortgage had an extraordinary year in 2020–21, making a return of more than 100% in 12 months, as the big technology stocks it has owned for years soared during the lockdown, but has since come back down to earth, with its market value falling by around a third over the past 12 months.

3i meanwhile has had a spectacular year for its size, with its market capitalisation more or less doubling as its largest holding, a Dutch retailer called Action, continued to expand and grow in value. This one trust now accounts for more than 10% of the investment trust sector's total market capitalisation, just as Scottish Mortgage did at its zenith. Whereas the latter has been hurt by the rise in interest rates and an unsettling public boardroom row, closely followed by the

TICKER	MARKET CAPITALISATION (M)	1MTH DAILY AVG VALUE TRADED (M)	1YR DAILY AVG VALUE TRADED (M)	5YR DAILY AVG VALUE TRADED (M)	% SPREAD
III	20,177	49.09	45.40	27.11	0.0%
SMT	9,414	25.65	19.33	26.47	0.1%
PSH	5,585	1.28	1.69	2.36	2.7%
FCIT	4,533	3.78	4.29	3.39	0.2%
UKW	3,245	6.08	6.36	4.72	0.4%
ATST	2,946	2.20	3.11	2.96	0.6%
RCP	2,867	3.03	4.25	3.70	0.3%
3IN	2,809	2.85	3.36	2.80	0.2%
PCT	2,752	4.02	4.32	4.28	0.4%
BBOX	2,661	6.45	9.07	10.40	0.4%
TRIG	2,648	3.46	5.08	4.83	0.4%
HICL	2,519	4.92	5.31	4.95	0.3%

departure of three directors, 3i has benefitted from its bold decision not to scale back on its holding in Action to reduce concentration risk in its portfolio.

The 20 largest individual trusts on this measure accounted for just under 40% of total industry market capitalisation. In contrast, nearly 100 trusts had less than £50m in assets, although this figure includes a large number of venture capital trusts, which are invariably much smaller on average. The largest trusts tend to have the best liquidity, meaning they are easier to buy and sell in size. The spread between bid and offer prices is typically well below 0.5%. Economies of scale also make it easier for the biggest trusts to accept reduced annual management fees, with Scottish Mortgage, boasting an OCF of just 0.36% again a prime example.

A majority of the largest trusts in the sector have been operating for many years, but newcomers can break in. Some of the largest newcomers, like Smithson (SSON) and Tritax Big Box REIT (BBOX), raised a lot of money but have dropped down the rankings this year. At the same time there are regular departures from the investment trust universe, as funds either close down or return capital to shareholders, typically (though not invariably) as a result of indifferent performance, or where the trust has a predetermined wind-up date. Once again the diversity of the investment trust universe is well demonstrated in this table.

Best long-term performers

10 years

COMPANY NAME	TICKER	AIC SECTOR	
3i Group	III	Private equity	
India Capital Growth Fund	IGC	India/Indian subcontinent	
Allianz Technology Trust	ATT	Technology and technology innovation	
Polar Capital Technology	PCT	Technology and technology innovation	
HgCapital Trust	HGT	Private equity	
NB Private Equity Partners	NBPE	Private equity	
JPMorgan American	JAM	North America	
VinaCapital Vietnam Opportunity	VOF	Country specialist	
VietNam Holding	VNH	Country specialist	
Scottish Mortgage Investment Trust	SMT	Global	
HarbourVest Global Private Equity	HVPE	Private equity	
CT Private Equity Trust	CTPE	Private equity	
Pacific Horizon Investment Trust	PHI	Asia Pacific	
JPMorgan Global Growth & Income	JGGI	Global equity income	
Lindsell Train Investment Trust	LTI	Global	
Mobeus Income & Growth VCT	MIX	VCT generalist	
Dunedin Enterprise	DNE	Private equity	
Oakley Capital Investments	OCI	Private equity	
abrdn Private Equity Opportunities	APEO	Private equity	
Oryx International Growth	OIG	UK smaller companies	
Gulf Investment Fund	GIF	Global emerging markets	
3i Infrastructure	3IN	Infrastructure	
European Smaller Companies	ESCT	European smaller companies	
Alliance Trust	ATST	Global	
Canadian General Investments	CGI	North America	
abrdn New India Investment Trust	ANII	India/Indian subcontinent	
Mid Wynd International	MWY	Global	
Worldwide Healthcare Trust	WWH	Biotechnology and healthcare	
International Biotechnology	IBT	Biotechnology and healthcare	
F&C Investment Trust	FCIT	Global	
Impax Environmental Markets	IEM	Environmental	
Fidelity Asian Values	FAS	Asia Pacific smaller companies	

MANAGEMENT GROUP	£100 INITIAL INVESTMENT (SHARE PRICE TOTAL RETURN)	ANNUALISED %	£100 INITIAL INVESTMENT (NAV TOTAL RETURN)	ANNUALISED %	RANK LAST YEAR
3i Group	832	23.6	888	24.4	1
Ocean Dial Asset Management	533	18.2	443	16.0	26
Allianz Global Investors	533	18.2	584	19.3	2
Polar Capital Holdings	501	17.5	575	19.1	7
Hg	449	16.2	546	18.5	11
NB Alternatives Advisers	431	15.7	403	15.0	6
J.P. Morgan Asset Management	415	15.3	421	15.5	16
VinaCapital Investment Management	407	15.1	340	13.0	5
Dynam Capital	404	15.0	343	13.1	8
Baillie Gifford	388	14.5	459	16.5	3
HarbourVest Advisers L.P.	376	14.2	487	17.2	10
Columbia Threadneedle	362	13.7	381	14.3	22
Baillie Gifford	360	13.7	355	13.5	19
J.P. Morgan Asset Management	353	13.4	327	12.6	25
Lindsell Train	329	12.6	449	16.2	15
Gresham House	328	12.6	278	10.8	17
Dunedin	325	12.5	261	10.1	New
Oakley Capital Investments	316	12.2	376	14.2	33
abrdn	313	12.1	400	14.9	30
Harwood Capital	310	12.0	376	14.2	12
Epicure Managers Qatar	309	11.9	261	10.1	46
3i Investments	308	11.9	375	14.1	35
Janus Henderson Investors	306	11.8	305	11.8	21
Willis Towers Watson	302	11.7	272	10.5	50
Morgan Meighen & Associates	301	11.7	301	11.7	68
abrdn	299	11.6	315	12.2	74
Artemis Investment Management	298	11.6	298	11.6	41
Frostrow Capital	295	11.4	316	12.2	14
SV Health Managers	292	11.3	265	10.3	20
Columbia Threadneedle	292	11.3	285	11.0	29
Impax Asset Management	291	11.3	279	10.8	13
Fidelity	291	11.3	279	10.8	63

COMPANY NAME	TICKER	AIC SECTOR
ICG Enterprise Trust	ICGT	Private equity
Princess Private Equity Holding	PEY	Private equity
Fidelity European Trust	FEV	Europe
Schroder Asian Total Return	ATR	Asia Pacific
JPMorgan Indian	JII	India/Indian subcontinent
Brunner Investment Trust	BUT	Global
Pantheon International	PIN	Private equity
Scottish American	SAIN	Global equity income
Pacific Assets Trust	PAC	Asia Pacific
Herald Investment Trust	HRI	Global smaller companies
Montanaro European Smaller Companies	MTE	European smaller companies
Invesco Asia Trust	IAT	Asia Pacific equity income
BlackRock Greater Europe	BRGE	Europe
Polar Capital Global Healthcare	PCGH	Biotechnology and healthcare
Caledonia Investments	CLDN	Flexible investment
JPMorgan US Smaller Companies	JUSC	North American smaller companies

Although there is always a significant turnover from one year to the next, a good number of trusts have survived long enough to have multi-decade track records. The next few pages summarise the best performing trusts over 10, 20 and 30 years. The results are measured as both the value of £100 invested and as a compound annualised rate of return, with dividends reinvested, on both a share price and a NAV basis.

Of around 380 trusts whose data is recorded by the AIC, around a third have been launched in the last 10 years. Another third have compiled 20-year records and only a fifth have survived long enough to have a 30-year record. There is a Darwinian process at work in the sector, with the weakest trusts eventually being either liquidated, taken over and renamed, or absorbed into another investment trust.

Until this year the average annualised rate of return achieved by the top trusts that have survived this long was higher over 10 years than over 20 or 30 years. Now they are more closely aligned. Because of the magical effect of compounding, any trust that can grow at 10% every year will at least double in value every seven years and quadruple every 14.

MANAGEMENT GROUP	£100 INITIAL INVESTMENT (SHARE PRICE TOTAL RETURN)	ANNUALISED %	£100 INITIAL INVESTMENT (NAV TOTAL RETURN)	ANNUALISED %	RANK LAST YEAR
Intermediate Capital Group	290	11.2	341	13.1	42
Partners Group	290	11.2	295	11.4	51
Fidelity	285	11.0	270	10.4	55
Schroder Investment Management	280	10.8	276	10.7	65
J.P. Morgan Asset Management	277	10.7	293	11.3	New
Allianz Global Investors	276	10.7	266	10.3	57
Pantheon Ventures	276	10.7	357	13.6	47
Baillie Gifford	275	10.7	302	11.7	59
Frostrow Capital	271	10.5	276	10.7	61
Herald Investment Management	269	10.4	272	10.5	44
Montanaro Investment Managers	268	10.4	272	10.5	53
Invesco Asset Management	263	10.1	259	10.0	64
BlackRock Investment Management (UK)	257	9.9	263	10.2	71
Polar Capital Holdings	252	9.7	276	10.7	New
Caledonia Investments	251	9.6	284	11.0	60
J.P. Morgan Asset Management	251	9.6	292	11.3	24

It is not wrong therefore to see the table toppers over 10, 20 and 30 years, those which have produced annualised returns of more than 10% per annum, as among the cream of the crop, although you need to take into account the higher risk of some specialist sectors, like smaller companies and single country funds. Despite the recent surge in inflation, note that inflation over the three periods has averaged 2.9%, 2.8% and 2.4% respectively, so a 10% annualised return is equivalent to a 7% real (=inflation-adjusted) return.

The sell-off in equity markets in 2022/23 has now brought the 10-year performance figures back down to those of longer periods. The 30-year period includes two very bad bear markets (2000–03 and 2007–09). The 2000–03 bear market has now dropped out of the 20-year figures. The current downturn brings to an end the long and impressive bull market which began in 2009 after the global financial crisis.

The table also shows how the better-performing trusts have changed position in the rankings. The top spot, held by Scottish Mortgage for several years, this year is held by 3i Group for the second year running. Indian and Vietnamese trusts appear prominently in the top ten this year, alongside the two largest technology trusts, which have bounced back after a tough year in 2022.

20 years

COMPANY NAME	TICKER	AIC SECTOR	
HgCapital Trust	HGT	Private equity	
Scottish Mortgage Investment Trust	SMT	Global	
3i Group	III	Private equity	
Lindsell Train Investment Trust	LTI	Global	
Polar Capital Technology	PCT	Technology and technology innovation	
Allianz Technology Trust	ATT	Technology and technology innovation	
British Smaller Companies VCT	BSV	VCT generalist	
abrdn UK Smaller Companies Growth	AUSC	UK smaller companies	
abrdn Asia Focus	AAS	Asia Pacific smaller companies	
European Smaller Companies	ESCT	European smaller companies	
BlackRock Smaller Companies	BRSC	UK smaller companies	
JPMorgan European Discovery	JEDT	European smaller companies	
Pacific Horizon Investment Trust	PHI	Asia Pacific	
CT Private Equity Trust	CTPE	Private equity	
Scottish Oriental Smaller Companies	SST	Asia Pacific smaller companies	
European Opportunities Trust	EOT	Europe	
BlackRock Throgmorton Trust	THRG	UK smaller companies	
Biotech Growth Trust	BIOG	Biotechnology and healthcare	
JPMorgan Global Growth & Income	JGGI	Global equity income	
Fidelity Asian Values	FAS	Asia Pacific smaller companies	
JPMorgan American	JAM	North America	
Fidelity European Trust	FEV	Europe	
JPMorgan Indian	JII	India/Indian subcontinent	
The Global Smaller Companies Trust	GSCT	Global smaller companies	
Finsbury Growth & Income Trust	FGT	UK equity income	
Montanaro European Smaller Companies	MTE	European smaller companies	
JPMorgan Emerging Markets	JMG	Global emerging markets	
Mid Wynd International	MWY	Global	

We have expanded the list of 20- and 30-year performers this year to show the number of trusts that have delivered double-digit annualised returns over two and three decades. Note for how many of these trusts the share price and NAV total returns are not that different. This is evidence of a general truth: over time the discount at which you buy the shares of a top-performing trust matters less than you think.

The return on invested capital of a well-managed trust is far more important than the entry price, which is one reason why a buy-and-hold strategy is sensible for long-term investors. While discount movements accentuate the volatility of share prices, those cyclical swings even out as time goes by: an important message to take away.

MANAGEMENT GROUP	£100 INITIAL INVESTMENT (SHARE PRICE TOTAL RETURN)	ANNUALISED %	£100 INITIAL INVESTMENT (NAV TOTAL RETURN)	ANNUALISED %	RANK LAST YEAR
Hg	2,267	16.9	2,012	16.2	1
Baillie Gifford	1,615	14.9	1,475	14.4	2
3i Group	1,603	14.9	1,416	14.2	29
Lindsell Train	1,535	14.6	1,598	14.9	9
Polar Capital Holdings	1,415	14.2	1,459	14.3	5
Allianz Global Investors	1,291	13.7	1,250	13.5	3
YFM Private Equity	1,251	13.5	670	10.0	23
abrdn	1,177	13.1	922	11.8	12
abrdn	1,177	13.1	1,230	13.4	7
Janus Henderson Investors	1,172	13.1	1,049	12.5	13
BlackRock Investment Management (UK)	1,150	13.0	964	12.0	11
J.P. Morgan Asset Management	1,147	13.0	974	12.1	14
Baillie Gifford	1,142	13.0	1,186	13.2	6
Columbia Threadneedle	1,117	12.8	1,124	12.9	62
FSSA IM	1,107	12.8	1,168	13.1	17
Devon Equity Management	1,098	12.7	1,020	12.3	21
BlackRock Investment Management (UK)	1,060	12.5	839	11.2	16
Frostrow Capital	1,035	12.4	826	11.1	4
J.P. Morgan Asset Management	1,030	12.4	818	11.1	42
Fidelity	1,016	12.3	976	12.1	28
J.P. Morgan Asset Management	1,013	12.3	916	11.7	36
Fidelity	989	12.1	852	11.3	44
J.P. Morgan Asset Management	987	12.1	1,054	12.5	8
Columbia Threadneedle	981	12.1	864	11.4	24
Frostrow Capital	978	12.1	902	11.6	34
Montanaro Investment Managers	976	12.1	-	-	15
J.P. Morgan Asset Management	976	12.1	918	11.7	19
Artemis Investment Management	972	12.0	759	10.7	39

Over 20 years the performance story is not that dissimilar to the 10-year data. Five of the top 10 this year appear in both lists, although in absolute terms their performance is better over the 10-year period. The 10th ranked trust now has a 20-year annualised share price rate of return that is roughly 1.5% per annum lower than this time a year ago and 2.5% below that of the tenth best performer two years ago.

It is worth noting the number of smaller company trusts that still feature in the 20-year list despite their recent derating. The final column shows how individual trusts have moved up and down the rankings. Notable risers include 3i and the British Smaller Companies VCT and fallers Biotech Growth Trust and JPMorgan's Indian trust.

30 years

COMPANY NAME	TICKER	AIC SECTOR	
HgCapital Trust	HGT	Private equity	
Rights & Issues Investment Trust	RIII	UK smaller companies	
ICG Enterprise Trust	ICGT	Private equity	
Fidelity European Trust	FEV	Europe	
European Smaller Companies	ESCT	European smaller companies	
Canadian General Investments	CGI	North America	
JPMorgan European Discovery	JEDT	European smaller companies	
Scottish Mortgage Investment Trust	SMT	Global	
Henderson EuroTrust	HNE	Europe	
Invesco Perpetual UK Smaller Companies	IPU	UK smaller companies	
TR Property Investment Trust	TRY	Property securities	
Henderson European Focus Trust	HEFT	Europe	
BlackRock Smaller Companies	BRSC	UK smaller companies	
AVI Global Trust	AGT	Global	
JPMorgan American	JAM	North America	
JPMorgan UK Smaller Companies	JMI	UK smaller companies	
North Atlantic Smaller Companies	NAS	Global smaller companies	
Pantheon International	PIN	Private equity	
Aberforth Smaller Companies	ASL	UK smaller companies	
Montanaro European Smaller Companies	MTE	European smaller companies	
Caledonia Investments	CLDN	Flexible investment	

Source: AIC/Morningstar, data to 30/09/23, excludes companies with <10% NAVTR annualised return in the period.

Over 30 years the best performers include two familiar names, HG Capital and Scottish Mortgage and several European trusts, as well as less-familiar names such as Canadian General Investments (the Canada equity market being just as good a performer over time as the US market) and Rights and Issues. The latter's manager, Simon Knott, has retired as manager of this idiosyncratic smaller companies trust. The trust's management has now been handed to Dan Nickols at Jupiter Asset Management, who has some big shoes to fill.

The 30-year period includes trusts from no fewer than 10 broadly different sectors, suggesting that these trusts do have something special about them, not just the good fortune of operating in the sectors that have performed particularly well. It is also a testament to the breadth and diversity of the investment company sector as a whole.

MANAGEMENT GROUP	£100 INITIAL INVESTMENT (SHARE PRICE TOTAL RETURN)	ANNUALISED %	£100 INITIAL INVESTMENT (NAV TOTAL RETURN)	ANNUALISED %	RANK LAST YEAR
Hg	6,611	15.0	7,154	15.3	1
Jupiter Unit Trust Managers	4,850	13.8	5,615	14.4	2
Intermediate Capital Group	3,471	12.6	4,193	13.3	3
Fidelity	3,405	12.5	3,394	12.5	5
Janus Henderson Investors	3,164	12.2	3,080	12.1	6
Morgan Meighen & Associates	2,863	11.8	2,297	11.0	15
J.P. Morgan Asset Management	2,746	11.7	3,043	12.1	7
Baillie Gifford	2,500	11.3	2,387	11.2	8
Janus Henderson Investors	2,500	11.3	2,347	11.1	14
Invesco Asset Management	2,338	11.1	2,057	10.6	11
Columbia Threadneedle	2,309	11.0	1,884	10.3	4
Janus Henderson Investors	2,197	10.9	2,279	11.0	17
BlackRock Investment Management (UK)	2,067	10.6	1,787	10.1	19
Asset Value Investors	2,014	10.5	1,880	10.3	13
J.P. Morgan Asset Management	1,945	10.4	1,754	10.0	18
J.P. Morgan Asset Management	1,796	10.1	1,793	10.1	16
Harwood Capital	1,781	10.1	2,291	11.0	9
Pantheon Ventures	1,684	9.9	2,415	11.2	22
Aberforth Partners	1,636	9.8	1,823	10.2	26
Montanaro Investment Managers	1,589	9.7	-	-	31
Caledonia Investments	1,540	9.5	-	-	24

Unsurprisingly perhaps the rankings in the list change less markedly than in the 10- and 20-year rankings. Note again how close the NAV and share price total return figures for each trust are to each other. Where there are differences, it can be a case of consistent performance producing an improvement in a trust's rating over time.

In cases where the NAV return is higher than the share price total return, indicating that there has been a derating over time, some of the smaller companies trusts again stand out, suggesting that if the trust's strategy and process remains unchanged, there may be bargains to be had by purchasing at today's levels.

The best 30-year performers are generally those that operate in growth sectors. Their returns are more volatile from one year to the next, but tend to come out on top in the end. While styles come in and out of fashion, as they have done this year, growth is usually the long-term winner for those who can tolerate the ups and downs along the way.

Z-scores

TOP 15 'CHEAP' FUNDS	TICKER	CURRENT DISCOUNT	AVERAGE DISCOUNT	Z-SCORE
abrdn China	ACIC	-22.4	-14.3	-4.4
Henderson High Income	HHI	-9.2	-0.7	-4.4
Brunner	BUT	-17.5	-12.1	-4.0
Law Debenture	LWDB	-3.5	1.4	-3.7
India Capital Growth	IGC	-15.7	-7.8	-3.4
Aquila Energy Efficiency - €	AEEE	-40.5	-24.2	-3.3
Mobius IT	MMIT	-11.1	-1.2	-3.3
Merchants	MRCH	-1.6	0.7	-3.3
IP Group	IPO	-65.6	-57.8	-3.2
Scottish American	SAIN	-9.7	-1.5	-3.1
City of London	CTY	-1.0	1.6	-3.0
Foresight Sustainable Forestry	FSF	-34.6	-5.5	-3.0
Altamir Amboise	LTA	-34.6	-25.4	-3.0
Augmentum Fintech	AUGM	-51.4	-37.0	-2.9
Hipgnosis Songs	SONG	-53.6	-43.6	-2.9
BOTTOM 15 'DEAR' FUNDS	TICKER	CURRENT DISCOUNT	AVERAGE DISCOUNT	Z-SCORE
Jade Road Investments	JADE	-53.1	-88.6	2.8
Athelney Trust	ATY	0.9	-9.0	2.7
Rights & Issues IT	RIII	-9.6	-15.8	2.3
Symphony International Holding	SIHL	-40.5	-51.4	2.2
Round Hill Music Royalty	RHM	-12.1	-36.2	2.1
Schroder Capital Global Innovation	INOV	-39.2	-49.5	2.1
Hansa Trust	HAN	-37.7	-41.6	2.1
Hansa Trust A	HANA	-40.1	-42.8	1.9
JPMorgan Multi-Asset Growth & Income	MATE	-0.5	-3.2	1.9
European Opportunities	EOT	-9.8	-12.4	1.7
Boussard & Gavaudan - £	BGHS	-13.3	-18.2	1.7
Fair Oaks Income 2021	FAIR	-9.4	-13.4	1.7
Castelnau Group	CGL	7.1	-0.8	1.6
Schroder British Opportunities	SBO	-28.5	-32.2	1.6
STS Global Income & Growth	STS	0.8	-0.9	1.6

Source: Deutsche Numis.

Z-scores measure mathematically how far a trust's current discount or premium has diverged from its volatility-adjusted average over some previous period (days, months or even a year can be used). Brokers and other professional investors calculate the figures regularly in order to look for trading opportunities or good entry/exit points. A minus figure for a z-score suggests that a trust looks 'cheap' relative to its past discount history; and a positive figure the reverse.

There may, however, be a good reason for the change in sentiment towards a particular trust, so they are a blunt instrument without specialist knowledge and should never be relied on by inexperienced investors. If you already have a specific investment trust on your watchlist and are looking for a good moment to buy, then checking the z-scores can be useful in timing your purchase.

Bear in mind however that discounts widen for a reason; if the z-score is looking attractive, it is often because there is some negative story or headline out there. By the same token, if you are thinking of selling part or all of your holding in a trust, then at the margin it makes most sense to do so when the trust's shares are showing up as 'dear' in the z-score rankings. Since most investors tend to hold the trusts they own for a number of years, these opportunities do not arise very often in practice.

The table of one-year z-scores shown opposite is for illustration only. The data was current at 25 October 2023, but remember that z-scores can be volatile and change quickly. Trusts in the upper part of the table, which look 'cheap' at that point, can easily appear in the 'dear' section of the table a few weeks later, having gained in price and seen the discount narrow in the interim.

Investment trusts are best held for the longer term. A consistent 15% return over 20 years, if you are smart enough to find such a thing, will be worth far more at the end of the period (nearly 19 times your original investment) than anything bought in the hope of gaining from a short-term z-score movement. Nevertheless they can help at the margin, both in identifying possible opportunities and good buying/selling points.

Issuance

Investment company fundraising

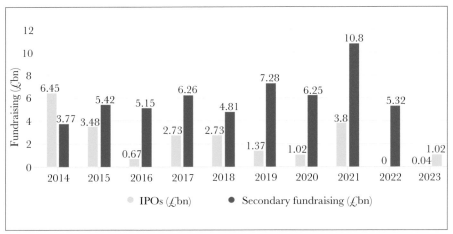

Source: AIC.

COMPANY NAME	SECONDARY FUNDRAISING 2023 (YTD) (£M)
BH Macro	315
JPMorgan Global Growth & Income	118
City of London Investment Trust	106
3i Infrastructure	102
Castelnau Group	57
Ruffer Investment Company	53
Gresham House Energy Storage	50
Merchants Trust	41
TwentyFour Income Fund	29
Law Debenture Corporation	25
CQS New City High Yield Fund	17
Henderson Far East Income	15
Personal Assets Trust	14
Ashoka India Equity	14
TwentyFour Select Monthly Income	12

Source: AIC, data as at 30/09/23. Excludes VCTs and company issuance from treasury. Company data for companies who have raised >10m in period only.

With the great majority of trusts moving to a discount it is no surprise that there has been very little issuance of shares in 2023. There has been no IPO (initial public offering) of significant size for the last two years and a number of planned issues have been scrapped because of poor market conditions. The only trust that has succeeded in coming to market this year, Ashoka Whiteoak Emerging Markets, managed to raise just £30m, at the bottom end of its target and well below the normal minimum size considered viable.

The IPO process runs to an irregular cycle. Some periods are characterised by a spurt of new issues in a particular segment of the market. Property trusts and hedge funds, for example, were hugely popular in the run up to the financial crisis in 2008. Income-generating trusts operating with alternative assets, notably infrastructure, renewable energy and specialist property sectors, have been particularly popular since then.

At any one time, there are always potential IPOs being worked on by brokers, of which only a handful will make it to the starting line. The current drought of IPOs follows a period of several good years in which increasing amounts of new capital were raised for new trusts. Broker Numis Securities noted last year that 2022 was the worst year for IPOs since they started recording the data in 2000 and this year has been equally as barren.

Secondary issuance is how investment trusts that have already succeeded in obtaining a listing can continue to grow their capital base. The figures for secondary issuance look, if anything, even worse on a 10-year perspective. By convention investment trusts can only issue new equity if their shares are trading at a premium and the small minority that have breached this convention in the past suffer reputational consequences that can last for years (I can only think of two examples in recent years).

The biggest issuer of shares this year was BH Macro, the hedge fund managed by Brevan Howard, which raised more than £300m in one go, from a placing in February. This followed a very successful year in 2022, which saw strong performance and its shares trading at a healthy premium. Since then, unfortunately, the shares have fallen by nearly 15% and the premium has disappeared.

Trusts can also issue shares on a regular basis if they continue to trade at a premium. Only a handful of trusts have been able to do this, headed by JPMorgan Global Growth and Income (JGGI) and City of London (CTY). The amount raised overall from share issuance, at £1bn, is the lowest for at least 10 years and below the amount of capital that has been returned to shareholders via buybacks, tender offers and exits.

Return of capital

COMPANY NAME	AIC SECTOR	TICKER	CAPITAL RETURNED 2023 YTD (£M) – TO 30/09/23	SPECIAL DIVIDENDS 2023 YTD (£M) – TO 30/09/23	CAPITAL RETURNED 2023 YTD (£M) INCLUDING SPECIAL DIVIDENDS – TO 30/09/23
NB Global Monthly Income Fund	Debt – loans and bonds	NBMI	115	-	115
Gulf Investment Fund	Global emerging markets	GIF	64	-	64
SLF Realisation Fund	Leasing	SLFR	61	-	61
Starwood European Real Estate Finance	Property – debt	SWEF	40	8	48
Diverse Income Trust	UK equity income	DIVI	33	-	33
Amedeo Air Four Plus	Leasing	AA4	28	-	28
ICG-Longbow Senior Secured UK Property Debt Investments	Property – debt	LBOW	10	16	26
BioPharma Credit	Debt – direct lending	BPCR	-	21	21
Tetragon Financial Group	Flexible investment	TFG	20	-	20
Riverstone Energy	Commodities and natural resources	RSE	18	-	18
Total			**390**	**44**	**434**

Source: AIC. Top 10 companies by capital returned. Currently excludes companies that liquidated in their entirety in 2023.

Buybacks and tenders by month over the last 13 months

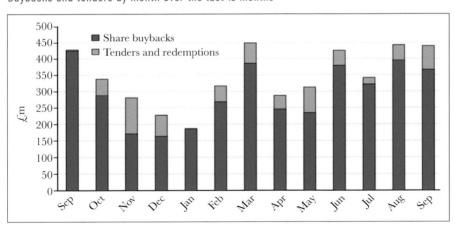

Source: Winterflood Securities, Monrningstar as at 30 September 2023.

Summary of delistings

YEAR	COMPANY	AIC SECTOR	TOTAL ASSETS AT TIME OF LIQUIDATION (£M)
Feb 23	**Blue Planet Investment Trust**	Global	7
Mar 23	**SME Credit Realisation Fund***	Debt – direct lending	7
Jun 23	**abrdn Latin American Income**	Latin America	41
Aug 23	**Secured Income Fund**	Debt – direct lending	10
Aug 23	**CT Property**	Property – UK commercial	325
Aug 23	**Momentum Multi-Asset Value**	Flexible investment	40
Aug 23	**Axiom European Financial Debt**	Debt – loans and bonds	85

Source: AIC.

*Returned £16.4m to shareholders via a redemption of shares in February 2023.

There can be a number of reasons why a trust decides to return capital to its shareholders. One is to try and limit the discount at which the shares in the trust are trading. Another is because a trust's board of directors has decided to liquidate or offer an exit to shareholders, typically after a run of poor performance. In some other cases a trust may decide to make a distribution of capital because of the sale of a significant asset that it owns.

Around 50 investment companies now have measures in place with which they attempt to control a specific level of discount and/or reduce discount volatility. Other trusts content themselves with a more modest statement of intent to keep the discount in mind. The measures include buying back shares in the market, making tender offers at periodic intervals (enabling those who wish to sell a chance to tender at least a proportion of their shares at a price close to NAV) and agreeing to hold a continuation vote at some date in the future, which if lost can lead to capital being returned or even a winding up.

It is fairly routine for investment companies to adopt the power to buy back their own shares. This requires shareholder approval at a general meeting and more than two-thirds of the companies in the sector have obtained this approval. In 1999 it became possible for investment companies to hold shares they have bought back 'in treasury', meaning they can be retained without being cancelled and so can be reissued later if and when demand for the shares has grown again.

Buybacks ran at an average rate of around £1.2bn a year over the past 20 years, but the trend picked up in 2022 and has accelerated in 2023 as discounts generally have widened, with £2.8bn bought back in the first nine months of 2023. Worldwide Healthcare (WWH), RIT Capital (RCP) and Smithson (SSON) head the list for amounts bought back year to date, followed by Capital Gearing (CGT), Polar Capital Technology (PCT) and Pershing Square Holdings (PSH).

Skin in the game

Why it matters

THE EXTENT TO which the interests of the directors and managers of a company are aligned with the interests of the shareholders is an important factor. Other things being equal, it is reassuring to know that those overseeing the company and managing its investments stand to gain or lose in the same way as those providing the capital for the business (which is what shareholders effectively do). Having 'skin in the game' matters; and trying to find out if a trust you are thinking of buying has such alignment should be an important element of your due diligence process.

Directors of investment trusts are required to disclose at least once a year in the company's annual report and accounts the extent of their holdings in the trusts on whose boards they serve. It is also a stock exchange listing requirement that they notify the market within 24 hours of any further dealings in their trust's shares. All significant shareholders must also notify the market if they own more than 3% of the share capital in any trust.

While directors' interests are always publicly available, it is unfortunately less easy to discover how much the managers of a trust's portfolio have invested themselves. Fund managers are only required to disclose their shareholding if it exceeds 3% of the total issued share capital of the trust. A number of managers do choose to do so voluntarily, but most do not – and that is information to which shareholders might legitimately feel they are entitled.

Alan Brierley, an investment trust analyst at Investec, periodically compiles a helpful comprehensive summary of the shareholdings of directors and managers (where the latter can be ascertained). His latest research on this topic, based on analysing 293 trusts, was published in June 2023. Earlier reports appeared in 2021, 2019, 2018, 2017, 2014, 2012 and 2010, making it easy to spot some of the most striking trends in board share ownership.

Needless to say, this bare information on its own lacks context. We don't know for example what proportion of a director or manager's overall wealth any given shareholding represents. Many fund managers are responsible for more than one trust and typically will be managing open-ended funds as well, in which they may also have some of their own money invested. Although precise figures are hard to come by, it is generally believed to be the case that managers of investment trusts typically have bigger shareholdings than their stakes in open-ended funds.

While it is easy to ascertain from an annual report how much an external fund management group will earn by way of management fees in any reporting period, knowing how much of that ends up in the pockets of the individual fund managers themselves, directly or indirectly (for example through a shareholding in the fund management company for which they work), is rarely if ever disclosed.

The same caveat applies to the information about directors. Modern preferred best practice is for all board members of a trust to be independent and non-executive (except in a small number of cases where trusts are self-managed or have a normal corporate business structure). Directors' fees are by definition normally only a small proportion of an individual board member's income and there is no legal requirement for them to own shares in the company on whose board they sit.

Nevertheless directors of investment trusts are typically encouraged to have a shareholding to help demonstrate that their interests are also aligned with shareholders, if only to a modest extent. The ultimate responsibility of an investment trust board in law is to safeguard the interests of shareholders, not least by overseeing and challenging the performance of the fund manager. (This does not always sit easily with another legal obligation, which is to help promote the company.)

Knowing that a fund's managers and directors may suffer financially, as well as reputationally, if an investment trust fails to perform well is undoubtedly valuable information for shareholders to know. In practice, however, as Alan Brierley has illustrated with his reports, there is considerable divergence across the investment trust sector in how far boards and management teams go when it comes to having 'skin in the game'.

His conclusion is that while there has been real progress towards greater disclosure over the past few years, "a significant number of managers are still unwilling or unable to disclose 'skin in the game'… We find this disappointing. For those that do not disclose, if they were at least to acknowledge that they have an unspecified investment, this would be a step in the right direction".

Headline findings

Ninety-five percent of boards are today deemed to be independent in corporate governance terms, meaning they have no business or close personal relationship with the fund manager of the trust. This is a big change from the past when boards were often very 'chummy', with many directors facing conflicts of interest that potentially inhibited their ability to act solely in the interests of shareholders.

The total investment by boards and managers as at the end of May 2023 was £4.2bn, down from £4.8bn the year before, but well up from £687m, the figure in the 2012 report. While changes in the number of trusts make comparisons of limited value, the comparable figure for 2019 was £3.4bn and £1bn in 2014.

Around half of the total was accounted for by less than half a dozen trusts with genuinely substantial personal or family holdings: led by Pershing Square Holdings (Bill Ackman and colleagues: £1,370m), RIT (Rothschild family: £549m), Tetragon Financial (£253m) and Apax Global Alpha (£199m).

Taking the headline figure at face value however, the aggregate loss of wealth experienced by boards and managers was of the order of 15% over the past two years, broadly in line with the extent of the derating across the trust universe. To this extent there has been a real alignment of interest with shareholders.

Fifty-three chairmen/directors had an individual investment in their trusts of more than £1m, while 89 managers or management teams had a personal investment of at least the same amount and 39 management teams had an aggregate investment in excess of £10m.

Managers with a personal investment in excess of £1m at 1 June 2023

COMPANY	DIRECTOR	VALUE (£'000)
RIT Capital Partners	The Rothschild family	549,099
Tetragon Financial Group	Reade Griffith	147,716
North Atlantic Smaller Companies	Christopher Mills	140,907
LXI REIT	Nick Leslau	94,251
Oakley Capital Investments	Peter Dubns	86,501
Literacy Capital	Paul Pindar	82,280
Pershing Square Holdings	Nicholas Botta	56,851
New Star	John Duffield	50,404
Tetragon Financial Group	Paddy Dear	43,497
Caledonia Investments	Will Wyatt	40,421
Literacy Capital	Richard Pindar	31,097
Hansa Investment Company	William Salomon	24,679
North Atlantic Smaller Companies	Peregrine Moncreiffe	16,126
Literacy Capital	Simon Downing	15,730
AEW UK Long Lease	Adam Smith	15,395
Global Opportunities Trust	Sandy Nairn	13,638
Warehouse REIT	Simon Hope	12,532
Warehouse REIT	Stephen Barrow	10,222
Rights and Issues	Simon Knott	9,445
Value and Indexed Property Income	Matthew Oakeshott	9,293
Caledonia Investments	Jamie Cayzer-Colvin	8,401
Lindsell Train	Michael Lindsell	7,976
Pantheon	John Burgess	7,398
Custodian REIT	Ian Mattioli MBE	5,523
JPMorgan Multi-Asset Growth & Income	Patrick Edwardson	4,928

COMPANY	DIRECTOR	VALUE (£'000)
Oryx International Growth Fund	Christopher Mills	4,165
Literacy Capital	Kevin Dady	3,333
EJF Investments	Neal Wilson	3,089
Personal Assets	Paul Read	2,546
Mid Wynd International	Alan Scott	2,038
Literacy Capital	Chris Sellers	1,936
Witan	Andrew Bell	1,921
Middlefield Canadian Income	Philip Bisson	1,907
Princess Private Equity	Felix Haldner	1,899
Personal Assets	Iain Ferguson CBE	1,852
Caledonia Investments	Mathew Masters	1,690
Urban Logistics REIT	Richard Moffitt	1,550
Oryx International Growth Fund	John Grace	1,547
NB Private Equity Partners	Wilken von Hodenberg	1,541

Source: Investec Securities analysis.

Eighty-five percent of directors have a shareholding in their trusts, while 15% do not. The latter includes 15 chairs, although this falls to seven if you exclude those only recently appointed. Fifty-four chairs with more than five years on the board still have shareholdings worth less than their annual fees.

Board's investment expressed as number of days' fees

COMPANY	AGGREGATE BOARD FEES (£, GROSS)	AGGREGATE BOARD SHAREHOLDING (£)	AGGREGATE BOARD SHAREHOLDING EXPRESSED AS DAYS FEES (GROSS)	AVERAGE BOARD MEMBER TENURE (YEARS)
abrdn Latin American Income	150,000	0	N/A	3
Axiom European Financial Debt	95,000	0	N/A	8
DP Aircraft I	160,650	4,461	11	8
Ground Rents Income Fund	170,000	16,011	34	3
JPEL Private Equity	100,000	10,510	38	5
Fair Oaks Income Fund	135,000	19,830	54	6
Fidelity Emerging Markets	167,500	25,617	56	3
abrdn China Investment Company	178,000	29,321	60	3
Baker Steel Resources	145,000	27,780	70	8
Target Healthcare REIT	216,500	50,469	85	1
abrdn Asia Focus	148,500	34,869	86	4
Schroder European Real Estate	175,000	47,566	99	7
abrdn Japan	117,500	33,885	105	6

COMPANY	AGGREGATE BOARD FEES (£, GROSS)	AGGREGATE BOARD SHAREHOLDING (£)	AGGREGATE BOARD SHAREHOLDING EXPRESSED AS DAYS FEES (GROSS)	AVERAGE BOARD MEMBER TENURE (YEARS)
CQS Natural Resources Growth and Income	136,500	39,670	106	6
Riverstone Energy	489,500	148,827	111	5
BlackRock Sustainable American Income	139,000	43,645	115	4
Crystal Amber	130,000	41,310	116	7
Harmony Energy Income Trust	225,750	72,101	117	2
Chelverton UK Dividend Trust	77,000	25,934	123	6
HOME REIT	163,000	57,456	129	3
Aquila Energy Efficiency	192,544	70,927	134	2
Weiss Korea Opportunity	127,500	47,410	136	4
CT High Income	123,500	45,979	136	3
Atrato Onsite Energy	163,000	61,612	138	2
HydrogenOne Capital Growth	173,250	67,012	141	2
AVI Japan Opportunity Trust	148,500	57,753	142	5
HICL Infrastructure Company	569,500	224,572	144	5
CT Capital & Income	155,500	62,000	146	5
GCP Infrastructure Investments	422,000	170,556	148	4
Life Science REIT	180,000	74,995	152	2
Triple Point Energy Transition	200,000	84,825	155	3
Triple Point Social Housing REIT	325,000	137,848	155	5
GCP Asset Backed Income Fund	253,500	109,596	158	7
Seraphim Space Trust	200,000	88,560	162	2
Round Hill Music Royalty Fund	285,000	127,689	164	2
River and Mercantile UK Micro	131,200	59,778	166	5
NB Distressed Debt	134,568	61,653	167	10
Invesco Bond Income Plus	191,000	88,399	169	3
Law Debenture Corporation	1,848,250	899,807	178	4
US Solar Fund	199,500	99,884	183	4

Source: Investec Securities analysis.

In this year's *Handbook*, to illustrate the range of experience, we include a table of those trusts where the board's aggregate investment in the trusts they oversee adds up to less than six months of their combined fees, as well as those where every single director has an investment greater than one year's fees.

Trusts where all board members have holdings worth more than one year's fees

abrdn European Logistics	Nippon Active Value Fund
Aquila European Renewables Income	Oakley Capital Investments
Ashoka India	Pacific Assets
BlackRock Income and Growth	Pantheon
Brunner	Pantheon Infrastructure
CC Japan Income & Growth	Personal Assets
Chenavari Toro Income	RTW Venture Fund
CT Private Equity Trust	Tetragon Financial Group
India Capital Growth	UIL Limited
Literacy Capital	Warehouse REIT
Montanaro European Smaller Companies	Worldwide Healthcare Trust

Source: Investec Securities analysis.

A number of trusts, mostly concentrated in the private equity, property and infrastructure sectors, are run as conventional businesses, including a CEO or executive director. In these cases their annual compensation is reported in the annual report.

Highest paid executive directors

COMPANY	EXECUTIVE DIRECTOR	APPOINTED TO BOARD	TOTAL REMUNERATION (£)	INVESTMENT VALUE (£)
North Atlantic Smaller Companies	Christopher Mills, CEO & Investment Manager	1984	3,230,000	140,907,218
BBGI Global Infrastructure S.A.	Duncan Ball, Co-CEO	2011	1,736,868	1,529,964
BBGI Global Infrastructure S.A.	Frank Schramm, Co-CEO	2011	1,593,421	1,459,881
Caledonia Investments	Jamie Cayzer-Colvin	2005	1,452,000	8,400,806
Caledonia Investments	Tim Livett, CFO	2019	1,087,000	111,653
Law Debenture Corporation	Denis Jackson, CEO	2018	1,048,000	695,764
BBGI Global Infrastructure S.A.	Michael Denny, CFO	2013	897,471	863,843
Picton Property Income	Michael Morris, CEO	2015	830,000	554,797
Taylor Maritime	Edward Buttrey, CEO	2021	744,000	391,229
Picton Property Income	Andrew Dewhirst, FD	2018	559,000	353,347
Witan	Andrew Bell, CEO	2010	476,142	1,921,000
Law Debenture Corporation	Trish Houston, COO	2020	464,000	39,781
Caledonia Investments	Matthew Masters, CEO	2022	450,000	1,690,013
Majedie Investments	William Barlow, CEO	2014	206,716	785,710

Source: Investec Securities analysis.

Discount control policies

COMPANY NAME	MANAGEMENT GROUP	
Capital Gearing Trust	CG Asset Management	
Invesco Select Trust	-	
Jupiter Green Investment Trust	Jupiter Unit Trust Managers	
Martin Currie Global Portfolio	Martin Currie Investment Management	
Personal Assets Trust	Troy Asset Management	
BlackRock Energy and Resources Income	BlackRock Investment Management (UK)	
AVI Japan Opportunity Trust	Asset Value Investors	
BlackRock Latin American	BlackRock Investment Management (UK)	
NB Global Monthly Income Fund	Neuberger Berman Europe	
VH Global Sustainable Energy Opportunities	Victory Hill Capital Advisors	
BioPharma Credit	Pharmakon Advisors	
abrdn Asian Income Fund	abrdn	
Balanced Commercial Property	Columbia Threadneedle	
CT Global Managed Portfolio	-	
CT UK High Income Trust	Columbia Threadneedle	
Fair Oaks Income	Fair Oaks Capital	
Finsbury Growth & Income Trust	Frostrow Capital	
Foresight Sustainable Forestry	Foresight Group	
JPMorgan Claverhouse	J.P. Morgan Asset Management	
JPMorgan Global Emerging Markets Income	J.P. Morgan Asset Management	
JPMorgan Global Growth & Income	J.P. Morgan Asset Management	
NB Distressed Debt	Neuberger Berman Europe	
North American Income Trust	abrdn	
Onward Opportunities	Dowgate Wealth	
Schroder Asian Total Return	Schroder Investment Management	
Schroder British Opportunities	Schroder Investment Management	
Schroder Oriental Income	Schroder Investment Management	
Starwood European Real Estate Finance	Starwood European Finance Partners	
Taylor Maritime Investments	Taylor Maritime	
The Global Smaller Companies Trust	Columbia Threadneedle	
Tritax Big Box REIT	Tritax Management	

AIC SECTOR	DISCOUNT CONTROL MECHANISM/POLICY	DCM/DCP TARGET
Flexible investment	DCP	0.0%
Flexible investment	DCP	0.0%
Environmental	DCP	0.0%
Global	DCP	0.0%
Flexible investment	DCP	0.0%
Commodities and natural resources	DCM	0.0%
Japanese smaller companies	DCM	5.0%
Latin America	DCM	5.0%
Debt – loans and bonds	DCM	5.0%
Renewable energy infrastructure	DCM	5.0%
Debt – direct lending	DCP	5.0%
Asia Pacific equity income	DCP	5.0%
Property – UK commercial	DCP	5.0%
Flexible investment	DCP	5.0%
UK equity income	DCP	5.0%
Debt – structured finance	DCP	5.0%
UK equity income	DCP	5.0%
Farmland and forestry	DCP	5.0%
UK equity income	DCP	5.0%
Global emerging markets	DCP	5.0%
Global equity income	DCP	5.0%
Debt – loans and bonds	DCP	5.0%
North America	DCP	5.0%
UK smaller companies	DCP	5.0%
Asia Pacific	DCP	5.0%
Growth capital	DCP	5.0%
Asia Pacific equity income	DCP	5.0%
Property – debt	DCP	5.0%
Leasing	DCP	5.0%
Global smaller companies	DCP	5.0%
Property – UK logistics	DCP	5.0%

COMPANY NAME	MANAGEMENT GROUP	
TwentyFour Select Monthly Income	TwentyFour Asset Management	
UK Commercial Property REIT	abrdn	
Biotech Growth Trust	Frostrow Capital	
RM Infrastructure Income	RM Capital Markets	
Worldwide Healthcare Trust	Frostrow Capital	
Allianz Technology Trust	Allianz Global Investors	
Blackstone Loan Financing	Blackstone Credit	
Chenavari Toro Income Fund	Chenavari Credit Partners	
F&C Investment Trust	Columbia Threadneedle	
STS Global Income & Growth Trust	Troy Asset Management	
Strategic Equity Capital	Gresham House Asset Management	
abrdn UK Smaller Companies Growth	abrdn	
International Biotechnology	SV Health Managers	
JPMorgan Emerging Europe, Middle East & Africa Securities	J.P. Morgan Asset Management	
Pacific Horizon Investment Trust	Baillie Gifford	
JPMorgan Asia Growth & Income	J.P. Morgan Asset Management	
JPMorgan US Smaller Companies	J.P. Morgan Asset Management	
abrdn Japan Investment Trust	abrdn	
Atlantis Japan Growth Fund	Quaero Capital	
Aurora Investment Trust	Phoenix Asset Management	
BH Macro	Brevan Howard Capital Management	
CVC Credit Partners European Opportunities	CVC Credit Partners	
Foresight Solar Fund	Foresight Group	
Greencoat UK Wind	Greencoat Capital	
Gulf Investment Fund	Epicure Managers Qatar	
JPMorgan Emerging Markets	J.P. Morgan Asset Management	
JLEN Environmental Assets Group	John Laing Capital Management	
NextEnergy Solar Fund	NextEnergy Capital IM	
Apax Global Alpha	Apax Guernsey Managers	
Atrato Onsite Energy	Atrato Partners Limited	
Brown Advisory US Smaller Companies	Brown Advisory	
Ceiba Investments	Ceiba Investments	
Fidelity European	FIL Investments International	
Fidelity Japan Trust	FIL Investments International	

AIC SECTOR	DISCOUNT CONTROL MECHANISM/POLICY	DCM/DCP TARGET
Debt – loans and bonds	DCP	5.0%
Property – UK commercial	DCP	5.0%
Biotechnology and healthcare	DCP	6.0%
Debt – direct lending	DCP	6.0%
Biotechnology and healthcare	DCP	6.0%
Technology and technology innovation	DCP	7.0%
Debt – structured finance	DCM	7.5%
Debt – structured finance	DCP	7.5%
Global	DCP	7.5%
Global equity income	DCP	7.5%
UK smaller companies	DCM	8.0%
UK smaller companies	DCP	8.0%
Biotechnology and healthcare	DCP	8.0%
Global emerging markets	DCP	8.0%
Asia Pacific	DCM	9.0%
Asia Pacific equity income	DCP	9.0%
North American smaller companies	DCP	9.0%
Japan	DCM	10.0%
Japanese smaller companies	DCM	10.0%
UK all companies	DCM	10.0%
Hedge funds	DCM	10.0%
Debt – loans and bonds	DCM	10.0%
Renewable energy infrastructure	DCM	10.0%
Renewable energy infrastructure	DCM	10.0%
Global emerging markets	DCM	10.0%
Global emerging markets	DCM	10.0%
Renewable energy infrastructure	DCM	10.0%
Renewable energy infrastructure	DCM	10.0%
Private equity	DCP	10.0%
Renewable energy infrastructure	DCP	10.0%
North American smaller companies	DCP	10.0%
Property - rest of world	DCP	10.0%
Europe	DCP	10.0%
Japan	DCP	10.0%

COMPANY NAME	MANAGEMENT GROUP
Greencoat Renewables	Greencoat Capital
Impax Environmental Markets	Impax Asset Management
Invesco Asia Trust	Invesco Asset Management
JPMorgan European Growth & Income	J.P. Morgan Asset Management
Montanaro European Smaller Companies	Montanaro Investment Managers
Rights & Issues Investment Trust	Jupiter Unit Trust Managers
Schroder AsiaPacific Fund	Schroder Investment Management
Witan Investment Trust	Witan Investment Services
Barings Emerging EMEA Opportunities	Baring Asset Management
Baker Steel Resources Trust	Baker Steel Capital

Source: Money Makers, from broker and other sources.

As mentioned earlier, a significant minority of investment trusts have formally adopted discount control policies designed to reassure shareholders that they will not allow the discount on the trust's shares to widen beyond a certain threshold. The targets vary from zero to 15%; and while some are firm commitments, others are more loosely worded to give boards some discretion to do nothing in 'abnormal' market conditions.

This table, a new one in the *Handbook*, lists the most important trusts that according to the Association for Investment Companies have identified a target discount level at which they will take some action. It is important to note that the conditions attached to each commitment vary a lot, so it is always worth checking the specific details.

The most common commitment is to buy back shares when discounts breach the target. A commitment to make a tender offer allowing shareholders to sell shares close to net asset value at a certain date is another method. Some boards agree to offer shareholders the chance to vote on whether a trust should continue or be wound up if performance falls below a certain target.

AIC SECTOR	DISCOUNT CONTROL MECHANISM/POLICY	DCM/DCP TARGET
Renewable energy infrastructure	DCP	10.0%
Environmental	DCP	10.0%
Asia Pacific equity income	DCP	10.0%
Europe	DCP	10.0%
European smaller companies	DCP	10.0%
UK smaller companies	DCP	10.0%
Asia Pacific	DCP	10.0%
Global	DCP	10.0%
Global emergingmarkets	DCM	12.0%
Commodities and natural resources	DCM	15.0%

For shareholders, the knowledge that discounts will not be allowed to become too wide can be an important positive factor in deciding whether to invest. It is worth looking for details of any such policy when researching a possible investment. As noted by several contributors to this year's *Handbook*, the widespread derating of trust discounts will put the strength of a number of boards' commitments under the spotlight.

Number of investment trusts buying back shares

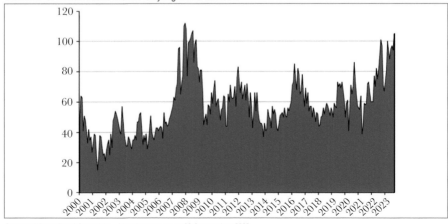

Source: Winterflood Securities, Morningstar as at 30 September 2023.

Enhanced income trusts

COMPANY	AIC SECTOR	DIVIDEND YIELD (%)	5YR DIVIDEND GROWTH (%) P.A.	DISCOUNT/ PREMIUM (%)	3YR NAV TOTAL RETURN	3YR SHARE PRICE TOTAL RETURN (%)
BBGI Global Infrastructure S.A	Infrastructure	6.23	2.85	-13.24	33.15	-15.43
BlackRock Latin American	Latin America	5.99	16.80	-15.09	54.05	43.63
Blackstone Loan Financing	Debt – structured finance	14.48	-4.36	-39.30	44.87	25.20
Chenavari Toto Income Fund	Debt – structured finance	14.26	-4.39	-31.24	22.04	29.29
CT Private Equity Trust	Private equity	5.97	12.91	-36.06	95.57	71.95
European Assets Trust	European Smaller Companies	7.55	-6.61	-8.93	-6.24	-4.69
International Biotechnology	Biotechnology and healthcare	5.61	6.42	-8.06	-11.87	-19.32
Invesco Asia Trust	Asia Pacific equity income	5.00	21.89	-14.17	12.12	10.99
Invesco Perpetual UK Smaller Companies	UK Smaller companies	4.64	-2.81	-7.19	-1.51	10.42
JPMorgan Asia Growth & Income	Asia Pacific equity income	4.76	0.00	-9.30	-4.46	-15.00
JPMorgan China Growth & Income	China/Greater China	6.07	31.34	-13.25	-50.32	-58.24
JPMorgan European Growth & Income	Europe	4.71	18.72	-10.98	50.12	55.91
JPMorgan Global Growth & Income	Global equity income	3.97	6.93	1.16	56.19	53.63
JPMorgan Japan Small Cap Growth & Income	Japanese smaller companies	4.78	n/a	-10.43	-31.00	-34.72
Montanaro UK Smaller Companies	UK smaller companies	5.34	15.49	-16.26	-12.52	-20.47
Princess Private Equity Holding	Private equity	7.53	5.45	-35.25	31.14	14.07

Source: Money Makers, various sources. Data as at 31 October 2023.

A small number of investment trusts have adopted a policy known as 'enhanced income' in recent years. In essence this means that they aim to pay out a fixed percentage of their net asset value each year as a dividend, whatever the NAV turns out to be. Typically this figure is around 4%. J.P. Morgan Asset Management is the fund management company most closely associated with this policy. Five of the 13 trusts it manages have a policy of this kind.

The origins of this practice date back to 2012, when it was decided to give investment trusts the flexibility to pay dividends out of any retained capital profits, not just from current year income and revenue reserves. To do this, a trust's articles of association need to be amended to give the directors power to make such distributions, with at least 75% approval in a shareholder vote.

Some well-known trusts, including Personal Assets (PNL) and RIT Capital Partners (RCP), have taken this route. However, a number have gone a little further by embracing what is called the enhanced income concept. Rather than just using capital profits to support a progressive dividend policy, they try to appeal to income-seeking investors by saying they will pay a fixed percentage of their NAV each year.

This means shareholders get the reassurance of knowing what the next year's annual payout rate will be, even if the amount of the dividend itself is not known, as that will depend on what the NAV turns out to be. With the rates on savings accounts having been pitiful (until recently), an enhanced income policy can broaden the appeal of a trust to income-focused investors while the extra demand for its shares can help narrow its discount.

The table lists those trusts which have adopted a fixed rate for determining their future dividend payments. These 17 trusts have around £8bn in assets, or about 3% of assets in the investment trust sector, but there are some sizeable trusts in the list. JPMorgan Global Growth & Income (JGGI) is the largest, followed by Bellevue Healthcare (BBH). It is a mixed bag, drawn from a wide range of sectors.

Few of these companies adopted this approach before 2016, so there was no rush towards it when the rules were relaxed in 2012. European Assets has had such a policy since 1999. It used to be a Dutch company, where different rules applied relating to distributions, and only migrated to the UK in 2019. BB Healthcare is the only trust on the list that adopted the enhanced dividend approach when it was first listed.

Almost all these trusts traded at discounts above 10% when they adopted the policy, clearly hoping the approach would allow them to stand out from their peer group. In most cases, the discount has since narrowed, although that could be for several reasons. Some of these trusts still trade on a double-digit discount, so it's certainly not a magic bullet, especially now that gilts and cash offer more attractive yields.

Investment trusts vs open-ended funds

SECTORS	1 YEAR		5 YEARS		10 YEARS	
	INVESTMENT COMPANIES	OEIC/UNIT TRUSTS	INVESTMENT COMPANIES	OEIC/UNIT TRUSTS	INVESTMENT COMPANIES	OEIC/UNIT TRUSTS
Global	106.68	109.19	121.48	136.33	258.81	243.55
Global equity income	107.93	109.81	126.59	136.33	258.81	243.55
Flexible	98.08	105.08	106.37	117.26	164.64	173.16
UK equity income	110.71	113.86	115.16	113.17	165.87	164.64
UK all companies	113.99	112.74	103.51	111.38	161.89	166.61
North America	104.69	110.97	155.41	152.60	274.15	320.51
Europe vs Europe ex. UK	123.97	118.19	133.61	129.96	228.19	213.35
Global emerging	116.17	104.03	123.31	111.34	164.30	157.98
Asia Pacific vs Asia Pacific ex. Japan	98.14	101.27	131.80	118.02	245.09	195.09
Japan	113.18	111.08	107.83	114.89	216.72	205.76
Property – UK commercial vs UK direct	91.45	90.15	89.24	98.48	120.10	135.59
UK small cap	108.30	101.90	100.82	98.99	172.43	184.83
TMT	103.20	119.15	167.46	169.32	516.57	469.44
European small cap	112.89	110.89	116.60	108.22	240.46	212.99
North American smallers	97.28	104.57	106.57	129.76	213.54	249.40

Source: AIC/Morningstar. All data to the end of September 2023. Sector averages are unweighted share price total return in pounds rebased to £100.

It is not uncommon for the investment managers of trusts to manage other funds outside the investment trust sector at the same time. In fact, a number of fund managers start their careers managing different kinds of fund (typically unit trusts and OEICs, though also hedge funds) and if successful are encouraged to take over or start an investment trust with a broadly similar investment objective.

Adding an investment trust to their responsibilities gives successful fund managers the opportunity to take advantage of the benefits of the investment trust structure, including the use of gearing and freedom from unhelpful forced selling as a result of fund flows. They can also use derivative securities such as futures and options for investment purposes.

These advantages show up regularly in comparisons between the long-term performance of investment trusts and that of open-ended funds with either the same manager or the same investment objective. Where trusts and similar funds can be directly compared in this way, trusts show up with superior performance records in most periods. Where a trust and an open-ended fund with the same mandate are managed by the same individual, it is rare for the trust not to do better over the longer term.

The degree to which comparable trusts outperform does vary markedly, however, from sector to sector and is not true every year. The table summarises the difference in the performance of directly comparable trust and open-ended equivalent sectors at 30 September 2023. The red-shaded cells show the periods over which trusts in each sector have outperformed, the blue cells when they have underperformed. The number of sectors which are underperforming open-ended equivalents has clearly increased as a result of wider discounts.

It is fair to point out that such simple comparisons can be criticised by statisticians on the grounds that the two samples are very different in size and also may display what is called survivorship bias. In 2018 academics at Cass Business School in London reported that a detailed analysis of investment trust returns between 2000 and 2016 appeared to support their superior performance. However, the study has now been abandoned because of 'data issues', principally the sample size and survivorship bias problems.

Who owns investment trusts?

Most bought investment companies in 2023 – ranked

NAME	SECTOR
Scottish Mortgage	Global
City of London	UK equity income
F&C IT	Global
Greencoat UK Wind	Renewable energy infrastructure
JPM Global Growth & Income	Global
BlackRock World Mining	Mining
Alliance Trust	Global
Fidelity European	Europe
Merchants	UK equity income
Renewables Infrastructure Group	Renewable energy infrastructure
Fidelity China	China equity
Fidelity Special Values	UK equity
Personal Assets	Flexible investment
Murray International	Global
Polar Capital Technology	Technology

Source: Deutsche Numis. Based on number of deals placed across platforms AJ Bell, Fidelity and interactive investor. Every month, for each platform the top-ranking fund is assigned a score of 10 and the score decreases until the 10th ranking fund, which is given a score of 1. The scores have been summed across each month (to September) to calculate a total ranking.

Private investors are becoming an ever more important market for investment trusts. Research by two specialist share register analysis and marketing firms (Richard Davies IR and Warhorse Partners) shows how the proportion of shares in investment trusts held by private investors has been rising over the past decade, thanks in part to the big platforms such as Hargreaves Lansdown, interactive investor and AJ Bell. The trend is slow but steady rather than dramatic, but evident nonetheless.

It is strongest in the traditional equity sectors of the universe, where few big institutions such as pension funds and insurance companies remain shareholders. They mostly now manage their investment portfolios directly themselves or by hiring the services of specialist fund managers on bespoke terms. The trend is somewhat less marked in the alternative asset classes.

The wealth management industry, traditionally the biggest buyer of investment trusts since the institutions departed, has meanwhile been consolidating and for a variety of reasons is no longer relying on investment trusts as mainstays of their client portfolios as much as they did.

Another survey by Warhorse and Dianomi in May 2022 revealed more about the private investor market for investment trusts. Investment trusts are predominantly owned by older investors; 80% are aged 51 or older. This group has the time to conduct research before investing and typically carefully research and review their investments.

They use a wide range of online and traditional sources of information, tuned to their individual preferences and needs. Half of investors use online platforms, such as interactive investor and Hargreaves Lansdown. Around 40% also use third-party websites, such as Trustnet and Morningstar, and read coverage in the national press, for example, the *Telegraph*, the *Times* and the *Mail on Sunday*. Older investors are typically less reliant on social media than younger investors.

Holdings vary significantly among investors. Half of investors have investment holdings valued at less than £250,000. However, over 30% have holdings between £250,000 and £2m. Most investors have multiple holdings of investment trusts. A quarter have 11 or more. Investment diversification is clearly a consideration in decision-making.

Fees

COMPANY NAME	AIC SECTOR
Life Settlement Assets	Insurance and reinsurance strategies
Petershill Partners	Growth capital
Regional REIT	Property – UK commercial
BH Macro	Hedge funds
Riverstone Credit Opportunities Income	Debt – direct lending
Tritax Eurobox	Property – Europe
Rockwood Strategic	UK smaller companies
Doric Nimrod Air Three	Leasing
VietNam Holding	Country specialist
Alpha Real Trust	Property – debt
abrdn Private Equity Opportunities	Private equity
Riverstone Energy	Commodities and natural resources
Pershing Square Holdings	North America
Oakley Capital Investments	Private equity
Phoenix Spree Deutschland	Property – Europe
JZ Capital Partners	Private equity
HydrogenOne Capital Growth	Renewable energy infrastructure
Symphony International Holdings	Private equity
PRS REIT	Property – UK residential
Marwyn Value Investors	UK smaller companies
Literacy Capital	Private equity
Schroder Real Estate	Property – UK commercial
Schroder European Real Estate	Property – Europe
Real Estate Credit Investments	Property – debt
AVI Global Trust	Global
abrdn Property Income Trust	Property – UK commercial
CT Global Managed Portfolio Income	Flexible investment
Doric Nimrod Air Two	Leasing
Weiss Korea Opportunity Fund	Country specialist
Pollen Street	Debt – direct lending
VPC Specialty Lending Investments	Debt – direct lending
Third Point Investors	Hedge funds
Volta Finance	Debt – structured finance
Crystal Amber Fund	UK smaller companies
CT Global Managed Portfolio Growth	Flexible investment
Triple Point Energy Transition	Renewable energy infrastructure
RTW Biotech Opportunities	Biotechnology and healthcare
Augmentum Fintech	Financials and financial innovation
Vietnam Enterprise Investments	Country specialist
RM Infrastructure Income	Debt – direct lending
Atlantis Japan Growth Fund	Japanese smaller companies
Ecofin US Renewables Infrastructure	Renewable energy infrastructure

TICKER	ONGOING CHARGE %	ONGOING CHARGE DATE	NET ASSETS (£M)
LSAA	7.10%	31/12/2022	90
PHLL	5.55%	31/12/2021	3,826
RGL	5.30%	31/12/2022	392
BHMG	3.35%	31/12/2022	1,502
RCOI	3.24%	31/12/2022	80
BOXE	3.15%	30/09/2022	714
RKW	2.85%	31/03/2023	50
DNA3	2.77%	31/03/2023	71
VNH	2.74%	30/06/2022	98
ARTL	2.74%	31/03/2023	126
APEO	2.73%	30/09/2022	1,160
RSE	2.70%	31/12/2022	587
PSH	2.68%	31/12/2022	8,812
OCI	2.66%	31/12/2022	1,168
PSDL	2.61%	31/12/2022	296
JZCP	2.56%	28/02/2023	248
HGEN	2.51%	31/12/2022	130
SIHL	2.45%	31/12/2022	324
PRSR	2.45%	30/06/2022	643
MVI	2.43%	31/12/2022	93
BOOK	2.41%	31/12/2022	293
SREI	2.28%	31/03/2023	318
SERE	2.23%	30/09/2022	157
RECI	2.23%	31/03/2023	338
AGT	2.22%	30/09/2022	1,031
API	2.20%	31/12/2022	316
CMPI	2.15%	31/05/2023	55
DNA2	2.08%	31/03/2023	199
WKOF	2.04%	31/12/2022	113
POLN	2.00%	31/12/2022	579
VSL	1.99%	31/12/2022	257
TPOU	1.98%	31/12/2022	500
VTA	1.97%	31/07/2022	204
CRS	1.97%	30/06/2022	81
CMPG	1.95%	31/05/2023	84
TENT	1.94%	31/03/2023	97
RTW	1.92%	31/12/2022	279
AUGM	1.90%	31/03/2023	271
VEIL	1.90%	31/12/2022	1,473
RMII	1.86%	31/12/2022	107
AJG	1.85%	30/04/2023	77
RNEW	1.80%	31/12/2022	104

COMPANY NAME	AIC SECTOR
Menhaden Resource Efficiency	Environmental
Boussard & Gavaudan Holding	Hedge funds
Tetragon Financial Group	Flexible investment
Miton UK Microcap Trust	UK smaller companies
Seraphim Space Investment Trust	Growth capital
EJF Investments	Debt – structured finance
CQS Natural Resources Growth & Income	Commodities and natural resources
HgCapital Trust	Private equity
Impact Healthcare REIT	Property – UK healthcare
Gabelli Merger Plus+ Trust	Hedge funds
Round Hill Music Royalty Fund	Royalties
Gulf Investment Fund	Global emerging markets
3i Infrastructure	Infrastructure
Princess Private Equity Holding	Private equity
Triple Point Social Housing REIT	Property – UK residential
Barings Emerging EMEA Opportunities	Global emerging markets
India Capital Growth Fund	India/Indian subcontinent
Chenavari Toro Income Fund	Debt – structured finance
Target Healthcare REIT	Property – UK healthcare

Source: AIC/Morningstar, data to 30/09/23.

The costs that investors have to pay for the privilege of having their investments managed by an investment company is a surprisingly important factor in determining the returns that they obtain. It is standard practice for a fund management firm to charge an annual management fee that is expressed as a percentage, typically somewhere between 0.3% and 2.0%, of the amount of the money they look after.

As a result, other things being equal, the larger the trust, the greater a fee the firm will earn, creating an incentive for the management firm to grow the size of the trust. In a rising market, the management firm also benefits from rising fee income even if they fail to outperform the fund's benchmark.

Deceptively modest percentage fees can quickly become big business; a trust with £500m of assets paying a management fee of 0.6% per annum will earn the manager £3m every year for its services, in addition to other administrative expenses, such as accountancy and legal fees. Some fund managers also charge a performance fee, an extra fee that is only paid if the trust beats a given target.

Given that only a minority of fund managers can consistently outperform a benchmark or passive fund equivalent, and the best rarely beat either by 2% per annum over time, the overall annual cost of owning any kind of investment fund can make a huge difference in determining whether they offer value for

TICKER	ONGOING CHARGE %	ONGOING CHARGE DATE	NET ASSETS (£M)
MHN	1.80%	31/12/2022	119
BGHL	1.77%	31/12/2022	286
TFG	1.74%	31/12/2022	2,041
MINI	1.72%	30/04/2023	55
SSIT	1.72%	30/06/2022	218
EJFI	1.70%	31/12/2022	100
CYN	1.70%	30/06/2022	141
HGT	1.70%	31/12/2022	2,165
IHR	1.67%	31/12/2022	469
GMP	1.67%	30/06/2022	55
RHM	1.67%	31/12/2022	432
GIF	1.67%	30/06/2022	95
3IN	1.64%	31/03/2023	3,100
PEY	1.64%	31/12/2022	899
SOHO	1.60%	31/12/2022	515
BEMO	1.60%	30/09/2022	73
IGC	1.59%	31/12/2022	166
TORO	1.55%	30/09/2022	173
THRL	1.51%	30/06/2022	689

money. Regulators have expended a huge amount of time and effort in trying to develop a standardised measure that will allow investors to compare the cost of competing funds.

The table lists trusts with the highest 'ongoing charge ratios' – the standard measure today – expressed as a percentage. It is an imperfect measure, but can at least give shareholders a first indication of whether a trust is worth paying for or not. Many firms these days charge tiered fees, meaning the percentage annual management fee declines once the size of a trust reaches a threshold.

Note that the table excludes most alternative asset trusts. The issue of how fees should be calculated and reported following the introduction of new regulations by the Financial Conduct Authority has become a live and contentious issue, as reported earlier. Open-ended funds (unit trusts and OEICs) are not subject to the same disclosure requirements, and many in the investment trust business feel that trusts are discriminated against by the latest changes, which has led to some wealth managers refusing to invest in certain trusts and some platforms refusing to list them.

Fees charged on market cap

COMPANY NAME	TICKER	AIC SECTOR
abrdn China Investment Company	ACIC	China/Greater China
abrdn Japan Investment Trust	AJIT	Japan
Alliance Trust	ATST	Global
Allianz Technology Trust	ATT	Technology and technology innovation
Artemis Alpha Trust	ATS	UK all companies
AVI Japan Opportunity Trust	AJOT	Japanese smaller companies
Baillie Gifford European Growth	BGEU	Europe
Baker Steel Resources Trust	BSRT	Commodities and natural resources
Bellevue Healthcare Trust	BBH	Biotechnology and healthcare
Biotech Growth Trust	BIOG	Biotechnology and healthcare
BlackRock Income & Growth	BRIG	UK equity income
Cordiant Digital Infrastructure	CORD	Infrastructure
Diverse Income Trust	DIVI	UK equity income
Downing Strategic Micro-Cap	DSM	UK smaller companies
Edinburgh Investment Trust	EDIN	UK equity income
F&C Investment Trust	FCIT	Global
Finsbury Growth & Income Trust	FGT	UK equity income
Harmony Energy Income Trust	HEIT	Renewable energy infrastructure
Hipgnosis Songs Fund	SONG	Royalties
India Capital Growth Fund	IGC	India
JPMorgan Asia Growth & Income	JAGI	Asia Pacific equity income
Keystone Positive Change	KPC	Global
Lindsell Train Investment Trust	LTI	Global
LXI REIT	LXI	Property – UK commercial
Majedie Investments	MAJE	Flexible investment
Mercantile Investment Trust	MRC	UK all companies
MIGO Opportunities Trust	MIGO	Flexible investment
Miton UK Microcap Trust	MINI	UK smaller companies
Mobius Investment Trust	MMIT	Global emerging markets
Montanaro European Smaller Companies	MTE	European smaller companies
Odyssean Investment Trust	OIT	UK smaller companies
Polar Capital Global Healthcare	PCGH	Biotechnology and healthcare
Round Hill Music Royalty Fund	RHM	Royalties
Schroders Capital Global Innovation Trust	INOV	Growth capital
TwentyFour Income Fund	TFIF	Debt – structured finance
TwentyFour Select Monthly Income	SMIF	Debt – loans and bonds

Source: AIC/Morningstar.

A separate issue is whether it is in the best interests of shareholders for management fees to be calculated as a percentage of net asset value or of market capitalisation. The table opposite lists the minority of trusts, about 10% of the total, whose fees are based on market capitalisation (or market capitalisation or net asset value, whichever is the lower of the two). Managers of the trusts whose management fees are calculated in this way will see their income decline when discounts widen, whereas those whose fees are based on net asset value will not. Fund managers argue that their job is to maximise the NAV while it is up to boards to manage the discount, so they think this is a reasonable approach. The alternative argument is that shareholders and managers should experience the same impact when discounts move, gaining when the shares are at a premium but losing when the discount widens.

Overall, the trend in management fees has been down in recent years, as the table below shows. Performance fees have become less popular, and a number of trusts have either reduced their base fee or agreed to tier them, so that the percentage fee charged by the management company reduces as the size of the company increases.

Fee changes

FEE AREA	ACTION	2018	2019	2020	2021	2022	2023 YTD
Base fee change	Reduced	41	38	31	23	12	8
Performance fee change	Reduced	5	1	4	2	2	0
Performance fee change	Removed	9	4	6	4	3	1
Tiered fee change	Reduced	16	6	9	10	4	6
Tiered fee change	Removed	10	16	11	7	9	8
	Total changes	**43**	**41**	**39**	**31**	**23**	**16**

Source: AIC. Please note that the breakdown above details the number of occurance of each type and will not add up to the 'total changes', e.g., a base fee reduction coupled with a performance fee removal will only count once in 'total changes' but the separate components of the amendment will appear in the relevant section.

Platform costs

PLATFORM	£5,000	£15,000
AJ Bell Youinvest	£52	£77
Barclays	£72	£72
Bestinvest	£50	£90
Charles Stanley Direct	£70	£99
Close Brothers A.M. Self Directed Service	£48	£73
Fidelity Personal Investing	£120	£120
Halifax Share Dealing	£74	£74
Hargreaves Lansdown	£70	£93
iDealing	£60	£60
IG	£128	£128
Interactive Investor (Investor Product)	£120	£120
iWeb	£120	£120
Sharedeal	£88	£88
Willis Owen	£50	£90
X-O	£24	£24

Source: AIC/the Lang Cat consultancy, data as at 08/02/23.

How much does it cost to hold shares in investment trusts on a private investor platform? The table gives an illustrative estimate for most of the largest platforms. The costs are shown as an annual percentage of the value of your portfolio, based on the amount you have invested. The data is collected by the Lang Cat consultancy and published on the AIC website. It is a valuable source of information, albeit with some important caveats.

It is important to note that your investment is assumed to be within an ISA tax wrapper. The figures shown only include ongoing platform fees, additional wrapper charges (if any) and trading charges (where applicable). Other charges, for example the management charges of the investment companies themselves,

	£25,000	£50,000	£100,000	£250,000	£500,000	£1,000,000
	£82	£82	£82	£82	£82	£82
	£72	£74	£124	£274	£524	£1,024
	£130	£230	£430	£1,030	£1,530	£2,530
	£134	£221	£286	£286	£286	£286
	£98	£161	£286	£661	£1,286	£2,286
	£120	£120	£120	£120	£120	£120
	£74	£74	£74	£74	£74	£74
	£93	£93	£93	£93	£93	£93
	£60	£60	£60	£60	£60	£60
	£128	£128	£128	£128	£128	£128
	£120	£120	£120	£120	£120	£120
	£120	£120	£120	£120	£120	£120
	£88	£88	£88	£88	£88	£88
	£130	£230	£380	£680	£1,055	£1,805
	£24	£24	£24	£24	£24	£24

are excluded. The data is based on publicly available charging structure information, with some details verified in conversations with platforms.

This table assumes you only hold investment trusts on the platform. A separate table on the website shows how the figure varies if you also hold open-ended funds on the platform. Their platform charges are generally higher, though only for larger portfolios (£50,000 or more). Bear in mind however that charges are not the sole, or even the most important, criterion for choosing a platform. The quality of the service – the range of options, the quality of the research and how smoothly and efficiently the platform works – are every bit as relevant.

AIC website

Sector breakdown for dividend heroes

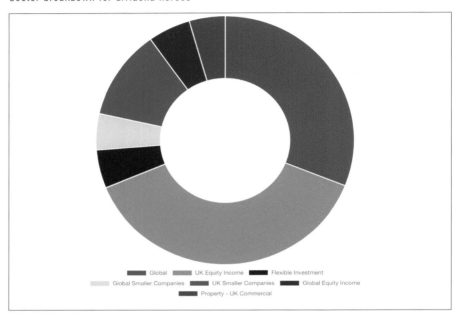

Source: AIC.

Dividend payments across 12 months to end of September 2023

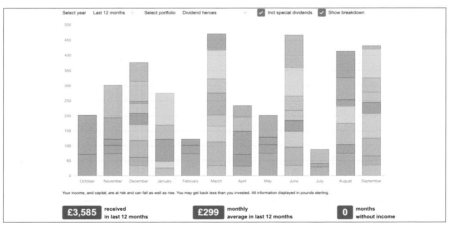

Source: AIC.

The AIC continues to make improvements to its website, which remains an invaluable resource for private investors looking to research and compare investment trust options. This year I would highlight the improvements that have been made to the income finder tool which was highlighted in the *Handbook* last year.

This has now been expanded and merged with a watchlist function to create a general portfolio and research management tool which allows you to track and analyse lists of trusts of any kind, not just ones you own for dividend income. (You can however continue to use the income builder or watchlist tools separately if you so choose.)

Once you have created a watchlist or portfolio, you can view and edit your holdings, and see the value of your portfolios at the last market close. If you have created a watchlist, you have the option to turn it into a portfolio by adding details of your holdings, entering either the number of shares you own or their value. It is possible to add a cash holding and see how that impacts the total.

You can also see charts breaking down your portfolios by company or AIC sector. Here is an example showing the breakdown by sector if you owned a portfolio that was made up exclusively of trusts that have earned 'dividend hero' status. As you would expect, they are concentrated in the global and equity income sectors.

The second chart shows how the dividend payments from this notional portfolio would have been spread across the 12 months to the end of September 2023. You can also create tables of data showing the frequency, payment dates and dividend cover of all the constituents, as well as the current discount and share price and NAV performance over different time periods.

This is not a fully fledged portfolio analysis tool therefore – there are more sophisticated commercial ones for which you have to pay a subscription fee that can run into hundreds of pounds per year – but it is accurate and of course free to use. It will certainly give you a useful broad overview of how your investments are faring.

Elsewhere on the improved website the AIC have added an expanded news and research section, where you can find, among other articles and interviews, links to the latest *Money Makers* podcasts (scroll down to the bottom of the page). It is important to note that the research is mostly paid for research from the likes of Edison, Kepler Intelligence and QuotedData, sponsored by the trusts they have covered, but useful nonetheless.

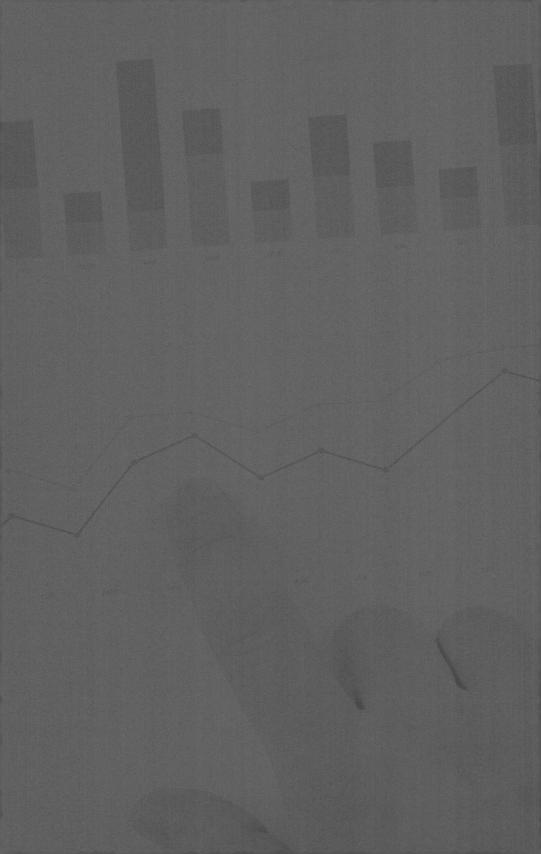

PARTNERS

About abrdn

If you're keen to capture the potential offered by global investment markets, turn to abrdn investment trusts. Managed by teams of experts, each trust is designed to bring together the most compelling opportunities we can find to generate the investment growth or income you're looking for.

At abrdn, we empower our clients to plan, save and invest for their futures. Through the expertise, insight and innovation of our teams, we aim to help clients create more ways for their money to make an impact. Our purpose is to enable our clients to be better investors and we set our sights on giving them more confidence to achieve their goals. We focus on delivering outcomes that are more than just financial – by investing sustainably to build a better world.

We're a global business. We manage and administer £495.7bn of assets for our clients, and we have around 5,000 employees globally (as at 30 June 2023).

For more information and to sign up for updates, please visit abrdn.com/trusts

The value of investments and the income from them can go down as well as up and investors may get back less than the amount invested.

AGT — nearly four decades of fundamental investing

AVI Global Trust (AGT) provides expertly managed exposure to the opportunities presented in various parts of the world.

The investment objective is to achieve capital growth through a focused portfolio of global equities.

The investment strategy identifies valuation anomalies to create a concentrated, unique, and diversified portfolio of stocks. The investment manager then engages with these companies to improve shareholder value.

How we achieve our investment objective

- We invest into a concentrated portfolio of stocks.
- We follow our distinctive long-only, fundamental value investment style.
- We seek out good quality, neglected securities trading at a discount to their net asset value.
- We improve shareholder value through active engagement.
- We build a contrarian benchmark-agnostic unconstrained portfolio.
- We provide diversification due to the nature of our holdings.

Our robust investment philosophy guides investment decisions

Emphasis is placed on three factors:

1. companies with attractive assets, where there is potential for growth in value;
2. a sum-of-the-parts discount to a fair net asset value; and
3. identifiable catalysts for value realisation.

A concentrated high-conviction core portfolio of c. 30± investments allows for detailed research which forms the cornerstone of our approach.

AVI took over the investment management of AGT in 1985. The experience gained from nearly four decades of following our unique investment style is key to our in-depth understanding of our universe of opportunities in a constantly changing environment.

AGT's long-term track record bears witness to the success of this approach, with a NAV total return well in excess of its benchmark. We believe this strategy remains as appealing as ever and we continue to find plenty of exciting opportunities.

 For more information visit
www.aviglobal.co.uk.

Baillie Gifford™
Actual Investors

Independent global investment managers

Baillie Gifford is privately and wholly owned by its partners. This is the crucial underpinning of our approach: we have no short-term commercial imperatives and no outside shareholders to distract us. We can simply do what's right for clients, and that's what has sustained our business since 1908.

We are the largest manager of investment trusts in the UK with a range of thirteen trusts. We have an extensive range of OEIC sub-funds and manage investments globally for pension funds, institutions and charities.

Some see the collective failure of active management as an argument to embrace passive. We see it as an opportunity to redefine our original purpose of deploying clients' capital into tangible, returns-generating activities. And we believe that redefinition is 'actual investment'.

Actual investment is not easy in our world of 24-hour news, where complexity and noise are confused with rational judgement. It requires the resolve to focus only on what really matters, to think independently and to maintain a long-term perspective. It requires a willingness to be different, to accept uncertainty and the possibility of being wrong. Most of all, it requires a rejection of the now-conventional wisdom that has led our industry astray: investment management is not about processing power, trading and speed. It is about imagination and creativity, and working constructively on behalf of our clients with inspiring individuals and companies who have greater ideas than our own.

The best investment ideas spring from thinking about future possibilities, not short-term probabilities. Our research covers the globe and we set no barriers to the imagination of our investors, encouraging fresh perspectives and the use of diverse sources of information.

We believe our approach to investing not only best delivers good outcomes for clients, but it also helps to develop great companies that provide for the needs and wants of people, thereby benefiting society as a whole. Investing responsibly for the long term is not counter to outperforming for clients, it's intrinsic to it.

About Columbia Threadneedle Investments

Columbia Threadneedle Investments is one of the leading investment trust managers, tracing its heritage back to 1868 when F&C Investment Trust, the world's oldest collective investment scheme, was launched. Today Columbia Threadneedle manages nine investment trusts with more than £10bn in assets, providing clients with a range of investment opportunities in equities, property and private equity.

Each trust is tailored to offer clients different aims and objectives with the option of capital growth, income or a combination of both, offered through portfolios with specific regional focuses or global remits. Clients can invest directly into Columbia Threadneedle's suite of investment trusts via its own savings plan or through a third-party provider.

Our nine trusts are F&C Investment Trust (FCIT), The Global Smaller Companies Trust (GSCT), CT UK Capital And Income Investment Trust (CTUK), European Assets Trust (EAT), CT Private Equity Trust (CTPT), CT Global Managed Portfolio Trust (CMPG and CMPI), CT UK High Income Trust (CHI), Balanced Commercial Property Trust (BCPT) and TR Property (TRY).

Columbia Threadneedle's investment trust business is part of its global asset management business, which is entrusted with £481bn on behalf of individual, institutional and corporate clients around the world. The business employs more than 2500 people, including over 650 investment professionals based in North America, Europe and Asia (all data as at 30 June 2023). Columbia Threadneedle Investments is the global asset management group of Ameriprise Financial, a leading US-based financial services provider.

To find out more information about any of our nine investment trusts, visit our website: **ctinvest.co.uk**.

*As well as looking at the potential rewards that investing can bring, it's important you're aware of the potential risks involved so that you can make an informed decision. The value of shares and the income from them is not guaranteed and can fall as well as rise due to stock market and currency movements. When you sell your shares, you may get back less than you originally invested. Our range of investment trusts invest in the stock market and some of them also invest in unlisted companies and funds and property. If they invest in emerging markets, unquoted securities or smaller companies, their potential volatility may increase the risk to the value of, and the income from, the investment. Investment trusts can also borrow money (gearing), which can then be used to make further investments and if markets fall, gearing can magnify the negative impact on performance. Each Trust has different risk factors. Please read our Key Features Document, relevant Key Information Document (KID) and Pre Sales Cost & Charges Disclosures before investing. For more information about investment risks, visit our website **ctinvest.co.uk**.*

About Fidelity International

Fidelity International provides world-class investment solutions and retirement expertise to institutions, individuals, and their advisers – to help our clients build better futures for themselves and generations to come.

As a private company we think generationally and invest for the long term. Helping clients to save for retirement and other long-term investing objectives has been at the core of our business for over 50 years.

We are responsible for total client assets of £423.9bn from over 2.8 million clients across the UK, Continental Europe and Asia Pacific.

Our UK investment trust business

Fidelity has over 28 years' experience managing investment companies and manages over £4.8bn in assets across six investment trusts. These are all focused on equity growth strategies.

As a major platform distributor, Fidelity is able to offer its own investment trusts and those managed by third parties to professional investors and retail investors alike through a range of different product wrappers. Fidelity also promotes its range of trusts directly to institutions and wealth managers through its highly experienced in-house sales teams.

We offer our own investment solutions and access to those of others and deliver services relating to investing; for individual investors and their advisers we provide guidance to help them invest in a simple and cost-effective way.

For institutions including pension funds, banks and insurance companies we offer tailored investment solutions and full-service asset management outsourcing. And for employers we provide workplace pension administration services on top, or independently, of investment management.

Source for all data: FIL International, 30 June 2023

India Capital
GROWTH FUND

About India Capital Growth Fund

Launched in 2005, India Capital Growth Fund looks to provide long term capital appreciation by investing predominantly in listed mid and small cap Indian companies. Investments may also be made in unquoted Indian companies where the fund manager believes long-term capital appreciation will be achieved. The company may hold liquid assets (including cash) pending deployment in suitable investments.

The closed-ended structure of India Capital Growth Fund is perfectly suited for the universe in which the team invest. The company invests in less liquid opportunities and takes a long-term approach, unencumbered by fund flows both in and out. The company is able invest in smaller, less well-known companies therefore shareholders are exposed to ideas that are unviable for larger fund houses. Often these ideas are identified in advance of our competition and usually allocated to on more attractive terms.

With specialist investment advisers and managers based on the ground in Mumbai and London, the team seek out innovative opportunities, identifying companies with sustainable growth at an attractive price. Given the nature of the companies in which we invest, the quality of the research we undertake is vital. Using a bottom-up approach the team meet the companies they invest in, undertake proprietary research and truly understand the business model of companies enabling them to invest with conviction.

India Capital Growth Fund adds a fresh dimension to any portfolio enabling shareholders access to the engine room of India via small and midcap stocks. Driven by a positive macro- and geopolitical environment, and favourable demographics, India is a fast-growing economy that cannot be ignored by investors.

India Capital Growth Fund has appointed Ocean Dial Asset Management, a River and Mercantile Company, as its investment manager.

About Invesco

Invesco is a leading independent global investment management firm with more than 8,400 dedicated people in over 26 countries. Our philosophy is about using our integrity, passion and expertise to solve the needs of our clients, helping them reach their goals.

We manage $1.5 trillion of assets (as at 30 June 2023), giving our clients the confidence of working with a partner with size, scale and stability. We offer a wide range of single-country, regional, and global capabilities across major equity, fixed-income, and alternative asset classes, including a broad range of ESG-related capabilities, delivered through a diverse set of investment vehicles.

Investment trusts by Invesco

We offer four investment trusts across a large and diverse range of seven strategies. Whichever one is right for you, each has the same commitment to investment excellence at its heart.

- Invesco Asia Trust plc (IAT), managed by Ian Hargreaves and Fiona Yang.

- Invesco Bond Income Plus Limited (BIPS), managed by Rhys Davies and Edward Craven.

- Invesco Perpetual UK Smaller Companies Investment Trust plc (IPU), managed by Jonathan Brown and Robin West.

- Invesco Select Trust plc (IVPU, IVPG, IVPB and IVPM), a multi-portfolio investment trust made up of four portfolios, each managed independently by expert managers.

For more information on our investment trust range, please visit our website: **www.invesco.com/uk/en/investment-trusts.html**.

Investment risks

Capital at risk. Invesco Bond Income Plus Limited has a significant proportion of high-yielding bonds, which are of lower credit quality and may result in large fluctuations in the NAV of the product. It may invest in contingent convertible bonds which may result in significant risk of capital loss based on certain trigger events. The use of borrowings may increase the volatility of the NAV and may reduce returns when asset values fall. It uses derivatives for efficient portfolio management which may result in increased volatility in the NAV.

Important information

As at 4 October 2023 unless otherwise stated.

The yield shown is an estimate for the next 12 months, assuming that the fund's portfolio remains unchanged and there are no defaults or deferrals of coupon payments or capital repayments. The yield is not guaranteed. Nor does it reflect any charges. Investors may be subject to tax on distributions.

This is marketing material and not financial advice. It is not intended as a recommendation to buy or sell any particular asset class, security or strategy. Regulatory requirements that require impartiality of investment/investment strategy recommendations are therefore not applicable nor are any prohibitions to trade before publication. Views and opinions are based on current market conditions and are subject to change.

*The Key Information Document is available on our website: **www.invesco.com/uk/en/ investment-trusts/invesco-bond-income-plus-limited.html**.*

Further details of the company's Investment Policy and Risk and Investment Limits can be found in the Report of the Directors contained within the company's Annual Financial Report.

If investors are unsure if these products are suitable for them, they should seek advice from a financial adviser. Invesco Fund Managers Limited. Invesco Bond Income Plus Limited is regulated by the Jersey Financial Services Commission.

PANTHEON

About Pantheon

Pantheon has been at the forefront of private markets investing for more than 40 years, earning a reputation for providing innovative solutions covering the full investment lifecycle in private equity, real assets, and private credit, from primary commitments to new funds, direct co-investments and providing liquidity via secondary purchases.

We have partnered with more than 1,000 institutional investors and professional clients of all sizes, including a growing number of private wealth managers, and have more than US$60bn in discretionary assets under management and a combined $93bn in assets managed or advised (as at 31 March 2023) through a range of pooled funds and bespoke separate accounts.

Our specialised experience is delivered by a global team of 130 investment professionals based in 12 offices across Europe, the Americas, and Asia.

Key facts:

- More than **40 years** of investing experience in private markets
- **US$60bn+** in discretionary assets under management
- **US$75bn+** committed to investments since inception in 1982
- **Serving 1,000+ clients**, including both institutional investors and private wealth clients

Pantheon's investment prowess is underpinned by deep relationships with hundreds of high-quality fund managers across all our asset classes. It is reflected in our investments in approximately 2,000 funds and seats on 625 advisory boards.

Pantheon has actively managed two London Stock Exchange-listed investments since they were launched in 1987 and 2021 respectively.

Pantheon International Plc (ticker: PIN) is a FTSE 250 investment trust and one of the longest-established private equity companies listed on the London Stock Exchange. It provides simple access to a high-quality, diversified portfolio of exceptional private companies all over the world by investing with many of the world's best private equity managers, which might otherwise be inaccessible to many investors.

Pantheon Infrastructure Plc (PINT) aims to provide exposure to a diversified portfolio of global infrastructure assets, via direct co-investments alongside high-quality fund managers sourced through Pantheon's global platform. Target assets typically have strong defensive characteristics, including contracted cash flows, inflation protection and conservative leverage profiles, with a focus on sectors with strong secular tailwinds.

About Polar Capital

Polar Capital is a specialist active fund management company offering investors a range of predominantly long-only equity funds, including three thematic investment trusts.

They have a fundamental, research-driven approach, where capacity is rigorously managed to enhance and protect performance.

The investment trusts are in the specialist sectors of technology, healthcare and financials. Polar Capital Technology Trust (PCT) was the first product managed by Polar Capital, founded in 2001 by fund managers Brian Ashford-Russell and Tim Woolley together with corporate partner Caledonia Investments. Technology remains at the core of the Polar Capital business.

Managed by a team of 10 dedicated technology specialists – one of the largest technology teams in Europe – PCT is a leading investment trust with a strong multi-year, multi-cycle track record. The managers have an active investment approach and seek to identify developing technology trends early and invest with conviction in those companies best placed to exploit them. PCT provides investors with access to the huge potential of companies globally within the technology sector, with a capital growth mandate.

The investment team has discretion on how much they allocate to any one region, to any size of company and to any subsector/theme. The assessment of future thematic growth coupled with rigorous fundamental analysis, has enabled PCT to deliver an impressive track record for nearly 25 years. As major new trends emerge, disrupting industries and companies across the world, PCT is well-placed to exploit these opportunities.

PCT provides an active, diversified, core approach to investing in this large and exciting investment sector.

Polar Capital's investment teams are mostly based in the company's principal location in London, with offices in the UK, US, Germany, Switzerland, France, Spain, Denmark, China and Singapore.

Schroders

About Schroders

As a global asset and wealth manager, Schroders delivers a broad range of investments designed to meet the diverse needs of institutions, intermediaries and individuals.

For over 200 years we have built principled partnerships with our clients, putting them at the centre of everything we do. They trust us to deliver sustainable returns through times of economic prosperity and of uncertainty.

We are a global business, managed locally. Our international presence supports us in understanding the needs of our clients and delivering them the right expertise from across the business.

As an active investment manager we believe that we have an important role to play in driving better outcomes for our clients and society as a whole. We bring together people and data to identify the trends that will shape the prosperity of individuals, businesses and future generations.

Schroders Investment Trusts

Schroders has been managing investment trusts since 1924 and has established a strong reputation. Our specialist teams draw on Schroders' extensive investment resources, combining global insights with local market knowledge.

We offer a range of investment trusts, focusing on the UK, Asia, real estate, private equity and renewable infrastructure. With clearly defined investment strategies, they help investors meet different financial objectives.

 Scan the QR code to find out more about our investment trust range.